KNOWLEDGE FOR WHAT?

The Place of Social Science in American Culture

LONDON: HUMPHREY MILFORD
OXFORD UNIVERSITY PRESS

KNOWLEDGE FOR WHAT?

THE PLACE OF SOCIAL SCIENCE IN AMERICAN CULTURE

ROBERT S. LYND

Co-author of "Middletown" and "Middletown in Transition"

PRINCETON

PRINCETON UNIVERSITY PRESS

1948

"And in this staggering disproportion between man and no-man, there is no place
for purely human boasts of grandeur, or
for forgetting that men build their cultures by huddling together, nervously
loquacious, at the edge of an abyss."

—*Kenneth Burke, in*
Permanence and Change

CONTENTS

FOREWORD

NO one is wise enough or informed enough to venture with assurance upon the large task here undertaken. The only reason for attempting it is that such efforts at appraisal of the present work and potentialities of the social sciences, however faulty in detail, seem clearly to be needed at the present stage in the development of social science and of American culture. And if it was to be undertaken at all, it seemed desirable to push the analysis straight through the network of diffidence and respect for one's colleagues that tends to shackle frankness within an academic fraternity. For, as the reader will see, in the judgment of the writer this is not a time in which urbanity, trial and error, and the unseen hand of progress can be relied upon to make all things work together for good.

The reader may be puzzled at first glance by the fact that two seemingly independent lines of thought are developed in this book: the one an appraisal of the present characteristics of American culture, with particular attention to elements of strain and disjunction; and the other a critique of current focus and methods in social science research. They are here included together because they so inescapably do belong together. Social science is not a scholarly arcanum, but an organized part of the culture which exists to help man in continually understanding and rebuilding his culture. And it is the precise character of a culture and the problems it presents as an instrument for furthering men's purposes that should determine the problems and, to some extent, the balance of methods of social science research. It is because the writer feels that our American culture presents acute problems demanding all the intelligence science can muster, and because social research appears to him to be falling short of meeting this need, that it has seemed essential to include here related analyses both of the culture and of the present state of our research.

Some of the single judgments made in these pages will almost certainly be proved invalid or subject to correction. But it is the hope of the writer that the central points at which the book drives will not be lost in the dust of umbrageous counter-charges. If the points appeal to the reader as in any respect well taken, it is hoped that he will correct them in detail and soften and modify the form of statement in whatever way will enable him to make constructive use of them. If this inadequate formulation succeeds in directing attention to the problems discussed and leads to a better statement and a more direct attack, it will have served its purpose.

The substance of this book was delivered in preliminary form as the four Stafford Little Lectures at Princeton University in the spring of 1938.

Columbia University R. S. L.

I

SOCIAL SCIENCE IN CRISIS

CONTEMPORARY social science contains within itself two types of orientation that divide it into two blocs of workers: the scholars and the technicians. Both work within the protective tradition of free intellectual inquiry; and both assume continuity and relevance between their respective realms in the common task of exploring the unknown. Actually they tend to pull apart, the scholar becoming remote from and even disregarding immediate relevancies, and the technician too often accepting the definition of his problems too narrowly in terms of the emphases of the institutional environment of the moment. The gap between the two, while not sharp or even commonly recognized, is significant for two reasons: important problems tend to fall into oblivion between the two groups of workers; and the strains generated by current institutional breakdowns are prompting sharp and peremptory scrutiny of the rôles and adequacy of the social sciences. Nazi power-politics has stripped the social sciences in Germany of their intellectual freedom, while professors-in-uniform in Italy have been forced to betray their heritage by solemnly declaring the Italian population to be of Aryan origin. This is a critical time for social science.

The scholarly bloc among social scientists is placed in jeopardy precisely by that leisurely urbanity upon which it prides itself as it looks out upon the confusions in the midst of which we live. The time outlooks of the scholar-scientist and of the practical men of affairs who surround the world of science tend to be different. The former works in a long, leisurely world in which the hands of the clock crawl slowly over a vast dial; to him, the precise penetration of the unknown seems too grand an enterprise to be hurried, and one simply works ahead within study walls relatively sound-proofed against the clamorous urgencies of the world outside. In this time-universe of the scholar-scientist certain supporting assumptions have grown up, such as "impersonal objectivity," "aloofness from the strife of rival values," and the self-justifying goodness of "new knowledge" about anything, big or little. Such a setting has tended to impart a quality of independent validity and self-sufficiency to the scholar-scientist's work. The practical man of affairs, on the other hand, works by a small time-dial over which the second-hand of immediacy hurries incessantly. "Never mind the long past and the infinite future," insists the clattering little monitor, "but do this, fix this—now, before tomorrow morning." It has been taken for granted, in general, that there is no need to synchronize the two time-worlds of the scholar-scientist and of the practical man. Immediate relevance has not been regarded as so important as ultimate relevance; and, in the burgeoning nineteenth century world which viewed all time as moving within the Master System of Progress, there was seemingly large justification for this optimistic tolerance.

Our contemporary world is losing its confidence in the inevitability of Progress. Men's ways of ordering their common lives have broken down so disastrously as to make hope precarious. So headlong and pervasive is change to-day that the scholar's historical parallels are decreasingly relevant as present guides, because so many of the variables in the situation have altered radically. The scholar-scientist is in acute danger of being caught, in the words of one of Auden's poems,

"Lecturing on navigation while the ship is going down."

Both scholar and technician are placed in a new and exposed position by the recent sharp shift in the relative importance of the social sciences. Until the great depression that began in 1929, they were poor relations of the natural sciences. In a world whose "progress" and "manifest destiny" were so generally accepted as dependent upon the production of goods, natural science and its technologies seemed to be the primary antecedents to general welfare. Edison, Ford, the Wright brothers—men like these, aided of course by American business enterprise, were the great creators, and American boys have placed such men with the traditional political giants, Washington and Lincoln, as the "great Americans." An increasing stream of able young scientists flowed into the private laboratories of General Electric, United States Steel, du Pont, and other corporations, there to develop new alloys and plastics. A world of enterprising businessmen which bought invention and efficiency by giving subsidies to science appeared to be the latest and happiest formula in that succession of lucky circumstances known as "the American way."

In this world, which had hitched its dreams to material progress, the social sciences moved less confidently. They were newer, afraid of being thought unscientific by their rich relations, and generally less venturesome. Dealing as they do with the familiar fabric of institutionalized behavior, they were especially exposed when they ventured upon novel hypothesis or prediction. If they erred, popular familiarity with their subject-matters, and their consequent lack of mystery, brought swifter ridicule from the man on the street than is generally meted out to the worker within the sheltered walls of a natural-science laboratory. Then, too, the monistic theory of progress through business prosperity rendered divergence from the customary suspect and extra-hazardous *ab initio*. "Radical" means one thing in a natural-science laboratory and something vastly different in the social sciences. So the social sciences were prone to content themselves with the retrospective look, or with describing and analyzing current trends, like a retailer taking inventory of the stock on his shelves. Such an astute critic as Parrington pointed out near the close of the 1920's that political science and economics have "largely joined the Swiss guards" protecting the inner sanctuary of the vested system.[1] This over-ready acceptance of the main assumptions of the going system has been a source of confusion and embarrassment to the social sciences as that system has become highly unmanageable since the World War, and particularly since 1929.

The depression has reversed the relative emphases upon the natural and the social sciences. The poor relation finds itself wealthy and important—or at least supposed to act as if it were—while the former rich relative finds itself in the unaccustomed position of being less important. For it is the intractability of the human factor, and not our technologies, that has spoiled the American dream; and the social sciences deal with that human factor. The de-

[1] "In the welter that is present-day America militant philosophies with their clear-cut programs and assured faiths are wanting, and many feel, as Matthew Arnold felt fourscore years ago, that they are dwelling between worlds, one dead, the other powerless to be born. The old buoyant psychology is gone and in the breakdown and disintegration of the traditional individualism no new philosophies are rising. Builders of Utopias are out of a job. Political and economic theory is in charge of paymasters and is content with the drab rim of the familiar landscape. Retainer-fees have blotted out for it the lovelier horizons that earlier thinkers contemplated. Academic political scientists and economists have largely joined the Swiss guards, and abdicated the high prerogative of speculative thought. It is the men of letters—poets and essayists and novelists and dramatists, the eager young intellectuals of a drab generation—who embody the mind of present-day America; not the professional custodians of official views." (V. L. Parrington, *Main Currents in American Thought* [New York: Harcourt, Brace, 1930], Vol. III, p. xxvii.)

pression has made us acutely aware of the fact that our brilliant technological skills are shackled to the shambling gait of an institutional Caliban. As a result—

". . . While man's effort to control the forces of Nature is accompanied by increasing success and mounting optimism, his efforts to regenerate society lead only to confusion and despair.

". . . We see no lack of fertile farms, of elaborate and fully equipped factories, no lack of engineers and technicians and mechanics to operate the factories and cultivate the farms. . . . Yet we note that the factories are running intermittently or not at all, that the farms are cultivated only in part. It is not that all have enough; for we see millions of men and women, lacking the necessities of life. . . . We see . . . other men, in obedience to governmental decree, refrain from planting wheat and plow growing cotton under ground. A survey of human history will often enough disclose millions of men starving in time of famine: what we see now is something unprecedented— millions of men destitute in the midst of potential abundance. . . .

". . . Mankind has entered a new phase of human progress—a time in which the acquisition of new implements of power too swiftly outruns the necessary adjustment of habits and ideas to the novel conditions created by their use."[2]

Some people have even clamored for a moratorium on inventions until the rest of our living can catch up; while NRA codes have struggled to slow down the introduction of more efficient machinery, and relief work has been done in many cases by hand in order to thwart the labor-efficiency of the machine. Were Thorstein Veblen alive, he

[2] Carl Becker, *Progress and Power* (Stanford University Press, 1936), pp. 88-91.

[5]

would smile sardonically at this evidence that our institutional sabotaging of machine efficiency has at last come of age as an officially sanctioned public practice.

The spotlight has turned with painful directness upon the social sciences. And it has found them, in the main, unprepared to assume the required responsibility. We social scientists have great arrays of data:

—data on production and distribution, but not the data that will enable us to say with assurance, as the experts dealing with such matters, how our economy can get into use all of the needed goods we are physically capable of producing;

—data on past business cycles, but not data that enabled us to foresee the great depression of 1929 even six months before it occurred;[3]

—data on labor problems, but not the data to provide an effective program for solving the central problems of unemployment and of the widening class-cleavage between capital and labor;

—legal data, but not the data to implement us to curb admittedly increasing lawlessness;

—data on public administration, non-voting, and politics, but not data for a well-coordinated program with which to attack such central problems of American democracy as the fading meaning of "citizenship" to the urban dweller and what Secretary Wallace has called the "private ownership of government" by business;[4]

[3] The final summary chapter of the authoritative cooperative study of *Recent Economic Changes*, written as late as the spring of 1929, shares, though guardedly, the general optimism of that period regarding the future of American business. There were a few single economists, like B. M. Anderson of the Chase National Bank and H. Parker Willis of Columbia University, who viewed the prospect in the late 1920's with apprehension, but these Jeremiahs were but a minor note in the general chorus of bold or cautious optimism.

[4] *New Frontiers* (New York: Reynal and Hitchcock, 1934), Chap. iv.

—data on the irrationality of human behavior and on the wide inequalities in intelligence, but not the data on how a culture can be made to operate democratically by and for such human components.

Is the difficulty, as the social sciences maintain, that they do not have "enough data"? Or do we have data on the wrong problems? Or are too many of our data simply descriptive and too infrequently projective and predictive in the sense of being aimed at deliberate planning and control? Or are they too atomistic, relying upon the "unseen hand" of circumstances and upon common sense to tie bits of knowledge together and to make them work? All of these are involved. The net result is none the less decidedly uncomfortable—for the social sciences and for our American culture which supports them.

A world floundering disastrously because of its inability to make its institutions work is asking the social sciences: "What do you know? What do you propose?" And, unfortunately for the peace of mind of the social scientist, these questions are not asked with complete dispassion; not infrequently they are loaded in the sense of, "Tell us what we want to hear, or else—!" For the social sciences are parts of culture, and it so happens that they are carried forward predominantly by college and university professors, who in turn are hired by businessmen trustees. The stake of these last in the status quo is great. That is why they are trustees. The social scientist finds himself caught, therefore, between the rival demands for straight, incisive, and, if need be, radically divergent thinking, and the growingly insistent demand that his thinking shall not be subversive. The solution of problems that beset the culture requires the utmost use of intelligence. And, as P. W.

[7]

Bridgman of Harvard University has remarked,[5] "The *utmost* exercise of intelligence means the *free* use of intelligence; [the scientist] must be willing to follow *any* lead that he can see, undeterred by any inhibition, whether it arises from laziness or other unfortunate personal characteristics, or intellectual tradition or the social conventions of his epoch. In fact, intelligence and *free* intelligence come to be synonymous to him. It becomes inconceivable that anyone should consent to conduct his thinking under demonstrable restrictions, once these restrictions had been recognized, any more than as an experimenter he would consent to use only a restricted experimental technique." But in a world rapidly being forced to abandon the sunny tolerance of individual trial and error under *laissez-faire*, "the utmost exercise of free intelligence" will be continually in jeopardy. And nowhere will the strain be so great as in the social sciences, for they deal with the white-hot core of current controversy, where passions are most aggravated and counsel most darkened.

Under these circumstances our university administrators—those who control the fates of working social scientists—are in some important cases wavering. They are concerned in their enforced daily decisions with the short-run "welfare of an institution," and this may be viewed as not synonymous with the long-run welfare of our American culture. To go ahead frankly into the enlarged opportunity confronting the social sciences invites trouble. Putting one's head into the lion's mouth to operate on a sore tooth has its manifest disadvantages. So we are witnessing today an active administrative espousal of the humanities, and controversies over the wisdom of the "liberal arts" emphasis as over against the "over-prac-

---

[5] "Society and the Intelligent Physicist," address before the annual meeting of the American Association of Physics Teachers in 1938, scheduled for publication in *The American Physics Teacher* for March 25, 1939.

tical" emphasis of the social sciences. "After all," runs the administrator's comment, in effect, "education should make rounded men. The university's job is not to solve problems but to turn out men with a liberal education, possessed of the great wisdoms of the past, ripe in judgment, and having the ability to meet the varied problems of life."

And so it is. It is not the intention in the pages which follow to deprecate the humanities or education in the liberal arts. The fact that most social science research must go forward in our culture within colleges and universities, however, makes the policies of educational administrators of direct relevance to the problems on which this research engages. Insistent public dilemmas clamor for solution. Decisions will be made and public policies established—because no delaying or turning back is possible in this hurrying climactic era. If the social scientist is too bent upon "waiting until all the data are in," or if university policies warn him off controversial issues, the decisions will be made anyway—without him. They will be made by the "practical" man and by the "hard-headed" politician chivvied by interested pressure-blocs.

The chapters that follow seek to appraise the present state of our American culture and of the social sciences as instruments for the analysis of its more critical problems and for the devising of indicated concrete programs of action.

A final word as to the social researcher as teacher: Most social science research is done by men who gain their main livelihood as teachers. The problems they select for research determine to a considerable extent what they teach. And what they teach determines to an important degree the outlook of their students upon technical problems and

[9]

related policies; and, in the case of those students who will go on to make a career of research, the teaching they receive will influence heavily the kind and acuteness of the problems they will eventually elect to investigate. Like everyone else, the teacher has given heavy hostages to fortune: he has a family to rear, usually on a not too ample salary; his income depends upon the academic advancements he can win, and these in turn depend upon "productive research"; he has been sensitized to research by his training, his head is full of projects he wants to get at, and yet research increasingly demands in these days that the golden sun of outside funds shine upon the would-be investigator. He lives in a world which, by and large, is not asking, "Is Smith trying to get at the facts? Is he trying to be fair and constructive at the same time that he is unwilling to pull his punch?" but which asks, "Are you for us, or against us?" Just because the need for acute, candid, fearless thinking is so great, the teacher-researcher of our generation carries perforce a heavy, inescapable responsibility. If he fails this oncoming generation at this critical moment—for reasons other than his sheer inability to comprehend, even as a so-called expert, the rush and complexity of the problems our culture confronts—his will be a desperate betrayal indeed. Upon those teachers who are on what is called, probably increasingly optimistically, "permanent tenure," there would appear to rest the special obligation to carry for their less-secure junior colleagues the main brunt of hard-hitting, constructive thought that spares no one, least of all themselves.

II

THE CONCEPT OF "CULTURE"

A PREVALENT mood among sophisticated persons today is a sense of helplessness in the face of the too-bigness of the issues we confront. This is no new experience for human beings, however wistfully we moderns may regard the quiet continuities of certain less mobile earlier eras or the earthy immediacies of the primitive peoples who inhabit the happy isles of the Pacific. Somerset Maugham's story of "The Fall of Edward Barnard" depicts the desire that men have felt intermittently, as they shuttled about amidst their compulsions, to escape into a world where life can be encompassed by one's bare hands, and where living goes forward to the rhythm of the tides and the seasons and in response to the heart's desire. But the sense of the augmented too-bigness and out-of-handness of our contemporary world is neither illusion nor merely another expression of this recurrent restlessness of man in civilization. While unprovable because of our inability to relive intimately the moods of the past, it appears probable that we today are attempting to live in the most disparate and confusing cultural environment faced by any generation of Americans since the beginning of our national life. In fact, Professor James T. Shotwell recently characterized "the anarchy we are living in today" as "the most dangerous since the fall of Rome."[1]

[1] In an address at the annual celebration of the Woodrow Wilson Foundation, broadcast by the Columbia Broadcasting System. See New York *Times*, December 29, 1938.

Ours is a world of division of labor and specialization. Each of us works, whether as scientist or businessman, on a narrow sector. This enhances our sense of helplessness, because, whatever we do, we feel ultimately coerced by larger forces not controllable within our immediate area of personal concentration. Herein lies one source of the sense of ultimate futility that haunts our private worlds, no matter how wide our knowledge, how acute our techniques, or how great our effort.

Modern science tends to be atomistic. Its drive is to isolate smaller and smaller variables and to study these in the greatest possible detail with the aid of minute controls. So vast is the universe of complexity presented by even these refined excisions from the total of phenomena in a given scientific field, that the specialist, far from feeling cramped in his isolated universe, tends to confront it with the enthusiasm of a small boy turned loose in a candy shop with a seemingly endless array of inviting opportunities before him. Countering this drive toward atomism has been another toward organization, which insists that the refined unit must be studied also as part of the functioning whole. Köhler, a member of the *Gestalt* school of psychologists, has pointed out that, while it is useful to study one hundred hearts together, a single heart has from a functional point of view more in common with a pair of lungs than it has with other hearts.[2] Likewise, William Stern, among the "personalistic" psychologists, has urged that, "The more exact an experiment is—that is, the more elementary and isolated the phenomenon, and the more constant the conditions—the greater is its artificiality, and the greater its distance from the study of the individual."[3]

---

[2] *Gestalt Psychology* (New York: Liveright, 1929), p. 351.
[3] Quoted from Stern's *Differentielle Psychologie* (3d ed., 1921, p. 12) by Gordon Allport in *Personality: A Psychological Interpretation* (New York: Holt, 1937), p. 20.

The several social sciences have aligned themselves in a variety of ways around this part-whole choice in emphasis. With the exception of that of history, the oldest emphasis is that of political science, law, and political economy. These three sciences have tended to treat the respective institutional complexes with which they deal as isolated, roughly self-contained systems; and from this grew their emphases upon such abstractions as "the political man" and "the economic man."

The presence of history as a separate discipline, claiming to give the total setting in any past era and the movement of the institutional whole over time, has reenforced this isolation of institutional areas. It has enabled the other social sciences to concentrate on their separate problems with the confident expectation that, as soon as today becomes yesterday, history will take over the task of joining parts into wholes. Thus history has served to an undue extent both as symbol and as surrogate for the other social sciences for the unifying of the entire field of human behavior. In passing, it may be noted that philosophy has played a similar rôle in the realm of the history and organization of ideas.

Another emphasis in this part-whole choice has come with the emergence of the science of psychology. This defined the part-whole issue not in terms of single institutions, as over against the total historical setting, but along the plane of the study of the individual, as over against the study of institutions. The development of such a separate social science concerned with the individual was welcomed by the other sciences, for somebody ought to study the individual, and now that psychology was doing it the other social sciences could continue with their accustomed work.

More recently, still another emphasis in this part-whole situation has arrived with the birth of the new sciences of sociology and anthropology. Sociology grew up well along in the nineteenth century as a form of protest against the abstractions both of the sciences studying separate institutional systems and of psychology preoccupied with the individual. Sociology was confessedly interested in the whole, and it attempted nothing less than to build a "science of society." This is but another way to state the common task of all of the social sciences. The fact that sociology overreached itself in its zeal to emphasize the interrelatedness of institutional behavior is not so much a reflection upon sociology as upon the isolation of the several social sciences which the new science sought to integrate. Anthropology has been more fortunate than sociology. Also a relatively late-comer among the sciences, the peculiarity of its subject-matter left it free (constricted only by the narrowness of training of its workers)[4] to put all social science to work on the functionally related whole of single cultures. It studied small, remote groups. These groups were "primitive," according to Western European standards, and therefore the older social sciences did not care much what anthropology did with them. Since these tribes did not have foreign exchange, banks, credit, labor problems, factories, Supreme Courts, and Jeffersonian and Hamiltonian traditions, the anthropologist was left free to walk in, look around, and ask such novel questions as "How does the life of these people hang together as a functioning whole?" He was a one-man expedition—literally all the social sciences there

[4] See, for instance, the statement by Professor Melville Herskovits, of Northwestern University, to his fellow anthropologists at the annual meeting of the American Anthropological Association in 1938, that anthropologists in general are lacking in insight, if not incompetent, when it comes to linking economics with anthropological research. When, he continued, an anthropologist thinks he is getting at the economic principles of primitive people, he usually is just skimming the surface of technology and sociology. (New York *Times*, December 29, 1938.)

were among the Baganda, the Todas, the Arapesh, the Trobriand or the Andaman islanders. What he didn't get, perhaps nobody else would.

A scholarly discipline wears a tough hide. The grip of habit is strong, even in a field allegedly dominated by "pure scientific curiosity." The failure of the social sciences to think through and to integrate their several responsibilities for the common problem of relating the analysis of parts to the analysis of the whole constitutes one of the major lags crippling their utility as human tools of knowledge. Our several specializations as social scientists play tricks with our scientific definitions of "the situation" and all too frequently prompt us to state our problems for research as if the rest of the situation did not exist.

It is a scientific commonplace today that all aspects of the behavior of an individual tend to hang together and to interact in some fashion, rational or irrational, and that on the institutional level, likewise, everything affects and is affected by everything else. The lines of connection may be illogical, and institutions may interact in functionally clumsy ways, but interact they do. We no longer feel at ease in talking about the "economic man," the "political man," and the "social man"; and we may even assert that "of course" and "in general," in a world of ramified institutional interdependence, we cannot hope to cope successfully with basic economic problems viewed solely as economic problems, with basic political problems viewed solely as political problems, or with urban, familial, or other problems viewed likewise within an artificially circumscribed field of institutional relevance. Thus the problem of the generally low state of municipal politics and government (including such phenomena as the growing indifference of urban voters, the unwillingness of the abler citizens to stand for local office, and the prevalence of administrative corruption) may not be viewed as solvable solely on the political level of analysis and action, by enacting new ordinances and state laws, by educating citizens in their civic responsibilities, and by exhorting better men to run for office. For these problems of municipal politics and government have long ganglia deeply imbedded in such things as the growing size of urban units in which citizens live as mobile, untied-in individuals, and in the extreme emphasis upon private money-making as the way to security and status.

This fact of the inescapable interrelatedness of the things with which the several social sciences deal is acknowledged by all. And yet, as Archibald MacLeish says in the foreword to *The Fall of the City*, "The argument [for the point he is making] is neither long nor sensational. It consists largely in asserting what everyone knows. *But such is the character of what everyone knows that no one knows it with enthusiasm.*" [Italics mine.]

So, despite our protestations that everything is interdependent, preoccupation with our specializations tends to put blinkers on us social scientists and to make us state our problems as if they concerned, in fact, isolated economic, or political, or sociological problems. And the fact that we strew the pages of our monographs with would-be exculpating phrases such as "other things being equal" and "of course, the many social [or economic, or political] factors also here involved should not be overlooked" hardly saves us and our data from the abstraction enforced by the original statement of our problem.

"Science," we like to say, "grows by accretion. None of us can solve the whole problem. Each must shape his bricks of data and place them modestly on the growing pile. Thus knowledge grows." Never before have our data been so imposing in quantity and refinement. And yet, never before have the lacunae been so devastatingly apparent. The comfortable old assumed process of separate scientific disciplines, growing each from its center outward toward its fellows and thus filling in the gaps, is either not working or not working fast enough to provide a social science corpus on which a floundering world can rely.

The recognition of this need is apparent in the growing insistence since the World War that the social sciences must "break down their disciplinary walls" and "cross-fertilize each other," so as to "fill in the gaps" and develop "neglected problem-areas";[5] but the slow movement in this direction has been to some extent checkmated by the counter-tendency within each of the social sciences to develop more refined quantitative measurements. Both the centrifugal tendency toward "cross-discipline" research and the centripetal tendency toward greater statistical refinement have been essentially healthy developments. The latter has managed largely to crowd out the former because the time-consuming process of developing statistical and related refinements in the handling of data has been employed by workers in each discipline predominantly on the analysis of the *old problems and concepts at the core of each discipline*. This has inevitably tended to distract their attention both from attempting to restate old problems in a wider context and from posing new problems lying in the terra incognita between the traditional disciplines.

Social science, as a part of culture, is carried in the habits of social scientists. Human beings seem to exhibit considerable resistance to making multiple radical changes at the same time. While subjecting themselves to the strain

[5] The organization of the national Social Science Research Council in 1923, with a constituent membership of the national associations of economists, political scientists, sociologists, psychologists, anthropologists, historians, and statisticians, is an evidence of this trend; as is also the elaborate study of *Recent Social Trends*, prepared under a committee set up by President Hoover, and published in 1931.

and risk of novelty in a given direction, they tend to hold everything else as fixed as possible. The status of the professional economist, political scientist, or other social scientist is deeply committed, by training and by the need for security and advancement, to the official concepts, problems, and theoretical structure of his science. Quantification and refined measurement carry heavy prestige, in part related to the reliance upon them by the authoritative natural sciences. When, therefore, these human beings who are social scientists were confronted simultaneously by the invitations both to experiment in the manifestly safe enterprise of quantifying their familiar problems and to engage in the more hazardous venture of faring forth into unfamiliar problem-areas, it is not surprising that they so predominantly elected the first of the two options. Admirable advances in quantitative techniques have resulted, but at a cost too little reckoned. In the case of social psychology, for instance, the ensuing situation has been penetratingly appraised by a leading social psychologist as follows: "Undoubtedly a large part of our trouble has been an over rapid development of research techniques which can be applied to the surface aspects of almost any social response and are reasonably sure to give a publishable numerical answer to almost any casual question. . . . Woe to that science whose methods are developed in advance of its problems, so that the experimenter can see only those phases of a problem for which a method is already at hand."[6]

Specialization and precise measurement must continue, for without them science cannot grow. But if human institutions form a continuum of sorts, all parts of which are interacting all the time, and if specialization and the re-

[6] Gardner Murphy, "The Research Task of Social Psychology" (Presidential Address before the Society for Psychological Study of Social Issues, 1938), *Journal of Social Psychology*, February 1939.

finements of measurement are not to continue to operate in effect to prompt us to ignore these vital continuities, there is need for an inclusive frame of reference for all the social sciences. Each specialist would then state his problems with reference to the inclusive totality in which they operate. This totality is nothing less than the entire culture.

It is here proposed, therefore, that the centripetal tendency in the several social sciences can be checked, and their much needed integration encouraged, by acceptance of the culture within which a given set of institutions operates as their common frame of reference. The concept "culture," as here used, does not refer to culture in the refined sense of *belles lettres* and sophisticated learning. It is used, rather, in the anthropologist's sense, to refer to all the things that a group of people inhabiting a common geographical area do, the ways they do things and the ways they think and feel about things, their material tools and their values and symbols. Cultures, the world over, reveal the same relatively few identical institutional clusters, though almost infinitely varied in emphasis, detail, and functional linkages. Everywhere men are engaged in getting a living, in living with the other sex and rearing young, in making group decisions and maintaining sanctions and taboos, in performing some sort of religious practices, and in carrying on patterned forms of leisure. It has been relatively easy for the anthropologist, studying the simpler ways of living of a compact tribe, to recognize and to stress the wholeness and interrelatedness of a culture. If we specialized social scientists, engaged in studying our own elaborate institutional world, have lost sight of our "culture" in our preoccupation with "prices," "production," "sovereignty," and "divorce legislation," it is not because our culture is basically different from other cultures, or because it is not a continuum. We have simply defined "the situation" differently from the way the anthropologist does; and by so doing we have allowed ourselves to lose sight of the fact that the specialties we have abstracted can be understood only as parts of the functioning total culture. That we have done so is undoubtedly related to the tradition which attributes a rationality to ourselves and our institutions which we do not vouchsafe to "primitive" man. This makes it easy for us to assume the presence of workmanlike automatic adjustments among the parts of our culture—adjustments which do not in fact exist.

If, then, we social scientists set ourselves the common task of understanding our American culture, nothing in American life escapes us.[7] Here our science and technology are caught and held in focus with our economic and political institutions, our educational and familial systems, our values and desires, our symbols, and our illiteracies. And if such a concept is inclusive horizontally throughout every area of living, it is no less inclusive vertically in the historical sense, since it forces attention to the fact that we live by habits of thought and action generated in and shaped by many different eras. Thus, while our machine technology derives largely from recent inventions, our labor policies straggle unevenly back to the English Poor Law dating from the age of Elizabeth and to the English Combination Acts of 1799; our Constitution dates from the pre-corporate eighteenth century; our sex mores from an era when sex was regarded as sinful; our habits of spanking children from an era that accepted the parental rôle as that of breaking the child's troublesome personality

[7] The emphasis here placed upon *American* culture is, of course, not intended to suggest that any sophisticated culture in our current world can be viewed in isolation. The same arguments for the viewing of a continuum within a single culture also apply to the inter-cultural continuum wherever cultural origins and intercommunication cross and recross national boundaries as they do today.

like a recalcitrant colt; and our religious ideologies from an era that believed in a punishing God and an imminent termination of this wicked world through a "second coming."

Thus, when we state our special research problems in terms of this continuously functioning whole, American culture, we sacrifice none of the sharpness in definition of problems and precision in techniques that science requires, while at the same time we force attention to all of the relevant parts of the total situation. By virtue of the very framework in which we conceive and state a given problem, the problem carries inescapably the whole context of our fumbling institutional past and of our but rudely coordinated present. The tendency of the specialist to abstract his problem from its context can never be wholly overcome. All that can be hoped for is to make it as difficult as possible for the economist to continue to say, "But *I* am interested only in phenomena that can be measured in terms of price"; for the student of government to say, "But *those* things are not my concern, for they belong to the sociologist"; or for the sociologist to protest that he is concerned only with the "social."

But the stating of specific institutional problems in their total cultural context is not enough, if the aim of social science is to understand the phenomena with which it deals. Analysis must also penetrate to a further level, if it is not to leave us with an unfortunate dualism. For description and analysis on the level of institutions and culture tempt us to accept culture as a self-contained universe; culture becomes another reified entity, like prices, social classes, money, society, the State, and similar objects of our current study. Over against this going cultural "system" is set the world of individual persons. The history of science exhibits many such once-assumed contrasting couplets—for instance, the long separation of mind *and* body. The acceptance of such dualisms, once entered upon, tends to encourage exaggeration of the separateness of their parts, as two groups of researchers draw apart in their preoccupation with exploring their respective wings of the artificially contrasted couplet. In the case of "the culture" *and* "the individual," the resulting procedure, typical of such cases, is apparent all about us:[8] Beginning with the useful discrimination between the culture (or the institution) and the person, we then proceed by imperceptible shifts in emphasis to treat culture as something *apart from* the persons who live by it; next, we slide over into the acceptance of culture as *independent of* the persons who live by it; and then we are tempted to move on to acceptance, overt or tacit, of *cultural determinism*, viewing culture as a self-contained force, operating by inner laws of its own to coerce and to shape people to its ends.[9] Now every one of these steps is war-

[8] The discussion at this point follows that developed by Professor Floyd H. Allport in his *Institutional Behavior* (Chapel Hill: University of North Carolina Press, 1933), p. 510.

The emphasis in the present volume upon the behavior of individuals as constituting cultural institutions diverges from the general point of view of Allport in important respects. The latter stresses the independence of individuals, disregarding the special qualities of behavior in group situations, and viewing institutions as derived from the behavior of individuals by a simple additive process. The present writer also does not share the underlying resentment of culture as interfering with "individualism" which Allport exhibits.

[9] Cultural determinism is widely accepted by implication throughout most of the social sciences. The culture is felt to be so massive as it bears down upon the individual that the latter is regarded as having, in fact, few alternatives but to adapt. This attitude, explicit or implicit, which regards man as so helplessly relative to culture, tends to block frank consideration by the social scientist of the human needs for drastic changes in the going cultural "system," and to prompt him to demand of the individual that he be an adjustive gymnast. As Gardner Murphy has pointed out, "In view of the general recognition of the infinite diversity of tensions and miseries traceable to the placing of man in an environment which does not satisfy him, there is surely little sense in continuing to speak as if man could adapt himself equally well to any environment. Here the concept of cultural relativism has done immense damage, indeed as great

ranted to a certain extent: the culture and the persons who live by it are different conceptual foci, and it is important to study culture-as-such and persons-as-such; and culture patently does things to persons in a highly coercive way, the culture of a metropolitan city, for instance, having a momentum *qua* culture to which most persons find it necessary to bend and adapt in order to survive in such a city. But the trouble comes for the social scientist when, in grappling with the monopolizing immediacies of his problem, he forgets that these useful conceptual discriminations are only true to a certain extent, as methodological tools—when he begins to accept them neat, without qualification.

For the most part, social scientists have lost "the person" below their horizon, as they move along busily ploughing their respective research furrows. Most of them just have not quite known what to do with individuals, dwarfed as the latter are by the magnitude and power of current institutions. Many, when their attention is called to individuals, shrug their shoulders and pass them off with a sigh of relief to the psychologist, trusting that the unseen hand of this disciplinary division of labor will eventually fit the jig-saw puzzle of science together. Others lapse into an economic or other determinism that dismisses individuals outright in the face of the inner teleologies of capitalism, social classes, and the like.

Obviously, this is an unsatisfactory situation for the sciences that deal with social institutions and, in their more expansive moods, speak of themselves as "the sciences of human behavior." For cultural institutions can continue to "work" only so long as people abide by and

damage, I believe, as the concept of an unchanging human nature. Both notions are blatantly at variance with the findings of the cultural sciences. If man is to be molded to society, society must also be molded to man." (*Op. cit.* above at footnote 6.)

[23]

support them; and the most patent aspect of many current institutions is that they are not working well, and people seem to differ in the degree to which they are willing to help to make them work. What appears to be needed is a recovery of persons-in-culture by social science.

It is here proposed, therefore, that the social sciences, in addition to viewing the institutions with which they work as parts of a total culture, take the further step of viewing culture as living in and operating as the learned habits and impulses of persons. This, like every useful conceptualization of a gross situation, can be overdone. It should not blind us to the facts that the culture and individuals interact; that culture does do things to people at the same time that people are doing things to culture; that a culture has at any given moment a coercive momentum that may usefully, for certain purposes of analysis, be regarded as "its own." Analysis must go forward on many levels. There is a rough, shorthand utility in lumping together the impacts of many specific individuals upon my decision to stop wearing an old suit to my office and to buy a new one, or upon my political views, or even upon such subtle things as my desiring to marry a pretty wife with money, and in saying that "the culture prompts me to do these things." Likewise, there is obvious utility in statistical prediction, on the basis of past experience, as to what masses of people will do, even though we do not know what individual persons will do; and the influence of inventions and other material aspects of our cultural environment may usefully be analyzed in many ways without forever stopping to stress the fact that these material tools are operative only because enough people have learned a meaning and use for them to keep them in operation. It is important to continue to study *the* price system, *the* securities market, *the* automotive industry, *the* family, *the* law, *the* tariff, *the* class structure, *the* city, *the* Federal administrative ma-

[24]

chinery, economic determinism, sequences in change in the cultural structure, and so on; for these things are necessary parts of our analysis. But, in so doing, the ultimate relation between persons and the culture must not be forgotten. The emphasis upon persons as the active carriers, perpetuators, and movers of culture performs for us the indispensable service of resolving the dualism of "culture *and* the person," and of placing the primary emphasis where it basically belongs, upon people. Cultural institutions occupy a derivative, though important and active, rôle as a set of learned instrumental ways of behaving with which human beings seek to realize their needs.

When one elects to state a research problem at this derivative, or institutional, level, one is working with a definition of the situation that will forever yield only crude or limited understandings until the analysis is *also* driven down to the level of the behavior of individuals. Understanding of institutions and social problems must be based upon analysis of what these institutions and problems *mean* to specific, differently situated people, how they look and feel to these different people, and how they are used. If, for instance, the same job means to one man security and to another a springboard to power, we are dealing with two different things under one label when we garble them together as a single institutional phenomenon.

The relatively small volume of current research on the level of the rich and varied individual behavior with reference to a given institution is directly related to the arduousness of such investigations. Careful interviewing involves enormous expenditures of time, and subjects have an annoying habit of proving intractable as one seeks patiently to delve into their personal behavior. It is far simpler and more convenient to deal with their behavior at several removes and with their differences assumed to "cancel each other out"—in the form of Census data, Treasury figures, election data, and so on. As Alfred Marshall remarks in connection with his discussion of statistics on consumption:[10] "It may be noted that the method of le Play's monumental *Les Ouvriers Européens* is the *intensive* study of all the details of the domestic life of a few carefully chosen families. To work it well requires a rare combination of judgment in selecting cases, and of insight and sympathy in interpreting them. At its best, it is the best of all: but in ordinary hands it is likely to suggest more untrustworthy general conclusions than those obtained by the *extensive* method of collecting more rapidly very numerous observations, reducing them as far as possible to statistical form, and obtaining broad averages in which inaccuracies and idiosyncrasies may be trusted to counteract one another to some extent."

The result of this choice of the simpler way is that whole sciences, e.g., economics, are built up virtually without acute knowledge of the dynamics of individual behavior around the institutions they profess to analyze. So heavy is the hand of custom in such matters that not only does each oncoming wave of young scientists follow the official pattern set by their elders, but some sciences tend to build up a defensive disparagement of the utility of refined data-gathering and analysis at the individual level. "Total bank clearings" sounds so much more authoritative than data on 250 individual cases that the tendency is to say, "What does a little sample study like that prove?"

It is not intended in the preceding discussion to disparage statistical treatment of mass phenomena in favor of studies of the behavior of individuals. Quite contrary, the emphasis is upon the indispensability of both procedures. One may begin with either approach and work

[10] *Principles of Economics* (London: Macmillan, 8th ed., 1920), p. 116.

into the other. Thus, large statistical studies disclose deviant groups, one can then single out crucial groups, and, by carrying the analysis to individual cases, discover the precise character of deviations and how they came to be. The point here made is that analysis is not usually carried to this further stage. The combination of the institutional and individual approaches may be seen in action in the fields of criminology and delinquency (see the work of the Gluecks and of Clifford Shaw); in the study of suicide; in studies of marital adjustment, child adjustment in home and school, and of family income and expenditure; and also in commercial market research.

Four distinct advantages may be gained from the proposed shift of emphasis from culture and institutions as basically impersonal "things," like specimens on a dissecting table, to emphasis upon them as existing and changing ✳ as the behavior of individuals:

(1) Maximum encouragement is given to recognition of explicit linkages among the data of all the social sciences. When "economic man," "political man," and "social man" are accepted as one and the same person, truly heroic abstraction is necessary if one is to view economic behavior apart from social behavior, political behavior apart from economic behavior, and so on. Motivation may not then be viewed as single and consistent, as economics tends to view it,[11] and such objects of study as citizenship, saving, conservatism, demand, occupation, marital satisfaction, social status, social classes, health, law observance, housing, and leisure break their dykes and flow together in the living persons whose behavior forms our institutions. It is not extravagant to say that scarcely any area of institutional analysis can fail to take on new meanings when

[11] Cf. below in this chapter at footnote 18.

set thus in the close context of the totality of individuals' living.

(2) When we view culture and institutions as the behavior of individuals, we are able to assign a normal place to deviations from "the" assumed normal way of doing a given thing in the culture. A chronic embarrassment of social science theory is the explanation of "exceptions to the general rule."[12] Some of these exceptions are so egregious as to defy explaining away by such qualifying phrases as "by and large," "in the main," and "other things being equal." The deviations refuse to "cancel each other out." In some cases these departures from the assumed norms are so striking that they have become standard "problems" with a semi-independent status as the object of research. As a result, social science is full of dichotomies composed of the norm and a prominent deviation from it: "competition *and* monopoly," "voting *and* non-voting," "law observance *and* crime," "marriage *and* divorce," or "*and* prostitution," "employment *and* unemployment," "free *and* administered prices," and so on. Even this overt recognition of departures from the norm belies the situation, for this Aristotelian emphasis upon classes and paired opposites hides the fact that one is dealing not with two contrasted poles but with a distribution of frequencies ranging from one extreme to the other.[13]

[12] Thus Alfred Marshall devotes a large share of his *Principles of Economics* to noting qualifying exceptions to the general laws of economics at points where the assumed general principle of "free competition" does not in fact operate.

[13] This point of view is succinctly set forth in the opening chapter on "Aristotelian and Galileian Modes of Thought" in Kurt Lewin's *A Dynamic Theory of Personality* (New York: McGraw-Hill, 1935). Lewin speaks of "the loss in importance [in modern physics] of logical dichotomies and conceptual antitheses. Their places are taken by more and more fluid transitions, by gradations which deprive the dichotomies of their antithetical character and represent in logical form a transition stage between the class concept and the series concept." (p. 10.) "What is now important to the investigation of dynamics is not to abstract from the situation. . . . Instead of a reference to the abstract average of as

The stubborn, unavoidable fact that confronts social science at every point is the presence, in every institutional trait that it seeks to analyze, of a subtly graded, unevenly distributed, and continually changing array of behavior. Individuals vary in their capacities and in their definitions of situations, and the pressures upon them to act in given ways or to depart from these ways of acting vary from moment to moment. The Securities and Exchange Commission is not so much concerned with honest and dishonest brokers as it is with an infinite variety of specific practices employed in some degree at one time or another by most brokers, which practices blur imperceptibly from "performing a highly useful social function" at the one extreme into "gross exploitation of the public" at the other. New and more realistic possibilities of analysis will follow upon the frank recognition that each institution represents a distribution of individual conformities and dissents, and that the whole array of behavior must be studied if we are to understand what the institution is.

Edward Sapir of Yale University has stated acutely this necessity for driving cultural analysis down to the level of — variant groups and individual differences:[14]

"It is no exaggeration to say that cultural analysis as ordinarily made is not a study of behavior at all. . . . Culture, as it is ordinarily constructed by the anthropologist, is a more or less mechanical sum of the more striking and picturesque generalized patterns of behavior. . . . [As such, these culture constructs] are not, and cannot be, the truly objective entities they claim to be. No matter how accurate their individual itemization, their integrations into suggested structures are uniformly fallacious and

many historically given cases as possible, there is reference to the full concreteness of the particular situations." (p. 31.)

[14] "The Emergence of the Concept of Personality in A Study of Cultures," *Journal of Social Psychology*, August 1934.

unreal. . . . If we make the test of imputing the contents of an ethnological monograph to a known individual in the community which it describes, we would inevitably be led to discover that, while every single statement in it may, in the favorable case, be recognized as holding true in some sense, the complex of patterns as described cannot, without considerable absurdity, be interpreted as a significant configuration of experience, both actual and potential, in the life of the person appealed to. Cultures, as ordinarily dealt with, are merely abstracted configurations of idea and action patterns, which have endlessly different meanings for the various individuals in the group. . . .

"The complete, impersonalized 'culture' of the anthropologist can really be little more than an assembly or mass of loosely overlapping idea and action systems which, through verbal habit, can be made to assume the appearance of a closed system of behavior. What tends to be forgotten is that the functioning of such a system, if it can be said to have any ascertainable function at all, is due to the specific functionings and interplays of the idea and action systems which have actually grown up in the minds of given individuals."

Professor Sapir concludes by suggesting the need for the close genetic study of the learning of a culture by individuals. "I venture to predict," he says, "that the concept of culture which will then emerge, fragmentary and confused as it will undoubtedly be, will turn out to have a tougher, more vital, importance for social thinking than the tidy tables of contents attached to this or that group which we have been in the habit of calling 'cultures.' "

Analysis of institutional phenomena which seeks to proceed in disregard of the patent fact of wide individual differences is inevitably superficial and distorted. The assumption that differences "cancel each other out" is unwarranted because these differences are not identical

quanta; they are qualitatively different; they carry therefore different weights, and they are thrown into the scales
in different combinations and at different moments. Look
at the range of these differences: In health we run the
whole gamut, and what we do and the way we think
is colored by how we feel when we get up in the morning
and at each succeeding moment during the day. The
energy of some of us is the despair of others. Some of us
are confident, while others swing uneasily to the tides of
anxiety and defensiveness. Some of us were born into a
favored race or class, while others are forced to live uphill
against set brakes because we belong to a minority group.
Some of us have attractive, forceful personalities, phy-
siques, and chins, while others must try "to win friends
and influence people" with less auspicious endowments.
For some of us "the future" runs reliably ahead, and for
others it is no longer than tomorrow, or the end of the
month. Then, too, as individuals we differ importantly
in our capacity to learn; and we learn seemingly common
things in a personal context that orients the thing learned,
if and to the extent that it is learned, in different ways.
We were all born little animals with unique endowments.
We have been "house-broke" in varying ways—gently or
roughly, consistently or erratically—by people bigger and
stronger than ourselves and able to exercise authority over
us. For convenience, we say we have "grown up," "become
socialized," "been acculturated." What we mean is that we
have learned, under the sharp sting of necessity, how to
"get by" and get what we want and avoid trouble in
terms of the habit systems of our coercive elders, who in
turn had picked up their habits from the retrospective
habits of their elders. What a social scientist deals with,
therefore, is not a unit institution carried evenly by all
persons, similarly learned in and responding to the institution in question. The problems that social science

wrestles with derive to an important extent from the fact that different individuals and masses of individuals react differently to supposedly common institutions.

The viewing of culture as the behavior of individuals is important because it helps to counteract the over-easy acceptance of the officially promulgated norms (legal and "right" ways of doing things) or of assumed central tendencies (usual or most frequent ways of doing things) as the operating reality of an institution. It helps to keep prominently in focus all types of varying behavior around the problem in question; it also breaks down the false rigidities between "the" normal and all deviants by substituting a continuum, all parts of which are normal behavior to the particular persons involved.[15]

(3) A third advantage, directly related to the preceding, is that this viewing of culture in terms of the behavior of individuals provides the basis for a more realistic and coherent theoretical structure for the social sciences. As already noted, one of the weaknesses of current social science inheres in the fact that much of its theoretical structure can be assumed to apply only "by and large," "other things being equal," and "under given [artificially simplified] conditions."

The situation in economics may be taken as a case in point. Twenty-five years ago Wesley Mitchell pointed out the need for a rapprochement between economics and the study of individual behavior to enable economic theory to regain a sense of reality. Professor Mitchell's paper, published in the *Quarterly Journal of Economics* in the year the World War began, was an appraisal of books by Veb-

[15] The significance of an investigation like Frederic M. Thrasher's *The Gang; A Study of 1,313 Gangs in Chicago* (Chicago: University of Chicago Press, 1927) lies in the fact that it shows how normal to the boy who lives it, under the circumstances in which he is forced to live, is this cultural form which is officially regarded as "abnormal" and "reprehensible."

len, Thorndike, Graham Wallas, and others, under the title, *Human Behavior and Economics: A Survey of Recent Literature.* It began as follows:

"A slight but significant change seems to be taking place in the attitude of economic theorists toward psychology. Most of the older writers made no overt reference to psychology, but tacitly imputed to the men whose behavior they were analyzing certain traits consistent with common sense and convenient as a basis for theorizing. By recent writers, on the contrary, non-intercourse with psychology, long practised in silence, is explicitly proclaimed to be the proper policy.

"This definite pronouncement has arisen from a somewhat tardy recognition that hedonism is unsound psychology, and that the economics of both Ricardo and Jevons originally rested on hedonistic preconceptions. Since hedonism is unsound, either we must admit that both the classical and the marginal analysis is invalid, or we must argue that the hedonistic preconceptions can be given up without compromising the validity of the analysis. The latter horn of the dilemma is chosen. Then we must choose again between providing a sounder psychological basis for our analysis, and holding that its psychological basis does not concern the economist. Again, the latter course is generally preferred. Thus, economic theory is said to rest upon the simple facts of preference or choice, and the psychological explanation of these preferences or choices is said to be a matter of indifference to our science. . . .

"Now, if economic theory really has no concern with psychology, perhaps a survey of recent literature upon human nature is out of place in this *Journal.* But that is not a necessary conclusion. For when economic theory has been purified so far that human nature has no place in it, economists become interested perforce in much that lies

[handwritten marginal note: the doctrine that pleasure or happiness is the highest good.]

outside their theoretical field. Further, it is possible that the effort to keep the study of human nature out of economic theory may break down. The admitted deficiencies of hedonism may stimulate future economists, not to disavow all psychological analysis, but to look for sound psychological analysis. It may even be that economists will find themselves not only borrowing from but also contributing to psychology. For if that science is ever to give a competent account of human behavior it seems necessary that economists should do a part of the work. . . .

". . . Nothing which we are doing ourselves along traditional lines concerns us more than these many-sided investigations of human behavior."

And Professor Mitchell closes his paper with the following paragraph:

"It was because hedonism offered a theory of how men act that it exercised so potent an influence upon economics. It is because they are developing a sounder type of functional psychology that we may hope both to profit by and to share in the work of contemporary psychologists. But in embracing this opportunity economics will assume a new character. It will cease to be a system of pecuniary logic, a mechanical study of static equilibria under non-existent conditions, and become a science of human behavior."

It is pertinent to note that, save for the appearance of a few books bearing such titles as *The Behavior of Prices* and *The Behavior of Money*—which use of "behavior" misses the point by applying the new word to the old institution—Professor Mitchell's admonition to his science has not been followed up.[16] So grandly constructed and

---

[16] Z. C. Dickinson's *Economic Motives: A Study in the Psychological Foundations of Economic Theory, with Some Reference to Other Social Sciences* (Cambridge: Harvard University Press, 1922) should be mentioned as an exception, though it unfortunately leaned heavily on the then current instinct theory. Thorstein Veblen, whose *The Instinct of Workmanship* was one of the books reviewed in

neatly joined is the neo-classical theoretical structure
handed on by Alfred Marshall that it has resisted modern-
ization by reason of its sheer perfection of design. Few
have dared to pull out the hedonistic stones in its foundation for fear of impairing its imposing superstructure.

To be sure, it is rather the fashion among empirical
workers nowadays to play down theory, to deny that their
work operates within any given theoretical system, or
even to urge that the old theories are inapplicable and that
the basis for a new theoretical structure is being laid down,
brick by brick, by empirical research. Many contemporary
economists, for instance, would deny that they are being
guided by the Marshallian system in their research. But
the grip of a reigning theoretical system upon the questions
which even the empiricist elects to set himself is not so
easily loosened. Why do these current researchers operate
so largely within the closed system of orthodox problems:
collecting data on prices, making indexes of manufacturing
output, analyzing foreign exchange, bank clearings, and
dollar totals of retail sales? Because these things are what
economics is.

But why is economics confined to such things? Why is
"labor problems" as a research field so heavily concerned
with labor legislation and with statistics of wage rates, of
wage differentials, and of unemployment, and so little
concerned with, e.g., analysis of labor actually on the job
and at home, of labor's motivations and frustrations,[17] and

Professor Mitchell's article, continued to stress economic behavior refreshingly
in his subsequent books, as he had in those that had preceded.

[17] R. B. Hershey, of the Wharton School of the University of Pennsylvania,
made an interesting try at this type of analysis in his *Workers' Emotions in Shop
and Home* (Philadelphia: University of Pennsylvania Press, 1932), as did Elton
Mayo, of the Harvard School of Business Administration, in his studies at the
Western Electric Company's Hawthorne (Chicago) plant. Carleton H. Parker
was also working along this line before his death. Whiting Williams's books,
beginning with *What's on the Worker's Mind*, represent impressionistic approaches to the same type of problem.

of the kinds of fresh operational theory that will include this living stuff of labor? Current price theory is derived from mass statistics and averages, without detailed step-by-step analysis of how executives in individual plants set their prices in specific cases. Generalizations about production, likewise following the path of mass statistics, fail to include the jungle of pertinent processes by which such factors in a specific plant as the durability, productivity, and automaticity of its machines and their flexibility in use are transformed into the "prices" with which the economist works. Theories concerning the investment market are derived with little or no detailed knowledge of how, and why, and equipped with what information, actual persons go into and out of the market; and we generalize freely about "the drying up of the capital investment market" because of the "withholding of capital" from investment at the present time, with little explicit knowledge as to who is withholding capital from what specific industries, and under what precise circumstances. Theories regarding capital accumulation are built with small knowledge of how and precisely why people save, and of the acute present confusion within many homes as to whether it is worthwhile to try to save at all. Likewise, the body of theory dealing with the distribution of goods depends largely upon such mass data as dollar-volume of production and of retail sales of different commodities, with little knowledge of the anxious choices involved in private consumption. All through the nineteenth century economic theory contented itself with viewing money simply as a neutral medium of exchange which does not affect the operation of the economy. Economists today are seeking to discover and to build into their theory the more active rôle that money is manifestly made to play in our economy; but they still work within their untenable basic assumption, belied by the facts of human behavior, that money measures of value afford an adequate basis for the understanding of economic behavior.[18]

All such procedures, lacking the vital interrupting thrust of close contact with individual behavior around the institution in question, tend to make for theoretical inbreeding. Concepts defined in ways essential to the going theoretical structure tend to be elaborated, rather than redefined. Such concepts are accepted as *facts*, and consideration of undercutting hypotheses is thereby discouraged. Thus "competition," for instance, as a subject of theoretical discussion, tends to be accepted unquestioningly as a thing fixed by the natural order; the problem for theoretical discussion then becomes the dualism of "competition *and* monopoly," and social science can turn its back on the relevant problem of the human costs in daily living of the competitive operation of our economy.

Failure to follow Professor Mitchell's thoroughly sound proposal of twenty-five years ago is in itself but an illustration of the fact that culture *is* the patterned habits of behavior of individuals, who in their teaching and research *are* current social science theory in action.

(4) A fourth advantage in resolution of the culture-person dualism by recognizing that the culture is the habits of individuals inheres in the fact that the realism involved in thinking about problems on the level at which they

[18] This cornerstone upon which economic theory is reared is reflected in Alfred Marshall's statement that "the claims of economics to be a science" rest upon the fact that it deals with "man's conduct under the influence of motives that are measurable by a money price." "The steadiest motive to ordinary business work is the desire for the pay which is the material reward of work. . . . The motive is supplied by a definite amount of money: and it is this definite and exact money measurement of the steadiest motives in business life which has enabled economics far to outrun every other branch of the study of man." "Being concerned chiefly with those aspects of life in which the action of motive is so regular that it can be predicted, and the estimate of the motor-forces can be verified by results, [economists] have established their work on a scientific basis." (*Op. cit.*, Chap. II.)

receive their dynamic push provides a sounder basis for analysis of cultural change, and therefore for prediction and control. "Social change" (cultural change) is a major complicating factor in our culture by reason of its increased prevalence, rapidity, and complexity, as well as the difficulties caused by the accompanying stubborn lags. The manifest need for planning and control grows with the pace and out-of-handness of the cultural changes all about us. Social scientists are busy studying "trends," "tendencies," "change." We may say that we are studying "how our culture works," or, more specifically, "the movement of prices," "trends in unemployment," "how demand changes," or "tendencies in Supreme Court decisions." We write books on *Recent Social Trends*, and *Economic Tendencies in the United States*. But with all our industry and technical refinements, we manage to be vastly more accurate in our descriptions of what *has* happened than in our predictions as to what *will* happen. This is not surprising, since effective prediction is difficult at best; but our relative ineptitude is caused to no small degree by the fact that we are so largely attempting to predict and control on the basis of only part of the necessary data, that derivative part obtained from analysis at the institutional level.

We watch culture change and say that "it changes." But culture does not "work," "move," "change," but is worked, is moved, is changed. It is *people* who do things, and when their habits and impulses cease to carry an institutional folkway, that bit of the culture disappears. "When one system of habits and mores is offered by one group to another, and the second refuses to adopt the new ones, there is a temptation to think in terms of a disembodied entity, a cultural pattern, which is incapable of 'assimilating' the new features. . . . The important thing is that it is *the Indians* that resist, and not their 'cultural pattern.' "[19] The Patent Office has registered thousands of changes that never "went" because people did not "take them up" and make them "go"; and the suppression of patents by corporations like the Bell Telephone Company shows the relative helplessness of useful patents ready to go when strategically placed people elect to suppress them.[20]

The culture does not enamel its fingernails, or vote, or believe in capitalism, but people do, and some do and some do not. When I give away a still warm and comfortable overcoat because it is beginning to look worn, I *feel* myself to be responding to people—my wife, my business associates, people at the club—and what they will think of me, and only incidentally and remotely, if at all, am I motivated by a non-personalized "cultural standard." When I stop my car at a red traffic light, it is an abstraction to say that I am "obeying the law"; what I *feel* in the situation is that *people* will do inconvenient things to me if I do not stop. Or to state this point from the viewpoint of comparative cultures: Objects and experiences that trip the trigger that releases a long line of associated actions in one habituated to a given culture may either be without meaning or have a different meaning to persons from another culture. A man in a blue uniform at a traffic intersection blowing a whistle when a light changes from green to red means to me as I drive toward him, "Stop my car—or else he

[19] G. and L. B. Murphy, *Experimental Social Psychology* (New York: Harper, 1931), p. 14.

[20] See Bernhard J. Stern's chapter on "Resistances to the Adoption of Technological Innovations" in *Technological Trends and National Policy*, a report by the National Resources Committee (Washington: Government Printing Office, 1937). Also, the same author's report on "Restraints upon the Utilization of Invention," prepared for the Committee on Freedom of Inquiry of the Social Science Research Council, and published in the *Annals of the American Academy of Political and Social Science* for November 1938.

will give me a ticket and I will have to lose time from my work and go to court and have to pay a fine and get on the court records as a traffic violator." But to an Eskimo he would mean none of these things. Likewise, a bank building with Corinthian columns would mean to an Eskimo only an extra-gorgeous shelter from wind and snow, while a calf-bound law book costing us fifteen dollars might mean to him a chunk of fuel, a nice chopping block on which to slice up fish, or perhaps an object to hurl at an enemy. Abstracted from the persons who live them, cultural institutions become dimmed, and often distorted, shadows on the wall.

From this point of view, such processes as motivation and learning within the individual become central to the analysis of cultural change. Here one sees the stark manipulative rightness of much modern advertising couched in terms of the needs of the individual personality;[21] also, the hopeless ineptitude of President Hoover's exhortation of people caught in the *sauve qui peut* of a great depression to "loosen your private purse-strings" so that "we may spend our way out of the depression." Here, too, one sees the common basis for the slowness of desired change that frustrates the reformer, and for the business-

[21] Characteristic of these are the halitosis advertisement headed "She couldn't bring herself to tell him"; the Camay soap advertisement headed "What men look for in the girls they marry"; the Lenthéric perfume advertisement picturing the break-up of a fashionable party, over the text, "Do they ask for your telephone number or say 'Pleased to have met you'? No one has time to get acquainted any more. People are introduced in mumbles, meet in snatches and disappear. First impressions must be quick and devastating. A dash of *Lotus d'Or* might be all that is needed for a rush and may save your hostess the trouble of asking her brother to take you home." Or the Steinway piano advertisement, headed "A song for parents," showing a winsome boy of ten learning to play on a Steinway, and telling parents: "These parents of modern children, their lot is not easy. . . . But the father who has in common with his son one great melody, one sweet, surpassing song, has not been left entirely behind."

man's concern over such things as the "increasing fickleness of consumer whim."

And here, also, one finds a resolution of the current Marx *vs*. Freud antinomy: For capitalism becomes more than an impersonal It grinding out the destiny inherent in Its nature; while the individual's inner conflicts are seen to be dependent upon a wider range of concrete factors in a specific cultural situation than Freud envisaged. Prediction and control in the social sciences built either around impersonal forces or around individual attributes regarded as independent of culture tend to prove in time unrealistic. Only as the too-inner drama of Freudianism – and the too-externalized drama of Marxism can meet and reenforce each other on the common ground of the behavior of persons-in-culture can either make its greatest contribution to a workable theory of cultural change. We lose no whit of the driving reality of economic determinism when we talk relatively less about what "capitalism does" and more about what men do under coercive pressures of capitalistic habits of thought, sentiment, and action. The nature of the apparently tightening class lines in the United States can be effectively grasped only as we seek to define them in terms of the complex web of felt loyalties and revulsions, expectations and thwarted hopes, limited freedoms and large coercions of individuals. Likewise, the particular forms of neurosis with which Freud is concerned can be fully understood only if they are seen as the outcome of a particular form of family life within a particular type and stage of economic development. One of the central problems of social science today concerns the discovery of where and to what extent the economic pressures analyzed by Marx are controlling, and where and to what extent the individual motivations studied by Freud operate.

The stress placed upon motivation and the learning process in the preceding paragraphs suggests the need for the working social scientist to grasp more clearly the intrinsic relationship between cultural processes (cultural change, diffusion, cultural lag, class stratification, social mobility, and similar things) and the processes of behavior within the individual. If it is useful to view culture as the behavior of the people who live it, it is likewise useful to view basic cultural processes as elaborations of basic processes within these persons. In this way cultural processes cease to occupy their present dubious position as Mohammed's coffins suspended miraculously between earth and sky. Three important processes deserve attention in the behavior of individuals: *rhythm*, *growth*, and *motivation*. These persistent tendencies in human behavior need to be kept constantly in view in the course of analysis of institutions, for they tend to write themselves large into the culture.

Rhythm on the biological level is the periodicity of energy storage and release; and on the level of the personality in culture it exhibits the further element of tension sustention prior to release. It involves such things as waking and sleeping, hunger and satiety, concentration and diffusion, work and play, living along and bursting forth in spurts of spontaneity. Each human organism has its own unique capacity for energy output and fatigue, and, around this, develops a rhythm of living which it tends to maintain as "feeling right to me," unless interfered with and coerced by an overriding counter-motivation.[22]

Around the central tendencies of these personal rhythms of living—running relatively free, or coerced by such intrusive counter-motivations as social approval, money-

[22] For a discussion of tensional problems within the person, see Lawrence K. Frank's "The Management of Tensions," *American Journal of Sociology*, March 1928.

making under the business-directed efficiency engineer's criteria, or the quest for power in a world of individualistic striving—the cultural rhythms tend to become patterned. These rhythms of living—both those that are altogether biological and those that are heavily institutionalized, as in the case of "three meals a day" or "one day of rest in seven"—swing within each of us through their urgent cycles of mounting tension in quest of release. We become like the mollusc, whose habits of burrowing in the sand and reappearing are conditioned by the movements of the ocean tide, and who, when removed from the beach to the laboratory, continues for several days in the same rhythm without the tide.

Many of the most acute problems in our culture derive from conflicts among rhythms, where the rhythms established in one institutional area of behavior coerce those in other areas. Thus the rhythms of family life, often including even sexual relations, tend in our urban environment to be constrained and interrupted by the monopolizing time and energy demands of work. While most of one's personal rhythms are highly adaptable, there tend to be limits of tolerance beyond which rhythms may not be interrupted without undue strain. Institutionalized coercion of inner rhythm, in many cases up to the brittle edge of human tolerance, has inevitable repercussions upon the private versions of the culture which individuals are continually building back into the total culture.[23]

[23] Our "efficient" rhythms of work within our type of economy involve extreme coercions of the spontaneous rhythms of the individual. The development and pervasive spread of money, as an impersonal medium of exchange by which work is measured, has dislocated work from "making things" to "making money." Riding the tide of this super-motivation of money-making, the machine process entered our culture and, under *laissez-faire*, was seized upon and utilized by the stronger money-makers primarily for their own ends. As Spengler has pointed out, money-making "subjects the exchange of goods to its own evolution. It values things, no longer as between each other, but with reference to

With the ground-swell of rhythm in the individual, the process of growth goes forward. This last involves processes of differentiation and integration (i.e., "finding oneself") and learning.

"Differentiation" (or individuation) is the process of substituting more precise adaptive behavior in place of gross or indecisive behavior. It goes hand in hand with the development of appropriate inhibitions. To the extent that the individual fixates on gross adaptations or develops erratic or imprecise inhibitions, his private version of the culture will be marked by crudeness and confusion. He may, for instance, adopt a decisive manner as a "front" for disposing of complicated matters with seeming assurance, or confuse means with ends, or flatten out the niceties of situations under the slogans of a Babbitt—and in each such case he contributes his quota to the imprecision of the culture. And the culture will accordingly do such things as treating corporations legally as individuals, branding divorce as a sin, passing laws to prevent crime, and confusing money-making with welfare.

itself." (*The Decline of the West* [New York: Knopf, 1928], Vol. II, p. 98.) The spontaneous rhythms of human beings are coerced more and more straitly to this end of private money-making. Extreme specialization and repetition are inimical to the natural rhythms of people of normal intelligence. The hours of the handicraft worker were long, but they allowed change of posture and the periodic substitution of large-muscle activity for small-muscle concentration; and the worker could interrupt the whole process to walk into his garden and smoke a pipe. (Cf. J. L. and Barbara Hammond, *The Skilled Labourer, 1760-1832* [London: Longmans, 1920], pp. 3-7.) The capacity of human beings to adapt their rhythms is great, but not so great as to make the 480 minutes of unremitting daily super-efficiency of the paint-sprayer, the tack-spitting upholsterer, or other similarly specialized, high-speed workers on an automobile assembly line "feel right."

Samuel Butler made the natives of Erewhon break up machines as hostile to human living. That such a procedure should appeal even to a sardonic Utopian, in view of the manifest utilities of the machine process, is a result of the fact that our culture has allowed money-making and its instrument, the machine, to impose progressively pathological rhythms upon the natural rhythms of human living.

"Integration" is that aspect of the growth process whereby the individual brings his various ways of behaving in different situations (i.e., his different selves) into a continuum of meaning relatively free from contradictions and disjunctions. Here two aspects of integration are important for the student of culture: the *degree* of integration and the *level* of integration. The individual who agrees to let certain of his selves disagree—e.g., his hard-boiled labor policy as an employer and his solicitous attitude toward his own children—is building a lack of integration into the culture.[24] As regards the level of integration, the individual who, through ignorance or intent, narrows his world to include but a part of its realities adds to the confusion of the culture. Gordon Allport[25] describes such a narrowed world of the country grandmother, remote from the world of abstract ideas and issues and possessed of only a few dominant habits and traits:

"She worries neither about the dictates of fashion nor the collapse of Capitalism; it is less important to her that the universe is wearing down than that her kitchen needs refurbishing. A few simple attitudes and rules of life serve her. She performs her daily duties, trusts in God, and drinks tea of herbs that she has gathered. Compared with an educated citizen of the world, buffeted about by discordant doctrines, torn by conflicts, personal and cosmic, her personality is not many-sided and rich, though in all probability it is better integrated."

[24] As will be pointed out in Chapter III, this dissociation of different selves within the individual—notably his business self from his personal or "real" self at home, at church, and so on—is becoming increasingly prevalent in our culture. We are by way of institutionalizing as normal this living as a split personality. The loss of independence by the familial, recreational, and religious sectors of living, as well as the widespread confusion of money-making as means with money-making as end, reflect the compulsive need of the individual to restore the feeling of integration by dragging the rest of living into line with the dominant money-making values.

[25] *Op. cit.*, p. 143.

Such grossly selective personal integrations, which ignore or subsume under slogans large areas of current reality, build the kind of culture in which common meanings and purposes are clumsy and ill-defined and the integration of the whole slight and unreliable. They also contribute an unwarranted rigidity to the fragments of reality in terms of which they are integrated; for both grandmother's belief in God and the Liberty Leaguer's blunt faith in property rights and the Constitution must be overstressed because so much of the structure of living in these individuals depends upon them.[26]

A final aspect of the growth process within the individual—the learning process—is crucial, as already pointed out, for the understanding of the dynamics of cultural change. When culture changes—a new law is passed, a custom falls into disuse, women wear shorts, anti-Semitism becomes a problem, or automatic machinery replaces human labor—it is the behavior of people that provides the dynamics of change. Neither a "culture" nor a "society" learns, but individual people do. A culture like ours, in which men assume basic equality in individual capacity to learn its complexities and in which the content and degree of learning of such a large proportion of the things one needs to learn are left so casually to the accidents of individual trial and error, is reckless to the point of being suicidal.

At birth there is the physical organism with a unique physical, temperamental, and learning potential, and with certain crude drives. Around it are other organisms—

[26] Under pressure of adverse circumstances, an individual may be forced off the level of integration he has been seeking to maintain and he may retreat, or regress, in some disorder to a cruder level. We are witnessing this today in the midst of the prolonged insecurity of the depression. It manifests itself in such things as renewed emphasis upon the literal finality of the Constitution, in anti-Semitism, and in the flight from the manifest need for more centralization and planning back to the more primitive level of reliance upon individual enterprise.

bigger, older, more authoritative—doing certain things, calling them "right," "legal," "necessary," "practical," and meting out disapproval or punishment to those who follow other ways of doing things. As the individual organism grows, it is guided into, stumbles on, and, as the personality develops, it increasingly selects out an array of tastes, interests, desires, and aversions relevant to its own emerging wants. Individual preferences—and so eventually the emphases of the culture—develop by a process of fixation: drives become fixated upon all manner of objects, persons, motives, values, and so canalized in directions that release or help sustain tensions and further satisfactions. This process involves not simply the implementing of biological needs by their association with biologically adequate stimuli, but also the substitution of biologically irrelevant stimuli of every conceivable sort. The selective processes of differentiation and integration ✳ tend to hook up together those things which have survival value to the individual personality as aids in getting ahead toward the goal or goals with regard to which that personality seeks satisfaction.

The process of learning in our culture is thus a mélange of somewhat fortuitous fixation and chance conditioning, erratically guided by institutional pressures, by sympathy, by the projection of others' hopes upon us and of ours upon them, and by suggestion of those we fear or love.[27]

Accompanying rhythm and growth, the motivations of — individuals are also built back into the culture. These are the directional orientations of living. Human life is lived *toward* things. The individual organism encounters experiences that, either directly and intrinsically, or indirectly by association in a chain of real or imputed in-

[27] For a detailed analysis of "The Learning Process in Social Situations" see Murphy, Murphy, and Newcomb, *Experimental Social Psychology* (New York: Harper, 1937), Chap. IV.

strumentalisms, release inner tension in a way that leaves the organism canalized to crave "more-of-this-thing-that-makes-me-feel-more-satisfied" as regards a given tension. These directional thrusts toward satisfaction are the things we call "motives." One's "personality" is the orientation to satisfactions and the methods of achieving them that one is thus continually working out in the environment. At any given moment each of us is a network of active and latent motives. A latent motive becomes active when, through external or internal stimulus, the individual finds himself on a tensional "hot spot"; it consists in a directional orientation to getting off that spot by a line of action associated with satisfaction in his experience.

Out of such unique networks of motives, the culture constantly acquires the standard sanctioned and tabooed directional orientations it exhibits. Thus we get the patterned tendencies in our own culture toward growing rich, belonging to the right clubs, living in the right neighborhood, knowing the right people, being regarded as a person with a nice sense of humor, winning one's letter in football, being the most popular girl at a dance, and so on through the infinite number of big and little "right" and "wrong" ways of behaving that give dynamic patterning to our culture.

And just as conflicts among rhythms generate problems, so do conflicts among motivations—toward being chaste *or* a "great lover," getting rich *or* taking time to be a good parent, being popular *or* being oneself, toward spending and living *or* saving and playing safe. Since each individual contrives his private version of the culture out of the interaction of his private urgencies with the roughly patterned behavior about him, it is of great importance for him and ultimately for the culture whether the motivations of those about him are largely similar or in conflict, whether they offer few or many degrees of option, whether they foster anxiety or confidence and repose, whether they encourage hospitality or resistance to adaptive change in ways of doing things.

In attempting, therefore, to find the "pattern" of American culture, one can never afford to lose sight of the fact that the pattern is what it is because of the rhythms, motivations, and processes of growth and learning of the dynamic individual creators and carriers of culture, struggling fiercely to feel "at home" with themselves and others in their world. These basic processes within individuals are inescapably the stuff out of which the culture is built. If the resulting pattern of the culture is found to lack strong and clear design, that is because malleable human beings, compulsively driving ahead under individualism and *laissez-faire*, with but few and casual maps and signposts, plunge down many sideroads toward vague goals. If the pattern appears contradictory and irrational, that is because so many struggling individual lives, caught in the immediacies of "today's decisions," lack a sense of direction, mistake means for ends, and know so little of "what it is all about" in a chaotic institutional world too big for them.

It is perhaps unnecessary to warn, in view of all that has been said above, that this linking up of cultural processes with the processes of individuals does not imply that the emphases of a given culture at any moment in time are fundamentally right merely because they are projections of processes normal to those persons who live the culture. Many traits in a rapidly changing culture like ours were better adapted to the circumstances of an earlier generation and have been carried over through inertia into our own era. Then, too, men do not build equal quanta back into their culture. Powerful individuals or classes may, through their power, dictate undue emphases useful to themselves but operating coercively to interfere with the normal life-demands of other individuals. These distortions, though in some cases highly pathological in their impact upon the individuals forced to accept them, may become in time so orthodox and generally accepted that they are viewed as "normal," "right," "inevitable," and "the American way." Only the recurrence of a "deplorable radicalism" among "the masses" or such danger signals as the mounting number of mental cases in hospitals trouble the official calm of the culture. But, sooner or later, one witnesses again the amazement and indignation of those in power as they view the "mistaken and obstinate" revolutions with which the human life-demands periodically seek to reassert themselves and to rebuild the culture closer to their desires.

When, therefore, in the light of all of the preceding, we define our common subject of study as "American culture," we do two things that sharpen our focus on reality. The explicit use of the concept "culture" compels overt recognition of the fact that all the jumbled details of living in these United States—automotive assembly lines, Wall Street, share-croppers, Supreme Court, Hollywood, and the Holy Rollers—are interacting parts in a single whole. Relative emphases in detail are not blurred but, rather, sharpened, as the separate traits are seen to fall into related clusters and patterns. And our focus is further unified and sharpened by viewing the place where this patterned culture *is* and *lives* and *changes* as in the habits of thought, sentiment, and action of individuals, who in turn tend to impart their rhythms, growth processes, and motivations to each other, and thereby to the culture. Without disparaging the continuing utility of the older type of studies which view institutions *qua* institutions, these studies are now seen to be but *one* level of analysis. The approaches are complementary and each is therefore indispensable. The newer one will utilize the older for the sense of orientation and direction which analysis of large masses of data at the institutional level yields; and the older approach will draw new hypotheses for its theories of "value," "prices," "sovereignty," "social classes," "community," and "social change" from the effort to understand these abstractions in action in the cultural microcosms, living individuals.

A substantial push in the direction indicated in the present chapter has been given by the emergence since the World War of the conceptual couplet "personality and culture." This has involved the posing of some new problems and a slow movement toward restatement of old problems in terms of the continuous reciprocal interaction ✳ of culture with individual personalities. Economics, political science, and history, the three oldest and most heavily entrenched of the social sciences, have paid little attention to this new development, though the work of Harold Lasswell should be noted as an outstanding exception. It has been relative newcomers—psychology, psychiatry, sociology, and anthropology—that have accepted "personality and culture" in varying degrees as a working frame of reference.[28] And it is an interesting commentary on the way even "scientific" human beings cling to their conventional, familiar ways of viewing their fields that the infiltration of this new approach has occurred most markedly in the study of children, notably at the nursery-school level. Here, in the pre-school period of childhood, was an area of life not preempted by any scholarly dis-

[28] A forerunner of this movement was the work of those psychologists and psychiatrists who had been making "personality studies," although these tended to underplay social conditioning. Biographers had been moving in this direction, too, and Lytton Strachey's *Queen Victoria* (1921) ushered in a "new biography" which directly related the personality of the subject to the cultural environment in which it developed.

cipline: no body of professors had established equities in theoretical systems, lecture notes, and text-books; and the institutions of business and politics made no vested demands as to what these little people should be made to buy or how they should be made to vote. In our culture the years before starting to school have been largely an institutional vacuum, with which only the individual home has been concerned. These years also offer the obvious point of departure for the genetic study of personality development. Into such a field, so largely unclaimed by science, new hypotheses could enter with relative ease.[29]

As this interest in personality and culture grew, the national Social Science Research Council picked it up as a new area for scientific exploration. This latter effort has proved largely abortive to date because of the scepticism of the older disciplines in the Council, and because the effort of the Council has been to view personality and culture as *another* (i.e., separate) field of inquiry. But the precise significance of personality and culture is that it is not an additional field for study but that *it is the field of all of the social sciences*. Here lies the key to the strengthening of social science by the "cross-fertilizing of the disciplines," which an agency like the Social Science Research Council was established to encourage.

At the present time a significant further change is occurring in the concept of personality and culture. Those

[29] The encouragement of interest in "personality and culture," beginning with studies of the pre-school child, is one of the most substantial achievements of the endowed philanthropic foundations. In the early 1920's, the Laura Spelman Rockefeller Memorial Fund began to stimulate this development, setting up research institutes to study child development at several universities. This child development movement undercut the preoccupation with remedial clinics and with research into isolated traits by forcing attention to the need to study as a continuum all the processes of growing up in a culture. It was a brilliantly conceived program which, starting as indicated above in an area little preempted by going work, has since spread far beyond the nursery school level and is today influencing even collegiate education and social science research.

employing it are looking askance at the dualism it implies; and they are beginning to substitute the wording "culture *in* personality and personality *in* culture." This involves the same unification of focus that the present chapter has sought to outline. If this as yet incipient movement succeeds in catching the imagination of working social scientists, and if it effects the needed changes in training which such a new point of view requires—a large assumption, but still within the range of possibility—the study of man in relation to his institutions will enter on an important new stage.

III

THE PATTERN OF AMERICAN CULTURE

WITHIN each single culture people tend to learn from each other many common ways of interpreting experience and defining situations. "The diversities in behavior and culture are the results of different interpretations of experience. . . . Different tribes define the same situation and pattern the behavior in precisely opposite ways."[1] In one culture the young members learn as they grow up that thunder is a sign that the gods are displeased; while in another culture they learn that it is an impersonal electrical disturbance. These different ways of interpreting situations do not affect only single traits and beliefs; they may translate themselves into large differences from culture to culture in relative emphases upon different functional areas of living. If we individuals in a given culture did not learn to accept substantially common meanings for a wide range of phenomena—from the physical universe to human gestures and institutionalized situations—we could not make sense out of accepting a piece of paper in repayment for a week's labor, or obeying the authority of a policeman, or putting sheets of engraved paper away in safety-deposit boxes, or voting, or submitting to eight or more years of compulsory schooling. Human behavior tends, as thus learned in any given geographical location, to assume a pattern—tight or loose, clear or blurred, but none the less a pattern of sorts.

[1] W. I. Thomas, *Primitive Behavior* (New York: McGraw-Hill, 1937), pp. 7 and 8.

Rhythms are adapted; motivations that have meaning to those about one are accepted.

Daily living, if it is to go on, cannot stop at each moment to scrutinize every word, concept, symbol, or other institutionalized device, but must take these largely wholesale, in patterns, and proceed to use them as given. These roughly common meanings for details and whole chains of details, thrust upon us by those about us, need conform to no system of logic or reason, for human beings are notoriously adroit in "thinking up good reasons" to explain what they habitually do. These meanings provide recognizable and dependable shorthand identifications which reduce complexity and enable us to live together. The fact that one can, in some measure, "feel at home in" — and trust the weight of one's hopes and plans to a culture is eloquent testimony to its patterning.

Sub-patterns appear: if we move from the Lower East Side in New York to Park Avenue, we change furniture and clothing in variety and expensiveness; we probably abandon pinochle and learn to play bridge; we probably spend week ends differently; we do not feel so comfortable socially if our job happens to be that of a mortician, a butcher, or a pawnbroker; we no longer feel comfortable sitting about home in the evenings in suspenders or without a necktie; *True Story Magazine* goes off the living room table in favor of the *New Yorker*, *Fortune*, and *Esquire*; and the length and detail of the future probably changes in subtle but identifiable ways.

A "pattern" is a somewhat misleading term for this element of identifiability in a culture, because it is over-explicit. Not only is the version of the culture carried by each individual unique, but the official or commonly alleged version of the culture may be a factually unreal description of what even the majority of people do.[2] It is an open question whether Americans today are "God-fearing," "law-abiding" (e.g., as regards income tax returns and support of the Wagner National Labor Relations Act), or "democratic."

One must, therefore, tread warily in attempting to characterize so complex a thing as the patterning of a culture. And this is particularly true in the case of our American culture, which stresses individualism, professes to run under *laissez-faire*, relates to a wide geographical region,[3] and includes such extremes as New York City and the Tennessee Mountains. To be sure, central tendencies are observable, but they are at best only tendencies in a wide and irregular distribution, and they may not even be counted upon to take the form of a comfortably smooth Gaussian curve. Furthermore, the emphasis in one institutional area, such as the family or religion, may conflict with that of another area, such as business. Rather, therefore, than resort to such over-all characterizations of pattern as Nietzsche's "Apollonian," and "Dionysian"[4] or Spengler's "Apolinian," "Faustian," and "Magian,"[5] the method will here be employed of describing a number of outstanding related characteristics of the contemporary American culture pattern.

Before attempting to characterize the pattern of our culture, it will be useful to set down briefly some of the

[2] See, in this connection, Chapter II at footnote 14.

[3] Regionalism is a real factor in American culture, not only as regards the composition of the population and the means of livelihood, but also as regards subtler things such as that suggested by the folk-saying that "Down South they ask, 'Who's your family?' Out West, 'What can you do?' And back East, 'How much money have you got?' "

[4] See *The Birth of Tragedy*. These terms are used by Ruth Benedict in her *Patterns of Culture* (Boston: Houghton, Mifflin, 1934).

[5] *Op. cit.*

principal guiding assumptions which many of its individual members have incorporated into their habits of thought, sentiment, and action, either as active principles guiding their conduct, or as truths tacitly accepted as "things that ought to be" or as "the way things work." Carl Becker[6] has called attention to the presence of such quietly omnipresent little keys to every era: "If we would discover the little backstairs door," he says, "that for any age serves as the secret entranceway to knowledge, we will do well to look for certain unobtrusive words with uncertain meanings that are permitted to slip off the tongue or the pen without fear and without research; words which, having from constant repetition lost their metaphorical significance, are unconsciously mistaken for objective realities. . . . In each age these magic words have their entrances and their exits." Around these magic words, assumptions grow up which are regarded as so much "of course" as hardly to require proof; they are passed readily from hand to hand like smooth-worn coins. They affect largely the weather of opinion in which we live; and as such they operate to fix the pattern of the culture.

Human beings employ these commonplace assumptions (and the emotionally evocative symbols elaborated around them) as gap-closers to make smooth the way before their feet. All cultures, even those of the so-called "simpler," "primitive" peoples, are more complex than we are wont to conceive them to be. Their complexities arise from many causes. They may arise from the richness and variety in ways of living offered by the culture. They may arise from lags and lack of coherence either within the several parts of a single institutional area or among the different institutional areas. They may arise from the extent to which the

[6] *The Heavenly City of the Eighteenth Century Philosophers* (New Haven: Yale University Press, 1932), p. 47.

emphases in the culture lean life away from the present into the future over prolonged swaying footbridges of instrumental action. The greater the number of disjunctions and the greater the frequency and prolongation of the instrumental lines of future contingency in a culture, the more of these gap-closing assumptions will be evoked to shore up and to impart a sense of seeming reliability to day-by-day behavior. And, just because our emotional need for security is so great, we tend to impute the utmost permanence to our assumptions. We like to think them rooted in "the will of the Almighty," "the Order of Nature," or "the immutabilities of human nature." As time goes on, as Veblen[7] has remarked, the underlying realities in these situations tend to "disappear in a tissue of metaphors."[8]

The deeply fissured surface of our American culture is padded smooth with this soft amalgam of assumptions and their various symbolic expressions; so much so that most of us tend to pass over the surface most of the time unaware of the relative solidities and insubstantialities of the several areas. In time, assumptions are built in on older assumptions, so that we have verbal clichés standing for clusters of underlying assumptions. Thus, "individual freedom" or "democracy" or "welfare" comes to stand for whole battalions of associated assumptions.

[7] *The Place of Science in Modern Civilization* (New York: Huebsch, 1919), p. 250.

[8] "The ideal conditions for thought arise when the world is deemed about as satisfactory as we can make it, and thinkers of all sorts collaborate in constructing a vast collective mythology whereby people can be at home in that world. Conflicts are bridged symbolically; one tries to mitigate conflict by the mediating devices of poetry and religion, rather than to accentuate their harshness. Such is man's 'natural' vocation. It makes for the well rounded philosophy of an Aristotle, who contributed much to the *Summa* of Aquinas. It seeks to develop attitudes of resignation whereby we may make the best of things as they are." (Kenneth Burke, *Attitudes toward History* [New York: New Republic, 1937], Vol. I, p. 34.)

As one begins to list the assumptions by which we Americans live, one runs at once into a large measure of contradiction and resulting ambivalence. This derives from the fact that these overlapping assumptions have developed in different eras and that they tend to be carried over uncritically into new situations or to be allowed to persist in long diminuendos into the changing future. Men's ideas, beliefs, and loyalties—their non-material culture—are frequently slower to be changed than are their material tools.[9] And the greater the emotional need for them, the longer men tend to resist changes in these ideas and beliefs. These contradictions among assumptions derive also from the fact that the things the mass of human beings basically crave as human beings as they live along together are often overlaid by, and not infrequently distorted by, the cumulating emphases that a culture may take on under circumstances of rapid change or under various kinds of class control. In these cases the culture may carry along side by side both assertions: the one reflecting deep needs close to the heart's desire and the other heavily authorized by class or other authority.

Wherever, therefore, such dualism in assumptions clearly exists, both assumptions are set down together in the following listing. The juxtaposition of these pairs is not intended to imply that they carry equal weight in the culture. One member may be thrown into the scale as decisive in a given situation at one moment, and the other contrasting assumption may be invoked in the same or a different situation a few moments later. It is precisely in this matter of trying to live by contrasting rules of the game that one of the most characteristic aspects of our American culture is to be seen.

[9] See W. F. Ogburn, *Social Change* (New York: Huebsch, 1922).

The following suggest some of these outstanding assumptions in American life:

1. The United States is the best and greatest nation on earth and will always remain so.

2. Individualism, "the survival of the fittest," is the law of nature and the secret of America's greatness; and restrictions on individual freedom are un-American and kill initiative.

But: No man should live for himself alone; for people ought to be loyal and stand together and work for common purposes.

3. The thing that distinguishes man from the beasts is the fact that he is rational; and therefore man can be trusted, if let alone, to guide his conduct wisely.

But: Some people are brighter than others; and, as every practical politician and businessman knows, you can't afford simply to sit back and wait for people to make up their minds.

4. Democracy, as discovered and perfected by the American people, is the ultimate form of living together. All men are created free and equal, and the United States has made this fact a living reality.

But: You would never get anywhere, of course, if you constantly left things to popular vote. No business could be run that way, and of course no businessman would tolerate it.

5. Everyone should try to be successful.

But: The kind of person you are is more important than how successful you are.

6. The family is our basic institution and the sacred core of our national life.

But: Business is our most important institution, and, since national welfare depends upon it, other institutions must conform to its needs.

7. Religion and "the finer things of life" are our ultimate values and the things all of us are really working for.

But: A man owes it to himself and to his family to make as much money as he can.

8. Life would not be tolerable if we did not believe in progress and know that things are getting better. We should, therefore, welcome new things.

But: The old, tried fundamentals are best; and it is a mistake for busybodies to try to change things too fast or to upset the fundamentals.

9. Hard work and thrift are signs of character and the way to get ahead.

But: No shrewd person tries to get ahead nowadays by just working hard, and nobody gets rich nowadays by pinching nickels. It is important to know the right people. If you want to make money, you have to look and act like money. Anyway, you only live once.

10. Honesty is the best policy.

But: Business is business, and a businessman would be a fool if he didn't cover his hand.

11. America is a land of unlimited opportunity, and people get pretty much what's coming to them here in this country.

But: Of course, not everybody can be boss, and factories can't give jobs if there aren't jobs to give.

12. Capital and labor are partners.

But: It is bad policy to pay higher wages than you have to. If people don't like to work for you for what you offer them, they can go elsewhere.

13. Education is a fine thing.

But: It is the practical men who get things done.

14. Science is a fine thing in its place and our future depends upon it.

But: Science has no right to interfere with such things as business and our other fundamental institutions. The thing to do is to *use* science, but not let it upset things.

15. Children are a blessing.
But: You should not have more children than you can afford.

16. Women are the finest of God's creatures.
But: Women aren't very practical and are usually inferior to men in reasoning power and general ability.

17. Patriotism and public service are fine things.
But: Of course, a man has to look out for himself.

18. The American judicial system insures justice to every man, rich or poor.
But: A man is a fool not to hire the best lawyer he can afford.

19. Poverty is deplorable and should be abolished.
But: There never has been enough to go around, and the Bible tells us that "The poor you have always with you."

20. No man deserves to have what he hasn't worked for. It demoralizes him to do so.
But: You can't let people starve.[10]

Assumptions like these are constantly and, as Becker remarks, "unobtrusively" changing. The very fact that a culture can tolerate such a wealth of contradictory assumptions is eloquent testimony to their lack of that "immutability" which men try to see in them. Assumptions and culture-pattern interact constantly upon each other: around such assumptions the culture assumes pattern and,

[10] In Chapter xii of *Middletown in Transition* (New York: Harcourt, Brace, 1937), dealing with "The Middletown Spirit," the author has attempted to set down a more extended list of these "of course" assumptions relevant to that particular city. With allowances for the heavily native-born, Protestant, small-city, Middle Western character of Middletown's population, most of the assumptions there set down would probably apply widely throughout the country.

in turn, the nature and degree of pattern in the culture at any given time gives rise to fresh assumptions that rationalize the pattern into solider meanings.

If, then, we use such folk assumptions as these as "the little backstairs door" to let us into more extended consideration of the patterning of our American culture, what do we see? The following characteristics are noteworthy:

1. *The process of patterning is basically casual.* Believing as we do in *laissez-faire*, the patterning of our culture has been left largely to chance. There are exceptions. Our written Constitution, inherited from the eighteenth century, is anything but casual, and its rigidity has created special problems as it has been employed in the fluidity of subsequent circumstances. Other minimum elements of deliberately designed pattern have been introduced by law, as noted below in discussion of the structuring of the culture. A pattern of religious observance has been taken over largely from the European background of the culture. Beyond such minima, our American culture tends to inch along into change, assuming such islands of patterning as it manifests largely as a kind of afterthought adaptation to the exigencies of specific situations thrust upon it by events. Casual fluidity is the "American way" and by long habituation "feels right."

This orientation makes sense to Americans because of their strong traditional commitment to three assumptions implied in those listed above:

(*a*) That people are rational, can and do know what is best for them, are free to choose, and will accordingly choose wisely.

(*b*) That "the greatest good to the greatest number" occurs when individual enterprise is left free from controls in the interest of any type of planned pattern.

[63]

(*c*) That any design and unity in pattern which is useful can be depended upon to develop automatically under the frictions of competing individual self-interests.

The question arises as to whether the characterization of a culture as "casually patterned" is not a tautology. Is not the essence of every culture that it just happens and grows? This tends to be true of cultures, unless urgent circumstances force the forsaking of casualness, because it is so largely true of the process of individual living, which is so largely preoccupied with "the next step." As John Dewey has pointed out,[11] men "stop and think" only when the sequence of doing is interrupted and the disjunction (a problem) forces them to stop and rehearse alternative ways—over, around, or through—which their past experience in collision with this problem suggests. Most cultures have grown and patterned themselves casually for the most part. And man's inveterate need to feel pride and rightness in his achievements has prompted him to honor the accidents of his past after the fact by describing them as "ordained by God" or as arising from the "inner genius" of his race, culture, or nation.[12]

But comforting parallels drawn from rationalization of the past or from contemporary primitive cultures must not be too readily embraced. Casualness may involve increasing hazards and penalties as the size and complexity of a culture increases. Numerous *ad hoc* pressure blocs have

[11] In *How We Think* (New York: Heath, 1910) and *Human Nature and Conduct* (New York: Holt, 1922).

[12] See Jacques Barzun's *Race: A Study in Modern Superstition* (New York: Harcourt, Brace, 1937) for a description of the extravagant lengths to which this attribution of a unique "genius" has gone in the case of the French people. The alleged magnificent competence of the English for "muddling through" is another contemporary case in point; and the racial pretensions of the Nazi propaganda machine present the spectacle of the deliberate manufacture of such myths on a large scale. (See Robert Brady's *The Spirit and Structure of German Fascism* [New York: Viking, 1937].)

developed to further the aims of more or less independent interests. And one of the most acute problems of our current world derives from the effort to reconcile and to operate together these highly organized institutional blocs within a tradition of general casualness. The "menace" some people discern in such institutions as the Catholic Church, the Communist Party, finance capitalism, organized labor, big business, and the totalitarian state derives in part from the coercive power of deliberate organization in the midst of a go-as-you-please culture. Big cities, big corporations, elaborate technology, nationalism —all such current ways of living—involve a situation the logic of which runs counter to *laissez-faire*. Furthermore, with planned totalitarian cultures in active and manifestly efficient operation, those cultures operating by casualness are as inevitably at a disadvantage as is the horse and buggy in a world of automobiles. Since the World War, Western cultures have apparently crossed a momentous mountain range, behind which they can never again retrace their steps to the *status quo ante* of liberal casualness.

2. Growing directly out of this casualness is the related aspect of the pattern which may be described as *the grossly uneven relative organization, or structuring, of the several functional areas of living*. Every culture develops its institutional structure around certain persisting life-activities of human beings: in getting a living, cohabiting with the other sex and making a home, training the young in their rôles, and carrying on common activities in governance, in play, in religion, and so on. It is to the relative degrees of supporting institutional structure around each of these persisting human activities that reference is here made. All of the functional areas of living are constantly interacting, and if one area is strongly organized and another weakly, this institutional situation invites the riding down of the

weaker by the stronger. A case in point is the overbearing elaboration of the institution of war in our present world, which tends to render all the rest of our living insecure. Or one may point to the coercion of our high school curriculum by the authoritative structure of university education.

The significance of structure for a culture may be suggested by the analogy of a Gothic cathedral, in which each part contributes thrusts and weights relevant not only to itself alone but to the whole. Such an analogy overemphasizes for our purposes here the fixity and rigidity of the separate parts. But just because of the need of human beings for certain vital freedoms to grow and to change, their dependence upon reliable, coordinated institutional structuring in the culture is correspondingly great, particularly in an elaborate and geographically widely based culture like ours. If such a culture is not to be unbalanced and unduly frustrating as the individual lives it, its structuring must extend through and support the entire chain of instrumental actions relevant to any given functional goal, and the linkages among the parts must be close, explicit, and dependable.

Within the general framework of devotion to *laissez-faire* individualism, our American culture has tended to make the following sub-assumptions regarding the process by which its structural form grows:

(*a*) It is assumed that as individuals feel the strain of trying to do any over-complicated thing alone, they will recognize, as free, rational persons, the need to join with their fellows and do something about it.

(*b*) It is assumed that when the institutional structure supporting one area of behavior, such as getting a living, becomes over-developed and begins to unbalance and to distort the rest of living, individuals will be aware of this and will automatically redress the balance.

The planned structuring built into the culture by its legal institutions as a minimum framework regarded as essential for its orderly operation consists in the following:

Political structuring along geographical lines which bestows upon the citizen the right to vote if he so chooses.

Structuring of a few highly selected functions such as lawmaking, taxation, policing, and the administration of such things as courts of justice, postoffices, national defense, and a public treasury.

Structuring of property rights.

Structuring of public education.

Structuring of the family to the extent of legalizing marriage, retarding divorce, and insisting upon the support of minor children.

Other types of structuring have been left to individual preference and the accidents of events. In the resulting welter are the Ford Motor Company and the unorganized Ford worker, the Catholic Church and the Seventh Day Adventists, Harvard University and the poverty of education in the South, the Cornell Medical Center in New York and the midwife, the Country Club and the neighborhood pool-room, and everywhere the isolated little units behind the closed front-door in the place we call "home."

The lack of balance and coherence in the culture structure is markedly apparent when one compares the elaborate structuring of property rights in our culture with the almost total lack of structuring of the rights of the individual worker to access to and permanence in the job upon which all the rest of his daily living must depend. As Harold Laski has pointed out, "America has been for so long a frontier civilization that its communal psychology . . . has remained intensely individualist even in an age where the primary assumptions of individualism were obsolete. It has lived under a constitution so organized as to minimize the power of popular will and to confront it with a body of safeguards for the rights of private property which has made it difficult to enact even the most elementary forms of social legislation."[13]

As a consequence in such a culture, operating under a theory of casualness, hypnotized by its material and technological growth, and viewing the way ahead as dependent upon maximizing production, a disproportionate structuring has developed around the institutions supporting property. The "center of town" is the business section; nine-to-five, our best waking hours, are devoted to work; the Chamber of Commerce or its equivalent dominates the policies of the city; while all our lives shiver or become buoyant with the dips and rises in "the market." This part of living thrusts up, like a skyscraper, above the generally low profile of the cultural structure. The family,

[13] The rest of Professor Laski's comment, following immediately after the above, is worth noting: "Until quite recently, moreover, the state, in its European substance, has hardly been necessary in American life; with the result that popular interest has never been deeply concentrated upon its processes. Now, when a state is necessary, the American people lacks that sense of its urgency which can galvanize it into rapid and effective action. It has been so long tutored to believe that individual initiative is alone healthy that it has no appreciation of the plane which must be reached in order to make individual initiative significant.

"The defects of the American political scheme are, to the outsider, little less than startling." Mr. Laski goes on to speak of the "paralyzing" checks and balances of our Congressional system, our anarchy of state rights, and the "dismal failure" of our city government. "Yet," he continues, "as soon as crisis came, it was obvious that the central American problem was no different from that of the European. It was the problem of planning the use of American resources for the total good of the community when the power to control them for private benefit was protected by the amplest constitutional safeguards any people has ever devised. The problem was rendered the more intense by the fact that long prosperity had persuaded the average man that the Constitution was as nearly sacrosanct as any such instrument might be. The disproportion in America between the actual economic control and the formal political power is almost fantastic. . . . There is in America a wider disillusionment with democracy, a greater scepticism about popular institutions, than at any period in its history." (*Democracy in Crisis* [Chapel Hill: University of North Carolina Press, 1933], pp. 44-6.)

the political state, education, religion, and recreation lean unevenly and insecurely against its base. And we are habituated to accept this unbalanced state of things, with one dominating and largely autonomous area of the structure dwarfing all others, as normal and inevitable. Because we regard the part of the cultural structure which has to do with business as primary, we are cumulating the resulting imbalance by adding more stories to the already over-balanced business structure. It is as if, in our preoccupation with driving ships faster and faster, we were filling the interior and decks with more and more machinery, leaving the passengers for whom the ships are run crowded forward in the steerage.

T. N. Whitehead, of the Harvard School of Business Administration, in a book which proposes the wrong remedies for a correctly diagnosed malady,[14] says of our present unbalanced and uncoordinated cultural structure:

"In a modern society, a part of the purposeful activities are, as before, performed as social living, and are regulated, though in a lesser degree, by social usage. But another part of these purposeful activities has become singled out for a very different form of organization. These activities have been withdrawn from the main stream of social living and are highly organized from the standpoint of technological efficiency. This fraction of the purposeful activities is known as industry, or, more broadly, as business. . . . The industrial organization is controlled without adequate regard for the social lives of those involved. . . . At the present time so much activity is industrial that society is becoming seriously and increasingly disorganized. . . .

[14] *Leadership in a Free Society* (Cambridge: Harvard University Press, 1936), pp. 78, 80, 165, 169.

"The business man's functions come near to disintegrating the society whose economic future he is providing for. . . .

"Every advance of industry has so far been accompanied by a corresponding impoverishment in social living. The rise of organized industry has reduced the importance of other institutions as integrators of society, without shouldering these functions itself. And the resulting social instability is so great as to threaten the industries themselves. . . .

"The connection between the general life of the community and the highly organized activities of industrial enterprise has become so slight that neither is concerned to support and assist the other. . . . Business organizations are the only widespread type of institution that has ever attempted to achieve stability as divorced from the main current of social living, and the result is exactly what might be expected in the circumstances."

The rhythms and cravings[15] of the individual organism provide some counter-drag against this mounting imbalance; but human wants are malleable, and in the rush and confusion of day-to-day decisions we tend to adapt ourselves defensively to the going emphases about us. Thus habit tends to constrict the rôle of fresh impulse as a governor on the cultural system.

It is this structural distortion, with the elements so unequal and out of balance that the sheer preservation of the going system becomes a monopolizing preoccupation, that presents one of the most striking aspects of our culture. To the resulting general sense of strain may be traced the compulsive overemphasis upon aggression rather than affectionate mutuality, upon action rather than upon repose, and upon doing rather than feeling.

[15] See Chapter v for a discussion of these.

Social legislation in a country like Sweden operates to build a more balanced structuring of the several parts of the culture, while Nazi Germany, Fascist Italy, and Soviet Russia are restructuring their institutions wholesale around one or another type of plan. Such instances are cited not by way of endorsing any of these existing plans as necessary models for American culture, but to suggest that the cumulating strains of structural imbalance in current culture are forcing nation after nation to undertake the contrivance of some more controlled organization of institutional parts into an inter-supporting whole. One may hazard the generalization that the functional strength of a culture may be gauged by the degree to which it satisfies the following requirement: Does it present to individuals a closely, explicitly, and dependably inter-supporting frame of behavior throughout the several institutionalized areas of living which provides the minimum of strain and the maximum of active assistance in the discovering and following of their own creative patterns of rhythm, growth, and motivation in living? ✳

3. The pattern of the culture *stresses individual competitive aggressiveness against one's fellows as the basis for personal and collective security*. Each man must stand on his own feet and fight for what he gets—so runs the philosophy of the culture—and in this way the common welfare throughout the entire culture is best achieved. In addition to thus explaining away the obvious crudities of aggression by identifying the latter with the common good, sheer anarchy is prevented by certain established rules of combat. If one dislikes the presence of a competitor's store across the street, one may not assault or threaten him, kill him, blow up his shop, or slander him, though one may ruin him and deprive him of his livelihood by underselling him, by buying up the property on which his store is

located and forcing him out, or by other devious means within the ample armory of business competition.[16]

Cultures differ in the rules of the game by which the individual acquires status. Broadly speaking, they tend to emphasize one or the other of two means: status by ascription (e.g., by reason of birth into a given family), and status by achievement.[17] Our culture stresses the latter, leaving the outcome almost entirely up to unremitting individual effort.[18] This forces upon the individual in our culture a restless ambivalence between his deep need to be affectionately and securely accepted by those about him as the person that he is, regardless of what he manages to achieve, and the cultural demand that he stick out his chest, square his jaw, and force those about him to yield him what he wants.[19] The most clearly patterned path out of this ambivalence is through concentration upon the achievement of success measured in terms of money. With the culture so little structured to encourage other lines of action, and with the need for security so great in a society of untied-in, offensive-defensive individuals, this general emphasis upon aggression involves a belittling of other paths to status. The shifting, anonymous world of the city mutes one's importance as a person by the peremptory demand that one demonstrate again and again what one can do in this

[16] See Chapter IV of Max Radin's *The Lawful Pursuit of Gain* (Boston: Houghton, Mifflin, 1931).

[17] Cf. Ralph Linton, *The Study of Man* (New York: Appleton-Century, 1936), p. 115.

[18] But see the regional differences noted earlier in this chapter at footnote 3.

[19] Dr. James S. Plant notes this ambivalence in the ceaseless quest by the person to secure answers to the two questions, "Who am I?" and "What am I?" By the first of these questions the individual in our culture seeks to discover who loves him, accepts him, gives him status without his having to struggle for it. The second question ("What am I?") involves the discovery of one's personal status-giving prowess in terms of one's aggressive capacities and the work one can do. (*Personality and the Culture Pattern* [New York: Commonwealth Fund, 1937], pp. 95*ff*.)

artificially narrowed world of striving for pecuniary success. This is apparent on every hand. Veblen described the prevalence of "conspicuous consumption" in his *The Theory of the Leisure Class*. People who meet in crowds, touch, and carrom apart, must accept and reject each other rapidly by obvious tags. Under these circumstances, the subtle, sensitive, and highly individuated person tends to become an isolate. The range of socially viable personality organizations is narrow, and even such relationships as marriage or friendship are not unaffected by demands for that kind of status which only the job can yield.

Over against any such summary characterization of American culture as this must be set the manifest fact that most of us Americans are not super-aggressors, most of us are not successes-in-a-big-way, and life consists for most people in just living along. This "just living along" — quality is a large part of American culture. But its numerical predominance does not render it either emotionally predominant or entirely emotionally self-contained. It represents, rather, in American life an enforced second-best, a coming to terms with the situation in which one finds oneself caught. At every point our young, optimistic culture thrusts forward its gains rather than its costs and losses. It plays up in print and symbol the pace-setting ways of life of its more successful members.[20] There is a general ten-

[20] Charles Horton Cooley saw clearly this fact that the dynamic values in a culture like ours tend to be set by a minority of the people: ". . . Pecuniary valuation is by no means the work of the whole people acting homogeneously, but is subject, very much like the analogous function in politics, to concentration in a class. . . .

"By virtue of this the power of the richer classes over values is far greater than that indicated by their relative expenditure. As people of leisure and presumptive refinement, they have prestige in forming those conventions by which expenditure is ruled. We see how cooks and shopgirls dress in imitation of society women, and how clerks mortgage their houses to buy automobiles. It is in fact notorious that the expenditure of the poor follows the fashions of the rich, unless

dency for people on all levels to struggle after these authoritative ways of living. Those who cannot get what they want do not generally commit suicide; they go on living, but their living takes place in a weather of coercive values and is marked by myriad little strains—between husband and wife, parent and child, merchant and merchant, and merchant and customer, among children in school, and among adults in their daily contacts. Neighborhood amenities may soften the struggle; and when nobody "south of the tracks" has a Packard, one may not crave a Packard. But there are always new Chevrolets, and small but real profits to be made by the little merchant by shrewd trading. The drama is simply reenacted in a humbler arena.

4. Growing directly from the preceding is the marked presence in the culture of *extreme differences in power*. This appears in many ways: in the dominance of urban industrial areas over rural areas in such matters as import tariffs; in the ability of business pressure-blocs to prevent the passage of legislation manifestly in the public interest —e.g., an adequate food and drug law; in the fact that 200 of the more than 300,000 non-banking corporations in January 1930 controlled 49.2 per cent of all non-banking corporate wealth;[21] in the ability of great corporations to command abler lawyers, to squeeze out small competitors, to control patents, and otherwise to dominate their fields; in the helplessness of the individual worker in the face of the labor policies of a Republic Iron and Steel Company; in the fact that ½ of 1 per cent of income-earners receive $15,000 or more and their incomes aggregate 20 per cent of

in matters of the most direct and urgent necessity, and in no small degree even in these." (*Social Process* [New York: Scribner, 1918], pp. 302-4.)

[21] See Berle and Means, *The Modern Corporation and Private Property* (New York: Macmillan, 1933), p. 28.

the total national income, while 81 per cent receive less than $2,000 and their incomes aggregate only 43 per cent of the total;[22] in the per capita annual personal income of $1,107 in the Middle Atlantic States as against $344 in the East South Central States;[23] and in such subtler things as the psychological pressures created by the high visibility of the habits and possessions of the rich because of increased mobility and intercommunication.

Despite a rising standard of living in the decades preceding 1929, including the growing mass ownership of automobiles and labor-saving devices in the home, there is a tendency for these disparities in size and power to increase. The ability of the barehanded individual to "get to the top" is declining.[24] The disproportionate amount of the national income going to the wealthy was actually continuing to increase in the decades preceding 1929.[25] And in yet another way the disparities grow. As material progress occurs and automobiles, electric refrigerators, and modern plumbing displace more primitive ways, the learning to live by new ways is left up to the individual in those cases where it is not commercially profitable to somebody to "educate" him. This means that in many important aspects of living the new displaces the old only partially, and the functionally most out of date persists alongside the new. Thus cold-water slum flats in New York and houses with backyard privies and no bathrooms in "Mid-

[22] These figures are for 1929 and are taken from Leven, Moulton, and Warburton, *America's Capacity to Consume* (Washington: Brookings Institution, 1934), p. 207.

[23] These figures are for 1929. *Ibid.*, p. 173.

[24] See the discussion of this at footnote 43 below in this chapter.

[25] "There has been a tendency, at least during the last decade or so, for the inequality in the distribution of income to be accentuated. That is to say, while the incomes of the masses of the people were rising during this period, the incomes of those in the upper income levels increased with greater rapidity." (Leven, Moulton, and Warburton, *op. cit.*, p. 126.)

dletown"[26] persist on into a world in which "the best modern practice" is leaving such primitive resources farther and farther behind. And the little tensions generated by these widening contrasts in those who must continue to live by the least adequate methods mount side by side with the satisfactions of those who have the newer devices.

In a culture which prizes "equality" as one of its foundation assumptions, this habitual and widespread tolerance of extremes of inequality in power requires the disguise of a formula. Two such convenient formulae are in wide use:

(a) The disparities at any given moment are regarded either as but temporary differences in a general progress in which "tomorrow can be different," or as due to the deliberate volition of the parties concerned—i.e., one has worked harder, or saved harder, or elected to be more enterprising and farsighted than the other. Bolstering such explanations is the related formula which equates closely the amount of one's personal wealth (and power) with the assumed antecedent contribution of that much welfare to the community. Veblen[27] has explained the course of the reasoning involved in this last formula: In early medieval times, he points out, work was overwhelmingly directed to the production of things needed for immediate use, i.e., food, clothing, shelter. Since no man produced everything, he depended in part upon his neighbor's contributions to the common store of needed goods under a system of division of labor. Thus the habits of life and thought under the handicraft and cooperative manorial systems tended to build the enterprise of the individual

[26] In 1935, 13 per cent of Middletown's families had no running water in the house, 37 per cent no bathtubs, 10 per cent no refrigeration, 18 per cent used backyard privies, 39 per cent cooked with kerosene, gasoline, coal, or wood, and 55 per cent heated their homes by stove. (*Middletown in Transition*, p. 195.)

[27] *The Theory of Business Enterprise* (New York: Scribner, 1904), p. 291.

rather solidly into the joint social enterprise. As business superseded the joint work of the manorial era, joint acquisition—or rather contiguous acquisition—was still regarded as *joint* work; and the older idea was carried over in the form of a belief that acquisition of property means not only the production of wealth but, as under earlier conditions, the production of common wealth, i.e., welfare. This continuation into modern times of the identification of work, property creation, property acquisition, and common welfare results in the businessman's being looked upon today "as the putative producer of whatever wealth he acquires. By force of this sophistication the acquisition of property by any person is held to be not only expedient to the owner but meritorious as an action serving the common good." In the early nineteenth century this identification was given new currency in the mystical doctrine of ethical hedonism, which lives on today in decrepit but venerable dignity.

(*b*) The second formula invoked to justify a special but crucial disparity in size and power, i.e., that between the individual and the corporation, is the convenient legal fiction which views a corporation as a person. Thus the Standard Oil Company of New Jersey, the Aluminum Company of America, the United States Steel Corporation, or R. H. Macy and Company is but a lone, humble person dealing with John Smith as laborer or consumer shoulder to shoulder in one of the oldest activities of man, the exchange of what I have for what you have. And if the United States Steel Corporation and John Smith go to court over their transaction, they are still conveniently assumed to be simply two equal individuals with equal access to the law as represented by their respective counsels.

But democracy still remains uneasy in the presence of this prevalent fact of giants and pygmies living side by side in alleged equality but manifest inequality. Competitive individualism sets few bounds to the power to which one has a "right," provided one is enterprising enough to win it. And machine technology finds ample justification for bigness in the yardstick of dollar efficiency. Over against such persuasive arguments for bigness stands the fact that many of the most emphatic controlling assumptions of the culture grew up in an era of small things, and the nostalgic bias of the culture is against "the curse of bigness" and in favor of "the little man." Our system of government derives from the familiar intimacy of the New England town meeting, where people knew each other and all preferences and objections rose easily to public consideration. Today the formulae remain substantially the same, but great cities are not New England villages; and the result is chaos and growing disillusionment in political behavior. The little-man philosophy which viewed any stalwart Cincinnatus as worthy to be called from his plough to direct public affairs lives on in popular resistance to the need to find a place in public administration for the big-man "expert." Master and workman, merchant and competitor, shop and home, as envisaged in the traditional symbols and assumptions of the culture, involved no such disparities in power as exist today.

Anti-trust legislation, while useful as a vote-catching device, dodges the central problem involved. "Bigness," large-scale operation and concentration of power, is a useful servant of modern man—when it is. Individual differences render differences in power as among individuals inevitable and socially desirable, and integrated industry is likewise an intelligent way to produce needed goods. But our system of wide differences in power, casually developed and casually tolerated, leaves unanswered the crucial questions: At what points in our institutional system is bigness useful? And how can such differences in power as are useful be made to serve rather than to disrupt the democratic process?

5. The pattern of our culture is one of *great individual mobility*, both horizontal and vertical, and consequently one in which *human beings tend to put down shallow roots*. This mobility involves positive gains in the access it gives to wider and more varied experience. But it is controlled primarily by the main chance to perform the instrumental activity of making more money, rather than by the varied needs of the whole personality. As machinery has taken over more and more of the learned skills of the worker, he has become increasingly a standard interchangeable part in the productive process, and his tie to a special craft, factory, or city has been attenuated. The individual in our culture is tending increasingly to "travel light"; he encumbers himself with fewer children, moves his place of residence more frequently, commits himself irrevocably to fewer things, often avoids making friendships with those who may become liabilities, and he even seeks subtly to disencumber himself from in-laws and the now vanishing lateral kinship degrees.

The dweller in a large American city tends to be a highly developed roving predatory animal. His culture resembles a frontier boom-town, with everywhere the clatter of new buildings going up and disregard for the niceties of living in pursuit of the main chance. He is free—free to swim or drown, free to bet all his life on "the big money," free to turn on the gas as a lost and beaten atom in the anonymity of his furnished hall-bedroom. "Man moving rapidly over the face of nature evades his destiny, which is himself.

[79]

Time loses its grip on space, and space on time. . . .
Plants that spread rapidly do not strike deep roots. . . ."[28]

6. It is a pattern of *increasingly large population masses, held together principally by the tie of the individual to his job, and with attenuated sentiments of community in feeling and purpose.* Ours is a culture of increasing mass-living in urban units. The portion of the total population of the United States living in urban places with 8,000 or more population has risen from 3 per cent in 1790, to 7 per cent in 1830, to 16 per cent in 1860, to 33 per cent in 1900, and to 49 per cent in 1930.[29] "By 1930 there were nearly 15 times as many rural people in the United States as there were in 1790, but there were more than 300 times as many urban people. . . . In 1929 there were concentrated in 155 [of the more than 3,000] counties containing the larger industrial cities, 64.7 per cent of all of the industrial establishments, 74 per cent of all industrial wage earners, 80.7 per cent of all salaried officers and employees. Moreover, 78.8 per cent of all wages and 82.9 per cent of all salaries in the country were paid in these [155] counties."[30] Not only does the urban pattern now dominate our culture quantitatively, but, with growing intercommunication and the concentration of sources of diffusion within large cities, the urban population is increasingly calling the tune for the patterning of the entire culture.

While this growing urbanization derives predominantly from economic causes, such as the concentration of industry in the "easy labor market" which a dense population affords and the resulting multiplication of retailing

[28] William A. Orton, *America in Search of Culture* (Boston: Little, Brown, 1933), p. 23.

[29] U.S. Census, *Population*, Vol. I, 1930, p. 9.

[30] *Our Cities: Their Rôle in the National Economy.* Report of the Urbanism Committee to the National Resources Committee (Washington: Government Printing Office, 1937), pp. 1-2.

and other service activities among such a dense population, the growth of cities has also been influenced by other factors. Urban living represents the most favorable environment for those wishing to benefit by the resources of the culture. On the personal side, the city presents the opportunity for rich, selective acquaintanceship in the pursuit of personal growth. On the material side, the overhead cost of providing desirable modern services—from labor-saving utilities to schools and the arts—can best be borne when widely shared. Without, therefore, by any means going to the extreme of Marx and Engels in speaking of "the idiocy of rural life," one may nevertheless say that the city is potentially a "natural" as a way of life for modern man. The inchoate character of urban life in our culture, which prompts some to characterize great cities as "wens of civilization," is not an evidence of the intrinsic weakness of urbanism, but rather of the pathologies that occur when urban units are allowed to develop casually as an adjunct to the individual scramble for wealth.[31] We

[31] It is important to bear in mind that the lack of common purposes under our type of culture is neither a new nor a transitory phase, despite its identification with the spirit of the passing frontier; but, rather, that it is dictated by the very structure of a culture which assumes that community emerges best from the conflict of private interests. Urbanism points up this tendency in the culture as sharply as it does primarily because cities embody most unrestrainedly the restless, predatory quality which the culture encourages. De Tocqueville described the resulting inevitable conflict a hundred years ago in words that are if anything more true today than when he wrote them: "Not only are the rich not compactly united among themselves, but there is no real bond between them and the poor. Their relative position is not a permanent one; they are constantly drawn together or separated by their interests. The workman is generally dependent on the master, but not on any particular master; these two men meet in the factory, but know not each other elsewhere; and while they come into contact on one point, they stand very far apart on all others. The manufacturer asks nothing of the workman but his labor; the workman expects nothing from him but his wages. The one contracts no obligation to protect, nor the other to defend; and they are not permanently connected either by habit or by duty. . . . Between the workman and the master there are frequent relations, but no real partnership." (*Democracy in America*, Vol. II, Part II, Bk. II, Chap. xx.)

have not as yet addressed ourselves to the task of building urban *communities*, in the social sense.[32] Fifty thousand families, paying their gas bills, mowing their lawns, jockeying their way through traffic to jobs in offices and factories, and sitting side by side watching movies, do not necessarily constitute "a community." Mumford remarks in his chapter on "The Insensate Industrial Town": "As for an expression of the permanent social functions of the city in the new type of plan [the rectangular gridiron plan of our American cities], it was utterly lacking. . . . There were no real centers in this urban massing: no institutions capable of uniting its members into an active city life. Only the sects, the fragments, the social debris of old institutions remained . . . a no-man's land of social life." The art of community living struggles unsuccessfully for a foothold in "these vast, inconsequential urban clottings."[33]

Whereas the close, personalized contacts of the neighborhood encouraged spontaneous social cohesion in the rural, village, and small-town matrix in which our culture took shape,[34] unguided spontaneity may not be relied upon to tie in the individual so securely as the population-base grows to city proportions. The rough generalization may be made that, as the size of a community grows arithmetically, the need for deliberate (as over against unplanned, casual) organization that weaves the individual into the group life increases in something like a geometrical progression. Urbanism in our culture has been almost entirely a matter of material change. As just pointed out, under the doctrine of casualness virtually no attention has been paid

[32] See Lewis Mumford's *The Culture of Cities* (New York: Harcourt, Brace, 1938).

[33] *Ibid.*, pp. 186, 191.

[34] Twenty-eight of the thirty-three urban places with a population of more than 2500 in the United States of 1790 had less than 10,000 population.

[82]

to the planning and perfecting of the non-material factor of social organization.

Many of those who migrate to our larger cities pride themselves on the fact that "Now, thank God, I don't *have* to know my neighbors, go to Rotary, belong to a church, or participate in an annual Community Chest drive!" And the big city does little to disabuse them of this attitude. Individuals can and do live comfortably in our large cities with no formal ties between themselves and the structures of the culture save the money tie between them and their jobs. One may or may not elect to exercise one's political right to vote; one may or may not own property, marry, or belong with anybody else to anything; but one must tie into the structure to the extent of getting money regularly. The culture puts an extreme reliance upon this money nexus between the individual and his job to hold the culture together. As jobs are given to individuals and not to families, the latter institution suffers. Urban folk delay marriage and in some cases elect not to marry; and kinship ties are narrowing and attenuating. Citizenship ties are weakening in our urban world to the point that they are largely neglected by large masses of people.[35] Neighborhood and community ties are not only optional but generally growing less strong; and along with them is disappearing the important network of intimate, informal social controls traditionally associated with living closely with others. Protestant religious ties are so optional and tenuous that the church has sunk to its weakest point in our national history as an active instrument of cultural structuring. Leisure ties are increasing in number but are highly unstable.

[35] In the mayoralty election of 1923 in Chicago, studied by Merriam and Gosnell in *Non-Voting* (Chicago: University of Chicago Press, 1924, pp. viii-x), only 723,000 of the 1,400,000 eligible electors bothered to go to the polls.

The individual's identifying tag derived from his job and the property it yields him tends to be heavily overworked as the fragile basis for social cohesion. The common focus is not on living together but on "the job." Old feelings of deep and diversified community are being displaced by slogans: "Buy in Akron!" "What's good for business is good for your family!"[36] This carelessness about common sentiment is part of the general orientation toward matter-of-factness in a culture stressing material development, personal mobility, and postponement of the subtleties of living. At point after point our culture plays down extensive, acute, and subtle feeling. To be "businesslike" is to be impersonal; in our moments of deep, personalized emotion we tend to retreat from others into ourselves or to the trusted tolerance of our immediate family; a businessman who is "artistic" may be somewhat suspect; being "romantic" or "idealistic" is regarded as an evidence of youth; and the person who "gets enthusiastic about things" is mildly disparaged as immature and "unsound." Human beings do not easily live so emotionally sterilized. So we burst out periodically in sex, drinking, hard-driving week-ends, and gusts of safe, standardized feeling at the movies and football games. Mickey Mouse and Charlie McCarthy tend to displace Uncle Sam and local symbols as repositories of common sentiment. They sweep the

[36] The decaying structure of American "holidays" as occasions continually rebuilding common sentiment is a mute and too little recognized evidence of this process of emotional disintegration. Washington's Birthday, Lincoln's Birthday, Decoration Day, the Fourth of July, and Labor Day have lost their ceremonial observations and are occasions for private holiday; while Thanksgiving is so sunk in football games and turkey-dinners that the annual Presidential proclamation has become a quaint curiosity.

It is not the loss of specific meaning of these holidays to which reference is here made. The point is, rather, that they formerly helped to contribute the binding mortar of common sentiment to the culture; and as their specific traditional meanings have worn thin to modern man, they have simply been abandoned and no emotionally rich substitutes put in their place.

country because there is so little else to feel about in common. They offer little identification of our personal rhythms of feeling with the deeper purposes of the culture as a whole and with our common goals as members of it.

No large society can long exist which is careless of this ✻ element of community in feeling and purpose. The tactics of a Hitler are profoundly right in so far as they recognize and seek to serve the need of human beings for the constant dramatization of the feeling of common purpose. In our own culture, the roots of the earlier forms of common sentiment were in certain structuralized forms of authoritarian security: church, nation, local community, and family. These latter, with the exception of nationalism, have weakened or disintegrated with the growth of historical criticism, science, and a mobile individualism. The democratic right of the individual to think—or to think that he thinks—has played its part in the discrediting of some of these earlier authorities that were wont to focus men's feelings. And democracy, interpreted largely as the right to be free to take or leave the world about one and to acquire private property, has afforded little new basis for deep common sentiment. The heavy current reliance upon a man's job (and the resulting offensive-defensive balance of property rights) to hold our culture together is due, not so much to the fact that people want only money, as to the fact that this is the clearest value that remains in a culture which has allowed other values to trickle away. The popularity of the disillusioned sophistication of a book like Thurman Arnold's *The Folklore of Capitalism* is an evidence of how little that is positive modern capitalist democracy has left us to work for and to feel strongly together about.

Nationalism remains, and it is taking over the rôle of creating common sentiment on a grand scale. But common sentiment sprayed over a population from the top down, and not living and growing richly at the grass-roots of a culture, loses its vitality. Human beings crave big, aggregating symbols on a culture-wide scale, but they also crave localized and highly personalized meanings. Human loyalties are largely built of an infinite number of shared purposes in commonplace daily acts.

Whatever one may think of the over-all rightness or wrongness of the Soviet Union, the social scientist cannot but approve the soundness of the social "activism" it encourages in individuals. A member of the Communist Party in the U.S.S.R. is expected to be active "politically, culturally,[37] and in his trade union." As a result, these individuals undertake responsibility for helping, through their active social participation, to build or to operate some small part of the social structure. This social activism spreads beyond Party members, though the Party remains the instigating nucleus. As a result, something over half[38] the entire adult population of the city of Moscow, for instance, is estimated to be actively engaged in some form of this socially integrative work. Children of our Boy Scout age begin to learn habits of socially directed participation in the Young Pioneer organization, while in the late 'teens and early twenties the Comsomols (junior Party members) undertake such work in earnest. Underlying such activism are the two assumptions that it is bad for a culture to allow its human participants to become socially lost in the

[37] "Culturally" here refers to reading and study and to participation in those aspects of life not comprised in the immediately political and economic. Cultural activism appears in the mounting consumption of books of all kinds, and in the vigorous and pervasive development of the arts, athletics, and other varied group activities in communities and neighborhoods of all sizes.

[38] This is a rough estimate made to the writer by a Soviet official in Moscow in the summer of 1938. The estimate includes all grades and degrees of activism, from the Party member to the non-Party person, e.g., including the housewife who assumes responsibility for seeing that the people in her apartment building know about a given group activity and are invited to participate.

shuffle, and that every human being has somewhere within him an active or potential interest in *something* which, if — shared with others, will make both him and the culture stronger. To a student of American urban living, any such organized effort to build a neighborhood, a city, or a collective farm socially around the common interests of individuals stands out in sharp contrast to our go-as-you-please in regard to such things. If cities and straggling countrysides are not to continue to isolate an unduly large number of individuals and to dissipate their potentialities for group living, some such fundamentally sound selective and organizational program of social activism will have to be adopted and pushed for all it is worth. Whether such a program can be developed within the divisive dynamics of private capitalism is another question.

We are today living through the end of that phase of our — cultural history which was dominated by the quest for the conditions of individual liberty. Heavily laden with institutions developed to that end, we are reluctantly moving into a new phase in which we must somehow manage to rewrite our institutions in terms of organized community of purpose. To this end we may no longer conceive of the state as simply a kind umpire over what Sir Henry Maine called "the beneficent private war which makes one man strive to climb on the shoulders of another and remain there through the law of the survival of the fittest."

7. The culture is patterned *to point life into the future*. The rhythms of tension and release within the individual organism orient living toward many short-run future consummations. One moves recurrently away from hunger toward food, away from fatigue toward rest, and so on. These raw physical drives become overlaid in every culture by a more or less elaborate congeries of institutionalized motivations toward future consummations. These may

involve becoming more popular, more successful, richer, more skilled, better informed, and so on, through scores of specific wants. Each of us grows up in a world of people exhibiting such motivations. We learn those that feel best in terms of our unique personality organization and environment or that we are coerced into accepting, and we live these private versions of orientation toward desired consummations back into the culture.

Thus every culture involves some tilt into the future. But cultures vary widely in the number of these future desiderata, the length of the chains of tension-sustention involved before the patterned goal is achieved, and in the relative preponderance of emphasis upon present, as over against future, consummations.[39] Our own culture, as a relatively young culture that grew up with the Industrial Revolution in an unusually rich physical setting, has gambled heavily on the future and written it into our institutional forms and the private lives of all of us. This gamble may have been largely justified during the expanding phase of our economy, but it also operates to confuse realism with hope.[40]

[39] Elderly people in our culture are frequently oriented toward the past, the time of their vigor and power, and resist the future as a threat. It is probable that a whole culture in an advanced stage of loss of relative power and of disintegration may thus have a dominant orientation toward a lost golden age, while life is lived sluggishly along in the present.

[40] This may be observed in the difficulty our democracy experiences in appraising the actual present human efficiency of its economic and political institutions. As already noted, we continually play up the asset side of our economy, neglect the appraisal of its human costs, and excuse inequalities by saying that "tomorrow will be better" or that inequalities are caused by personal slothfulness. As regards the operation of our political institutions, we have allowed the fact that their operation in the past has happened to coincide with and to be closely identified with a highly favorable economic era to dull our critical sense. The Methodist chapels of England in the first half of the nineteenth century were welcomed by factory owners because they filled the lives of overburdened laborers with high hopes of a better world to come in Heaven. In the same way, the hope encouraged by the accidents of past experience deadens us today to

It has been remarked that the Industrial Revolution gave the Western World the option of having more leisure, more babies, or a higher standard of living—and it "chose" to trudge up the long sandy slope represented by the last of these. This choice was rendered more or less inevitable by its past experience: by the historic prominence of scarcity as an inveterate enemy of men living in northern climates where winters are long and the earth's yield often niggardly or precarious; by the Christian emphasis upon the future; by the stern Puritan emphasis upon developing one's character through careful, thrifty stewardship; by the enthusiastic endorsement by capitalism of unceasing individual acquisitiveness; by the frontier tradition of a world to conquer, in which one was endlessly building a better tomorrow out of a crude present. The nineteenth century's discovery of the doctrine of evolution gave a thumping endorsement to this devotion to "progress," while the stupendous technological inventions completed the process of hypnosis. Ours was a culture which appeared to have the world by the tail with a downhill drag.

While the degree of flamboyance of assertion varied from person to person, few Americans doubted this basic thesis of progress prior to 1929. They were ready to give heavy hostages from the present to achieve this future. And they did. Parrington characterized Americans, living in a welter of instrumentalisms, as "a generation that had gambled away the savor of life." We violated our individual rhythms, bound ourselves out in service to fatigue and shoddiness provided it yielded a chance at "the big money," stretched our motivations ahead to the point of frustration, accepted meagre differentiations and stereotyped integrations of our personalities, and postponed

present undemocratic realities and encourages a probably quite unwarranted expectation of the future.

until our individual energies were spent the asking of the momentous question, "What doth it profit a man?"

In the face of this heavy institutionalization of the future, the inveterate craving within the individual for spontaneity, for living in the present, struggles for expression. Many of the deep habits engendered by the culture demand "Wait!" "Postpone!" "Save!" But spontaneity, egged on by salesmanship, urges "Now!" Spontaneity inevitably escapes into expression in some form, but in a culture which plays down the expression of sensitive feeling, it tends to be displaced to the grosser and more superficial level of stereotyped expression. We may channel our whole personality into the smashing aggression of our sales talk, and then when we have clinched the sale we may explode into boasting of "the big deal I put over," "how I beat down his price," or we may fare forth to celebrate expensively. In a culture that tends to harness the present instrumentally to the future, time must not be wasted; and the art of spontaneity verges on idleness unless the speedometer shows at the end of the day that we have had a good time in a big way.

The lack of patterning, of doing and feeling in terms of mutual group ends, discussed above, tends to channel behavior in terms of oneself as an aggressive-defensive agent. We view the behavior of those about us warily and tend to answer the recurrent inner question, "How am I doing?" not so much in terms of our personal spontaneities as of our comparative position in the competitive game. We lose sensitivity to the voice of our deeper and more personal cravings which asks in weaker and weaker tones as we live ahead, "Is this really what I *want?*"

It isn't fun to live so cagily behind a defensive wall of careful calculation.[41] Sympathy, for instance, is one of

[41] See the characterization of this status-preserving "wall of fear" in Plant,

man's deepest emotions, but it is incompatible with aggressive exploitativeness. Stretched as we are in our culture to the long future of achieving success, we tend to steady ourselves amidst our conflicts by a "hardening process," involving the development of "depersonalizing mechanisms."[42] We set up screens between ourselves and those about us. We do not want to know the personal frustrations of our employees, of the elevator man who takes us to and from our office or apartment, of the tired faces that pass us on the street. We curb our sympathies and build our walls because all these unhappy things about us would "take it out of us" and "slow us up"; they would tend to destroy our freedom and keep us from getting ahead. And we, in turn, seek to put a brave face on the basic human loneliness which the walls of those about us force upon us.

At present the culture shows signs of break-up in the pervasiveness of its heavy traditional orientation to the long future. The emphasis upon success—to be achieved in the future and measured largely in terms of money accumulation—still remains. Insecurity remains and has been heightened by the depression. But there is a growing emphasis upon "living while you live," which has been characterized as "the pleasure basis of modern living." This has been encouraged by the weakening of religious sanctions, a rising standard of living, shorter work hours, the rise of the vacation habit, the high and continuous visibility under modern intercommunication of the envied ways of living of the wealthy, and the commercially sponsored diffusion of automobiles and commercial recreation. This emphasis on living in the present is permeating to all income levels, though unevenly from level to level.

op. cit., p. 122. Much of modern literature, in particular the novels of D. H. Lawrence, represents the assertion of basic human desires against the cramping defensiveness of modern life.

[42] Plant, op. cit., pp. 156, 201.

An even more important evidence of cleavage in our traditional patterned orientation toward the future appears to be developing along class lines. The chance for the enterprising lone workman to "get ahead in a big way" is diminishing. Plant units are larger, machine technologies are holding more workers on a semi-skilled level, and in the impersonality of large-scale operation it is easier for the individual worker to get lost in the shuffle. The distance between the floor of the shop and the boss's big leather chair is lengthening. The chance to break away and start a modest shop of one's own is lessened by the high initial costs of machinery, the difficulty of securing credit on a shoestring, and the enhanced competitive advantage of existing big corporate units. All of this means that the gilt is wearing thin on the old formula that "The sky is the limit for any man who works hard, saves his money, and watches his chances"—and the little fellow is beginning to realize it.[43] As a result, the following distinction appears warranted. The businessman still tends to point his life up the long slope of the future to a relatively distant goal; whereas the workingman and many white-collar workers are accepting themselves as stuck where they are and forced to wrest such meaning as they can out of life on a dead-level. One emphasis on the future remains, however, even for the latter: the hope of sending the children to college. With this exception, if one represents the future as it feels psychologically to the businessman as a prolonged line sloping upward, it is probably safe to depict the sense of the future of a growing mass of workingmen as a horizontal line with incidental little waves of recurrent good times such as "getting out in the car *this* Sunday" and "going uptown to the movies *tonight*." The predominant time-focus in the one case is relatively long,

[43] Cf. in this connection *Middletown in Transition*, pp. 67-73.

a matter of years; and, in the other, short, from week to week or month to month. No research has been done on this cadence of life with regard to the future; but if, as seems likely, this differentiation is taking place, it presents a formidable disjunction in the American pattern of culture.

8. The pattern *places strong emphasis upon children, and, in adult life, upon youth in women and the years of greatest energy output in men.* Activities tend increasingly to be structured according to age groups. Whole-family work and recreation have given way to specialized groupings cross-cutting the population by age-level. Certain age-periods occupy preferred positions, the years of youth and early middle life being most highly valued. The care and nurture of children is a major concern, and institutions for their education are second only to economic institutions in cultural emphasis. The stress upon mobility rather than upon deep-rooted continuity, upon action and scientific technique rather than wisdom, upon change rather than growth, upon winning and holding status rather than receiving it freely granted at the hands of one's fellows, tends to displace men and women of advanced years in favor of their juniors. In such a culture "venerability" has lost its meaning and old age its function. Even in the professions gray hairs are becoming a liability to a man, while the rise of beauty parlors and growing cosmetic sales are evidences of the battle women are fighting to postpone becoming "motherly looking."

This skewing of life to the younger side has involved real gains in freedom for youth, and also an increment in vigor for the culture. But the total impact on the individual may be more negative than positive. The longest rhythm of life is the biological one of slow physical growth to maturity, the plateau of the middle years, and senes-

[93]

cence.[44] On the psychological side, the traditions of our culture do not prepare us to expect that the sense of achievement in the middle years will be followed by denial of fulfilment and loss of status. The stream will run more quietly, to be sure, but not, we are led to hope, without beauty. In fact, a culture like ours which encourages us to live instrumentally toward a long future, through years of self-denial and oversustained tensions, encourages us thereby to accumulate a heavy weighting of expectations for the years beyond fifty: "*Then* I'll take it easier"; "*Then* I'll do a lot of things I don't have time to do now"; "*Then* I won't have constantly to prove to people that I'm good, because they'll *know* it." These become the years of mandatory fulfilment; and, when the fact denies the promise, the frustration becomes one of the bitterest experiences of life. It is noteworthy, too, that at the other end of maturity those emerging from their teens are meeting today with formidable and socially reckless barriers to finding themselves in useful work.

Growing urbanism has emphasized the increasing disparity between the symbol and the reality of old age. The aged lose in a shifting urban environment the validating asset of long and continuous recognition. They suffer perhaps more than any others from the "hardening" and the barriers which busy urban dwellers develop. If old-age-security legislation represents a more realistic orientation to the problem of old age, the fact remains that our current culture has not developed a realistic, positive philosophy of the rôle of that part of the population possessed of the widest experience in the art of living. For the present, we content ourselves with leaving the race to the

[44] See Charlotte Bühler's *Der Menschliche Lebenslauf als psychologisches Problem* (Leipzig: Hirzel, 1933) for an interesting study of the life cycles of persons in diverse occupations, projected upon this curve of physical maturation and senescence.

strong, the new, the most adaptable. And by this neglect of the old we stiffen their resentment of the new and diminish thereby such contribution as they might be able to make. The gradual increase now taking place in the average age of our population will tend to accentuate this problem.

9. The character of the culture *encourages considerable (and possibly increasing) conflict between the patterned rôles of the two sexes.* As already pointed out, growing urbanization is forcing a separation of the worlds of job and of home; and the job world tends to run under rules of its own, largely divorced from the rest of living.[45] This entails not merely a division of labor, but a basic split in the structure of values by which men and women live. The fact that many women are going into jobs and professions means less the merging of the patterns of the two sexes than the adoption of a difficult dual pattern by these women; for the demands upon them to be feminine remain, even though they must live during their hours of work by the values of the men's world. Both sexes accept the traditional assumption of the culture that, fundamentally, the values for which the home stands—sympathy, understanding, mutuality, gentleness, treating persons as persons, cooperation rather than aggression—are ultimate and therefore more important. But the job world of the men, operating as it does to such a degree independently of the rest of the culture, demands more and more channeling of the personality into impersonality and aggressive dominance. The rôle of the male in the family is also constricting as the separateness of his job world diminishes his activities as parent. The status of the father as a family member is narrowing to that of "a good provider." At the

---

[45] Cf. above in the present chapter at footnote 14.

same time, increased popular awareness of the importance of good, positive sex-adjustment—an awareness heightened by the relaxing of religious condemnations of sex, the rise of mental hygiene, fiction written under the Freudian influence, and the great lovers on the cinema screen—has strengthened the demand on the male that he play an emotionally more subtle rôle as husband and lover. Likewise, new knowledge is making fresh demands of him to be an active, constructive person as a parent; which demands neither his training nor his time and energy resources help him to meet. The result is an intermittent sense of personal inadequacy in a situation from which, biologically and emotionally, he should draw strength and security.

The old, secure dominance of the male in the home is changing. The demand of the wife to be treated as a person has shifted the earlier tandem structure of marriage, with the man confidently in the lead, to a looser, more voluntary partnership, in which—

> *Though in wedlock*
> *He and she go,*
> *Each maintains*
> *A separate ego.*

The changes in woman's rôle in recent generations have been far greater than those in man's rôle. Bound by fewer children and less housework than formerly, women find themselves with greatly increased options. The very presence of wider options entails responsibility to choose wisely and to become "a person in her own right"; and this in turn involves more opportunity but, also, more uncertainty and mutual tension for both marital partners. Even if the man wants his wife to be independent, he is apt to perpetuate, in his busy preoccupation with the demands of his job, the emotional stereotype of his mother as constant helpmate and backer-up of his own father. While on the job, he is conscious of strains and insecurity; and, when he returns home, he is frequently unable to lay aside his 9:00-to-5:00 attitudes like a coat. In his weariness and perplexity he frequently feels inadequate as a person in his own home.

The tacit or open recognition by the male of the superiority of the values for which the home stands, as over against the values to which he perforce devotes his best energies on his job, tends to render him by turns fiercely defensive of his own world and erratically demanding that women outdo themselves in standing for all the "finer" things that the world of business denies. Women are thus made to carry as surrogates for the men wellnigh the entire burden of the subtler values in the culture. Upon the intimate and delicate marital relationship the man unloads most of his pent-up needs for intimacy and understanding at the fagged end of the day, and many marriages break under a load which they would not have been forced to carry in a more integrated culture. Karen Horney[46] describes, as a psychiatrist, this compulsive overweighting of the artificially narrowed love-relationship in our culture:

"All these factors together—competitiveness and its potential hostilities between fellow-beings, fears, diminished self-esteem—result psychologically in the individual feeling that he is isolated. Even when he has many contacts with others, even when he is happily married, he is emotionally isolated. Emotional isolation is hard for anyone — to endure; it becomes a calamity, however, if it coincides with apprehensions and uncertainties about one's self.

"It is this situation which provokes, in the normal individual of our time, an intensified need for affection as a

[46] *The Neurotic Personality of Our Time* (New York: Norton, 1937), pp. 286-7.

remedy. Obtaining affection makes him feel less isolated, less threatened by hostility and less uncertain of himself. Because it corresponds to a vital need, love is overvalued in our culture. It becomes a phantom—like success—carrying with it the illusion that it is a solution for all problems. Love itself is not an illusion—although in our culture it is most often a screen for satisfying wishes that have nothing to do with it—but it is made an illusion by our expecting much more of it than it can possibly fulfill. And the ideological emphasis that we place on love serves to cover up the factors which create our exaggerated need for it. Hence the individual—and I still mean the normal individual—is in the dilemma of needing a great deal of affection but finding difficulty in obtaining it."

✳ At no point more than in the family are the disjunctions of our culture and the worlds of different values they embody more directly and dramatically in conflict. Rich familial and marital adjustments are at best difficult of achievement because of the subtleties of personality demands. These adjustments are rendered more complex in our culture by the lack of strong, clear institutional structure supporting family life. As a result, family members are thrown back upon each other as a small group of over-dependent personalities who must work out a common destiny in a family situation which has lost many of its functions and, hence, forces them to rely overmuch upon intimacy. When the values of a culture are split into two sharply conflicting systems, with each sex assigned the rôle of carrying one system, the family becomes perforce, as Horney points out, the battleground not merely for the resolution of differences among the individual personalities of family members but also for the attempted resolution of the larger conflicts of the entire culture. Too little stress has been laid upon this toll which the casualness of our culture exacts of persons at the point of greatest potential richness in personal intimacy.

10. It is a pattern that *assumes that achievement of man's values will follow automatically from material advancement*. Our national history, as already pointed out, has happened to coincide with an era of amazing advance in material prosperity. As men have devoted themselves to business and industry, unparalleled wealth has resulted, and a share of this wealth has gone into a very tangible increase in the general level of welfare. Through the bottleneck of the price-system we have managed to get better medical care, better education, better housing, more leisure, less heavy toil in the home, and many other desirable things. Nobody planned all this, and apparently there had been no great need to plan, for these things seemed just to happen. They happened, in fact, because of our rich natural resources, the discovery and swift development of machine technology, and the presence of a vast frontier to settle and develop; but, to the average citizen, it seemed enough to say that they happened because men had been left free to make money. To be sure, there are many things we yet lack that we want—such things as still more leisure, better housing and diet for those who still have inadequate incomes, less unemployment, preventive medicine, child welfare programs, more adult education, and more security all along the line in living. But these things "will all come in time." The formula is deceptively simple: Welfare is a more or less automatic by-product of money-making; and if men will but apply themselves to the instrumental activity of earning more and more money, that is the best and surest way to achieve the qualitative ends of living we are all after.

Under this theory of indirection, the rest of the culture tends to be bent to serve the ends of business. Nothing escapes. Even the qualitative ends of living themselves are exploited in the service of money-making. Freedom is invoked to defeat a child-labor amendment. Liberty is used by a privately owned "free press" to defeat the effort to control misleading food and drug advertising in the public interest. Justice is invoked to protect the rights of property against the efforts of workers to organize. Education in the public schools is made to exclude consideration of economically unorthodox subject-matter and is used in other ways to indoctrinate ways of thinking useful to the status quo. Love of country and religion are exploited to the ends of better business. And "free" public opinion, a prized check on the misuse of democratic processes, is continually bought and paid for by using public relations counsels whose services are for sale for the private ends of the highest bidder. Such things befuddle men's view of their values. The upshot of this inversion of means and end is that, as R. H. Tawney has remarked, our Western culture resembles nothing so much as a giant hypochondriac so immersed in the processes of his own digestion that he is unable to get ahead with the activities normal to human beings.

11. Growing out of all the preceding, a final characterization of our culture pattern runs somewhat as follows: It is a pattern of *markedly uneven change, of unprecedented rapidity in some traits and of marshalled resistance to change in others, and tolerating at many points extreme disjunctions and contradictions.* Our culture has grown up during one of the eras of most rapid cultural change in the history of the Western World. The pace has been set by scientific discovery and by technological invention. With the process of change ruled by private enterprise, unchecked by any clear philosophy of control in the public interest, it has been a helter-skelter affair. The accumulated

momentum of change in certain areas is such that we now have no option but to recognize the need for extensive accompanying change in the many areas of life upon which changes already accepted impinge. The problem that confronts us is what to do about the confusions created by the unevenness of the process of adjustive change throughout the whole field. For we exhibit marked hospitality to certain types of change—for instance in our technologies—while the strain of adjustment to these large and rapid changes makes us conservatively resistant to undergoing the tension of change at other points; and we also complicate the situation by leaving interested private power-blocs free to obstruct needed change at many points. The resulting disjunctions and contradictions within the culture are humanly costly; but we excuse ourselves from recognizing the need to do anything about this situation because of our optimistic belief that "things are getting better" and "all these things will straighten themselves out in time."

The preceding pages have itemized many of these disjunctions and contradictions. What these conflicts do to personality is suggested by Dr. Horney:[47]

"When we remember that in every neurosis there are contradictory tendencies which the neurotic is unable to reconcile, the question arises as to whether there are not likewise certain definite contradictions in our culture, which underlie the typical neurotic conflicts. . . .

"The first contradiction to be mentioned is that between — competition and success on the one hand, and brotherly love and humility on the other. On the one hand everything is done to spur us toward success, which means that we must be not only assertive but aggressive, able to push others out of the way. On the other hand we are deeply

[47] *Ibid.*, pp. 287-9.

imbued with Christian ideals which declare that it is selfish to want anything for ourselves, that we should be humble, turn the other cheek, be yielding. For this contradiction there are only two solutions within the normal range: to take one of these strivings seriously and discard the other; or to take both seriously with the result that the individual is seriously inhibited in both directions.

— "The second contradiction is that between the stimulation of our needs and our factual frustrations in satisfying them. For economic reasons needs are constantly being stimulated in our culture by such means as advertisements, 'conspicuous consumption,' the ideal of 'keeping up with the Joneses.' For the great majority, however, the actual fulfilment of these needs is closely restricted. The psychic consequence for the individual is a constant discrepancy between his desires and their fulfilment.

— "Another contradiction exists between the alleged freedom of the individual and all his factual limitations. The individual is told by society that he is free, independent, can decide his life according to his own free will; 'the great game of life' is open to him, and he can get what he wants if he is efficient and energetic. In actual fact, for the majority of people all these possibilities are limited. What has been said facetiously of the impossibility of choosing one's parents can well be extended to life in general— choosing and succeeding in an occupation, choosing ways of recreation, choosing a mate. The result for the individual is a wavering between a feeling of boundless power in determining his own fate and a feeling of entire helplessness.

"These contradictions embedded in our culture are precisely the conflicts which the neurotic struggles to reconcile. . . ."

Jung made this same point of the inevitable carry-over of conflicts in the culture to the private arena of conflict within the individual: "We always find in the patient," he says, "a conflict which at a certain point is connected with the great problems of society. . . . Neurosis is thus, — strictly speaking, nothing less than an individual attempt, however unsuccessful, at the solution of a universal problem."[48]

One can elaborate Dr. Horney's list by the addition of many other contradictions: between saving and spending; between playing safe and "nothing ventured, nothing gained"; between "you've got to look like money in order to make money" and spending your money for the things you really want; between (if you are a woman) having "brains" and having "charm"; between things that are "right in theory" and "wrong in practice"; between change and stability; between being loyal and "looking out for Number One"; between being efficient and being human; between being democratic and "getting to know the right people."[49] Human beings are, as Freud has pointed out, inevitably ambivalent at many points, but a culture which encourages unnecessary ambivalence is recklessly careless of the vital energies of its people.

In some cases, the disjunctions and contradictions go beyond ambivalence and actually set up a blocked situation from which there seems no line of escape. The harassment of living for the thoughtful citizen of a democracy in these post-Munich days derives from the fact that there seems to be literally no way out which intelligence can sanction. In this context it is of interest to note the research by N. B. F. Maier of the University of Michigan, awarded the 1938 annual prize of $1,000 for the outstanding paper presented before the American Association for the Advancement of Science. Professor Maier taught rats

[48] C. J. Jung, *Two Essays on Analytical Psychology* (New York: Dodd, Mead, 1928), p. 23.
[49] See in this connection the list of contrasting assumptions presented earlier in the present chapter.

to respond to a given situation and then proceeded to confuse the animals by not allowing the expected conditions to occur. The result was that the rats no longer knew what to expect. At the same time, by playing a strong stream of compressed air upon them, he placed them in a situation in which they had to do something but in which no avenue of action presented itself. In this situation the rats soon developed very noticeable symptoms of hysteria, as we know it in man. Such blockages in the face of the necessity to "do something" appear not only in the current international situation, but also in such situations as those involved when the head of a family loses his job during hard times. And the result in us human beings is essentially the same as in Professor Maier's rats.

— Confronted by such ceaseless contradictions in a world which demands of us a great show of outward confidence and decision, we Americans tend to do two things: In general we "play safe"—a little of this and some of that—keeping a foot in both camps. This makes for arrested differentiation within the personality (and consequently within the culture); we do not allow ourselves to "find" ourselves far enough in terms of our personal uniqueness to lay us open to attack from the counter point of view. We follow the middle of the road and vote the "regular fellow" ticket straight—and then we feel ourselves misunderstood when somebody calls us Babbits. Thus we live in ambivalence much of the time. But our tingling persons, thus checked, yearn for the clean release of unequivocal action. And so we have resort to the other alternative, and we are startled to find ourselves periodically going in for slogans with a whoop of enthusiasm. It is, for instance, because war offers such a cleansing projection down a single unswerving path that it presents such a seductive way out to men laboring in the midst of dilemmas and frustrations. Hitler employs anti-Semitism adroitly to the same end. And, on a less spectacular plane, modern merchandising manipulates our hunger for a way out, a fresh start, by selling us a new car, an Easter bonnet, or an electric razor as a momentary splurge into authoritative certainty.

Such, then, is the pattern of our American culture: A pattern of opportunity and of frustration, of strength and of careless disregard for patent weaknesses; a pattern which presents, from the vital point of view of liveability defined in terms of the satisfaction of individual rhythms and growth, a large measure of inversion of emphasis between means and end; a pattern of competing individuals struggling singlehanded in exaggeratedly big and little, and structurally defective, ant-heaps; of rootless people wandering from farm to city in quest of gain; with youth favored but frustrated, and sex rôles in conflict; believing in a future which for most of them will never happen; searching for "the way," which recurrently turns out to be an unmarked fork in the road; and relying on the outworn dogmas of "rational human choice" and the automaticity of "whatsoever things are good and true" to bring them to the Promised Land. It is in the main a pattern of lack of pattern, marked by the disorder and the substitution of doing for feeling that characterizes a frontier boom town. For the individual it is a pattern of extreme complexity, contradictoriness, and insecurity.

And yet, such is the nature of the world we live in that Thomas Mann and other thoughtful persons hail our American culture as the one remaining culture where freedom has a chance of survival. We are a young culture, rich in material resources, and strong even in the midst of our confusions. Our alleged freedoms are at point after point actual realities. We still have our democratic traditions, to which we can appeal in seeking to make them more wide-spread realities. And our people still hope—which is much. Travellers abroad during recent years cannot fail to have been impressed upon their return to the United States by the relative vitality that still persists in our tradition of liberty. Here there is still at least some chance to use our liberties to make real our hopes.[50]

But it is less than candor to fail to recognize that our freedoms move within the tightening grooves of the contemporary world scene. We are inescapably a part of this larger scene in a world which has shrunk space and finds its institutions linked together. So great is our confusion and so rapidly do our disabilities cumulate, that it appears probable that only forthright and extensive change can recapture our culture for the basic ends of human living.

A central problem that the pattern of our culture presents is the gross imbalance between what we are able to know and the limited extent to which we have institutionalized this knowledge in the service of living. Carl Becker has caught this situation brilliantly in the closing pages of his *Progress and Power*:[51]

"... Never before have men made relatively greater progress in the rational control of physical force, or rel-

---

[50] Time may prove that, despite our present greater freedoms, only the Soviet Union among contemporary great nations is building for basic liberties. Many aspects of the confused Russian situation are special to its traditions, to the threatening international chaos around it, and to the resulting wasteful but enforced speed with which it is having to build from very primitive beginnings. Like us, the Soviet Union is a young culture, it has great natural resources, and its people hope. Unlike us, it is stating its problems positively and straining its resources to build toward new goals. No such bold effort can be dismissed when there is so much about it that is humanly profoundly right. But this is not to say that the re-structuring of American life should be dictated by or should seek to follow the details of the Soviet pattern. One of the weak aspects of left-wing reform in our own culture is the insistence upon the rightness of Soviet precedent, and the basic disregard, despite the "new Party line," of the necessity to rebuild American culture in terms of our own special conditions.

[51] *Op. cit.*, pp. 91-6.

atively less in the rational control of social relations. The fundamental reason for this discrepancy is clear: it is that the forces of Nature have been discovered and applied by a few exceptional individuals, whereas every effort to ameliorate human relations has been frustrated by the fact that society cannot be transformed without the compliance of the untutored masses. . . . It is therefore not enough that a few exceptional individuals should have discovered the advantages to be derived from rational social arrangements; in addition the masses who compose society must be persuaded or compelled to adapt their activities to the proposed changes, and the means of persuasion or compulsion must be suited to the apprehension of common men. The result is that those who have, or might acquire, the necessary matter-of-fact knowledge for adjusting social arrangements to the conditions created by technological progress have not the necessary authority, while those who have the necessary authority (representatives elected by the people, or dictators who act with their assent) must accommodate their measures to a mass intelligence that functions most effectively at the level of primitive fears and tabus.

". . . Until recently the chief function of the sophisticated, the priests and scribes, has been to stabilize custom and validate social authority by perpetuating the tradition and interpreting it in a manner conformable to the understanding of common men. During the last three hundred years this functional connection between the sophisticated and the unsophisticated has been broken, since there has emerged a new class of learned men, successors to the priests and scribes, whose function is to increase rather than to preserve knowledge, to undermine rather than to stabilize custom and social authority. . . .

"The exceptional few move with assurance and live at ease in an infinitely expanded time-and-space world. . . .

But within this enlarged frame of reference common men are not at home. . . .

". . . While the mastery of the physical world has been effected by scientists whose activities, unhampered by the conscious resistance of their subject-matter or the ignorance of common man, have been guided by matter-of-fact knowledge and the consciously formulated purpose of subduing things to precisely determined ends, the organization of society has been left to the chance operation of individual self-interest and the uncertain pressure of mass opinion, in the expectation that a beneficence not of man's devising would somehow shape the course of events to a desired but undefined good end."

Two final appraisals may be suggested:

1. The knowledge which the sophisticated experts possess in our culture is growing at a rate far more rapid than the rate at which it is being institutionalized in the habits of thought and action of the mass of our population. This increasing disparity arises from our heavy reliance upon casual adjustment, assumed to occur automatically wherever it is rationally relevant; from our over-exclusive reliance upon commercial exploitation to diffuse any new knowledge throughout the population; and from the freedom granted to interested power-blocs to suppress patents, obstruct change, and bend new knowledge to their private ends.

Progress is a heady drink. As Becker remarks, "by locating perfection in the future and identifying it with the successive achievements of mankind, [the doctrine of progress] makes a virtue of novelty and disposes men to welcome change as in itself a sufficient validation of their activities."[52] In such an era of rapid change as our genera-

[52] *Ibid.*, p. 81.

tion is experiencing, there is a hypnotizing tendency to concentrate attention upon sheer movement and upon the things achieved to date—the widespread ownership of automobiles, bathrooms, and electric labor-saving devices, the declining infant and maternity death rate, the shortening of the work day and week, prolonged education, and the amazing increases in productive output by industry. Yet if one paraphrases Thomas Hobbes's statement that "The utility of moral and civil philosophy is to be estimated not so much by the commodities we have from knowing those sciences as from the calamities we receive from not knowing them," one may say that the utility of progress is to be estimated not so much by the commodities it gives us as from the disabilities we receive from the partial and imperfect application of progress to the whole round of daily living.

The second appraisal, a broader formulation of the preceding, runs as follows:

2. As a culture, we are cumulating our disabilities and the resulting strains incident to daily living at a rate faster than social legislation, education, and all the agencies for "reform" are managing to harness our new knowledge in the reduction of these disabilities. We are becoming culturally illiterate faster than all these agencies are managing to make us literate in the use of the potentialities of the culture.

This may be envisaged if one conceives of two lines sloping up with the passage of time from a horizontal base-line, the one line (representing our cumulating perplexities) rising at a steep slope, and the other line (representing adjustment, reeducation, and reform) rising much more gradually. The gap between the ends of the two lines, i.e., the failure of adaptation to keep up with the rate of development of new problems, is widening with the passage of time. It seems not unreasonable to suggest that, if "progress" means anything, the gap should be narrowing rather than widening.

In order to visualize the tortuous, creeping process of adaptation to ways of living that are regarded as modern and socially desirable, one has only to look at such things as the following: the prolonged and still inconclusive fight for a child-labor amendment to the Federal Constitution against the opposition of vested private interests; the ragged disparities among the marriage and divorce laws of the several states; the belated recognition of venereal disease as a thing the culture can "do something about"; the bitter opposition of the American Medical Association to socialized medicine; the power of the Catholic Church in blocking the public sanction of birth control; the chronic blocking by sectional interests of anti-lynching legislation; the increasing subtlety of domination of our media of information by business, as witnessed in the attitude of the press in the 1936 national election; the reluctance of the courts to develop a positive and socially constructive interpretation of "the public interest"; the resistance to the right of labor to organize and bargain collectively; the confusion in consumer purchasing, including the opposition of business to the kind of testing and grading which is routine practice in purchasing by the Federal government and by large corporations; the lagging adaptation by public education to non-traditional areas of needed learning; and the weakness of structuring of agencies to transmit to the mass of the population new knowledge about homemaking, marital adjustment, child care, leisure, and the techniques of mental adjustment and skilful interpersonal relations. The culture pays little heed to the curve of individual intelligence, which reveals the sharp limitations on the ability of many of our people to learn a large number of complicated things. And wherever it is to the private interest of any person to oppose cultural change, our institutions allow, if they do not actually encourage, him to do so to the limits of his resources. This anarchistic philosophy tends to reduce change of a non-commercial sort to a trickling minimum. Our culture ✳ includes no positive philosophy regarding change and the techniques for achieving it. Each effort at education and reform involves a protracted, haggling campaign, usually by a weak minority group, to budge habits with ganglia extending throughout the whole culture. The "disillusioned reformer" is a man who has given up trying to create change in the hardest possible way, i.e., by piecemeal attack upon isolated symptoms. Meanwhile, as suggested above, as this ragged line of simplification, reeducation, and reform creeps upward, the upper line (representing new elements of perplexity) rises much more sharply.

A very strong case can be made for the statement that we are drowning today in the sea of disabilities which progress, so raggedly mediated to us, has created. In the midst of our great freedom we are free, as Anatole France remarked, under the majestic equality of the law to sleep on park benches—and, with mounting unemployment, more and more of us are exercising this freedom. Our freedom and equality are exercised in a world which has been described as run on the doctrine of "'Each for himself and God for all of us,' as the elephant remarked as he danced among the chickens"—and the elephants are getting bigger and bigger.

The objection is immediately made to this characterization of our perplexities as outstripping our adjustments that it is one-sided in that it plays down the significance of adjustments actually achieved. The standard of living was rising—up to 1929; business and industry are more efficient; housework entails less heavy drudgery; schools are better and schooling is prolonged; medical science knows more about how to keep us well and saves lives formerly lost through ignorance; urban living involves new variety, comforts, and other advantages; we are learning to take a more sensible attitude toward divorce where marriage is unsatisfactory; people can buy an amazing range of pretty and useful things at the "five-and-tens"; and there is certainly something to be said in favor of a realistic awareness of the complexity of our problems, as over against blanketing them under oversimplified clichés. Such factors on the asset side of the ledger are undeniable. But the assets and liabilities are strictly relative—and relative not to a theoretical scale of efficiency, but to how they total up in individual human lives. Every gain in knowledge and efficiency and every outworn symbol or causal explanation displaced by more realistic analysis is potentially a gain in ease and richness of living. But when this new knowledge is not put to work in the service of all the people, when it is only partially applied to those able to "pay for it" or bright enough to learn it unaided, or when it is used by those with power in order to exploit others, this knowledge may be either largely barren or, worse, it tends to become a disruptive factor.

Only as a culture sedulously builds its gains into the balanced system of the whole of its people's lives can the net heightening of strain through social change be avoided. People's susceptibility to strain in a given case varies inversely with the following ratio:

$$\frac{\text{What they are \textit{personally} able to do about a given problem}}{\text{What they know about what \textit{anybody} can do about it}}$$

If little is known about a problem or about how to meet it, cultures tend to build up religious or natural explanations that exculpate the individual. In an era when infant mortality was a little-understood fact of Nature, it was rationalized by the comforting belief that "God took the little one to his bosom"; and while there was anguish over death, there was less of the modern parents' retrospective self-reproach that they had not made it their business to know more about infant diet, had not been more careful, or had not felt themselves able to afford a specialist in time.

Science has brought many new securities to those able to pay for expensive specialized services, and some to those who cannot pay. But it is also creating vast popular awarenesses of new problems as it seeks to discover how to make the hitherto unpreventable preventable. To cite but two commonplace examples, a generation ago thumb-sucking by infants was something they "just got over," and enuresis was handled by telling the child he was naughty and shaming him out of it; but today the whole intricate world of childhood tensions in relation to parental tensions, as antecedents to subsequent adult maladjustment, has opened up before parents. At point after point in daily living the demand for the application of specialized knowledge increases. One cannot know everything, and "everything costs so much money" in a world in which most people have too little money. Almost the entire ⚹ burden of adaptation is left to the individual by the culture, since the latter recognizes so little responsibility to structure new knowledge into the institutional forms that will encourage and render easy the use in daily living of the best we know. Hence the sinister partial impotence into which progress has led us, despite the fact that ours is physically the most superbly endowed culture on earth.

If the preceding analysis of the pattern of contemporary culture is even approximately correct, it presents a formidable task to the social sciences.

IV

THE SOCIAL SCIENCES AS TOOLS

"Concern for man himself and his fate must always form the chief interest of all technical endeavors. . . . Never forget this in the midst of your diagrams and equations."—Albert Einstein.

A MARKED characteristic of our culture is its emphasis upon the acquisition of knowledge. This emphasis arises from two things: ours is a culture with an honorific history of thought and deed copiously preserved in readily transmissible form; and, second, our culture recognizes knowledge as useful to do certain things that human beings want done. The presence of an upper class, proud of its traditions and solicitous for the refinements of "polite" learning, has helped to keep alive the scholarly wisdom of the humanities,[1] while the need to cope with problems generated by the world about us has encouraged the development of the other type of knowledge that we call science. However great a part "pure curiosity" and "the *disinterested* desire to know" may have played in the acquisition of scholarly knowledge and

[1] As Professor Cooley pointed out: "We very inadequately realize, I imagine, how much our modes of thought, and hence our valuations, are dominated by English social ideals of the seventeenth and eighteenth centuries. We get these not only through the social prestige, continuous to our own day, of the English upper classes, but through history, literature and art. Speaking roughly, the best European literature, and especially the best English literature, was produced under the dominance of an aristocratic class and is permeated with its ideals. Thus culture, even now, means in no small degree the absorption of these ideals." (*Op. cit.*, pp. 304-5.) See also in this connection Cooley's description of the rôle of the well-to-do in setting values for all other persons, quoted in footnote 20 in Chapter III above.

natural science, it has been the *interested* desire to know in order to do something about problems that has predominantly motivated social science, from the *Wealth of Nations* down to the present.[2] The social sciences have developed ✳ as instruments for coping with areas of strain and uncertainty in culture. Man would have sung and he might have developed the scholarly humanities and charted the stars in the Garden of Eden, but it would not have occurred to him to trouble his head to create social sciences. The aim of this chapter is, accordingly, to attempt an appraisal of each of the social sciences—its focus, boundaries, and something of its achievements—in terms of its serviceability in helping man solve the problems generated by living in his culture.

The serious young student approaching the social sciences tends to be hypnotized by their front of authoritative doctrine and extended bibliographies. In view of the manifest signs of acute strain in the culture, there is good reason for taking the social sciences seriously. But there is a deceptive quality about calling a body of theory and data a "science." Brilliant technological achievement and extension of our knowledge of the physical world have made science a word loaded with kudos; and there is a constant tendency to overplay the assuredness of the social sciences. They are relatively young as sciences go, and, compared with the natural sciences, they deal generally with things less easily objectifiable. Since they are sciences, the very urgency of the culture's need for help and assurance in the midst of its insecurities tends to thrust premature certainty upon them. Thurman Arnold notes in *The Symbols of Government* "the social pressure for an abstract science of law."[3] The same pressure is felt by

[2] The confusion that exists between "disinterested" scholarship and "interested" scientific knowledge is dealt with at greater length in Chapter v.

[3] New Haven: Yale University Press, 1935, p. 52.

each of the social sciences, for in disorder men clamor for law, and in uncertainty they insist upon certainty.

Each social science is but a characteristic bit of the total culture in and by which it lives; and each is carried in the habits and moulded by the personality needs of its professors. As such, social science is heir to all the strengths and weaknesses that human beings and their cultures exhibit. In the very process of its precise ordering of data, it displays cultural lags, distortions of emphasis, blind spots, and a propensity to play safe at exposed points. Its objectivity tends to be impaired by the fact that it is bent and moulded by the very thing it must try to objectify. In a culture like ours, which is casual as to its structuring and integration, it is not surprising, therefore, that the social sciences are not integrated; or that, in a culture patterned to oppose changes in fundamental rituals and beliefs, social scientists manifest some hesitation as regards forthright teaching and research on problems explicitly concerned with fundamental change.[4]

Like all casually developed culture-crystallizations, thrown up by the exigencies of past situations, the social sciences present but a spotty coverage of the field of man's problems. They have developed in different eras. Matter-of-fact thinking about government arose before similarly secularized thinking about money-making was considered necessary. Psychology has broken off from philosophy and, within the memory of men now living, become a separate experimental science. Sociology as an empirical science is still younger. And, quite as important, new sciences are

[4] This point may be illustrated by the relatively short shrift which Karl Marx receives from the social scientists in our universities. A professor of economics remarked before the annual meeting of the American Economic Association in 1937 that, despite the fact that what Marx wrote makes more sense and is more nearly correct at a number of points than many of the things economists actually teach, the latter go on teaching these other things because they cannot afford to commit *hari-kari*.

still emerging around the problems of the family, child-development, leisure, population problems, urbanism, consumption, and similar areas of study heretofore largely overlooked. We are, therefore, viewing a stage in a fluid cultural development, rather than the finished product which the authoritative term, "social science," tends to suggest. Furthermore, the respective bulk and prestige of the several social sciences has been largely influenced by the accidents of their affiliations with the rest of the culture; and they do not necessarily reflect a rational or scientific weighting of resources on the basis of the human significance of the problems involved. Thus economics as a science has ridden the broad tide of business advancement, while psychology and anthropology have had to struggle for funds by which to grow as empirical sciences. Here again, therefore, one must guard against the halo of adequacy which the term "science" gives to the social sciences.[5]

[5] A close parallel to this casual development of the social sciences appears in the evolution of our Federal government. In this case, as in the case of science, there is a folk bias in the direction of feeling that the existing picture is substantially complete and right for all time. The current conservative resistance to "revising the Constitution" and to "administrative reorganization" in Washington derives in part from a basic faith in the finality of "the American way" as it has been handed on to us. And yet one has only to look candidly at the development of the Federal machinery to recover a strong sense of the cultural casualness that has dominated this development. After the original establishment of the Departments of State, War, Navy, Treasury, Post Office, and Justice, nearly half-a-century elapsed before establishment of the next Federal department. This newcomer, the Department of the Interior, was called into being to handle such problems as the settlement of our vast public lands. Then another wait, until the first dominant vocational pressure-group, the farmers, got themselves a Bureau of Agriculture, later to be turned into a full Department of Agriculture. Then, as industry began to overtake agriculture, pressure groups injected an agency to care for Commerce and Labor; and this, in turn, yielding to the marshalled pressures of interested voters, changed into the separate Departments of Commerce and of Labor. The dominant grip of the Department of Commerce upon Washington under Secretary, and later President, Hoover was nothing ordained in the Constitution or in the minds of the Founding Fathers.

When a part of culture is thus singled out and capped and gowned with symbols of authority and prestige, it tends to play the rôle expected of it. As a result, the social sciences have tended to emphasize data gathered rather than data needing to be gathered, normative theory rather than the full range of refractory phenomena, and to stress Knowledge and Order rather than the vast areas of the Unknown and Chaotic. Their prestige as sciences rests upon their profession to see order in the disorderly sequences of daily living. And this bias in favor of the manageably known is intrinsic in the academic culture: We professors were trained by our professors, who were in turn trained by their professors, to enter *a discipline*, i.e., an artificially abstracted and fenced off area of our culture. The result has been a very human tendency to emphasize, by implication and focus of emphasis if not by overt insistence, the conservative core of data and abstractions that are accepted by tradition and by the bibliographies of our colleagues. Here, in each social science, is the centripetal tendency to shrink away from the marginal area where insistent reality grinds against the central body of theory. Consequently, each social science tends to be a floating island of more or less internally coherent but partially unreal theoretical and factual certainties in the vast sea of living uncertainty. What we tend to teach our students is the limited cartography of our respective islands, paying scant attention to the *mare incognitum* of surrounding behavior.

It was a direct result of pressures by powerful, interested people who, in a culture of unplanned *laissez-faire*, rode and utilized the accidents of cultural development. Likewise, the absence of—shall we say—Departments of Family Life, Leisure, Education, Population and Human Resources, and Consumption in Washington is in no sense an ordained part of "the American way," but, rather, evidence of the lack of organized pressure groups and of the monopolizing of public attention by other allegedly more important concerns.

John Dewey remarks in his opening essay in *The Influence of Darwin on Philosophy* that one aspect of this influence was to make philosophy "humble"; and it did this through undercutting the preoccupation with many of the traditional esoteric problems privy to the old philosophy and giving philosophy a new responsibility in the common task of understanding and directing daily human behavior. Some such imminent recapture of social science by the world of reality is now painfully in process, as specialists armed with monetary and other theories have trouped to Washington to "solve the problem of the depression," only to return to their universities discomfited, as yet other specialists stressing yet other theories have displaced them.

The suggestion that the social sciences are not already "humble" will strike many social scientists as a bit of effrontery. Whole schools of social scientists are devoted to patient, unpretentious empiricism. A great research body like the National Bureau of Economic Research proudly claims to eschew "theory-building" in favor of data-gathering and fact-finding around workaday problems. In this way, it is claimed, we will in time lay the factual groundwork for a sounder and more realistic theory.[6]

The emphasis upon empiricism in the social sciences needs no defense. But there is a seductive quality about

[6] The following characteristic statement of this abstemious scientific position is made by Wesley C. Mitchell in his foreword to Leo Wolman's *Growth of American Trade Unions, 1880-1923* (New York: National Bureau of Economic Research, 1924):

"In determining the facts on these heads as accurately as the materials permit, the National Bureau is following its policy of providing men of all shades of opinion with objective knowledge of the conditions which confront them. As in all our work, so here: we confine ourselves to stating the facts as we find them. With opinions about the promise or the danger to American life from the growth of trade unions we have no concern as an organization of investigators."

this close empirical description of how things work. To carry it on one usually places oneself inside the going system, accepts temporarily its values and goals, and sets to work at gathering data and charting trends. Such provisional acceptance of an *ex parte* definition of the situation may involve small risk in the case of an ethnologist at work on a primitive tribe, because he comes from a confessedly more sophisticated culture and expects to return to it with his data. The situation is quite different, however, when, for instance, an economist accepts provisionally the definition of the situation by the business world. For in this case everything around him shouts at the economist, "This is important. Here is where the money comes from that makes *your* civilization possible." Time is long, the data are never all in, the situation is changing, and, as the "objective" analyst finds more in the situation to record, he tends to be drawn deeper within the net of assumptions by which the institutions he is studying profess to operate. The changing situation requires the gathering of more data, the charting of more trends. So "the description and analysis of what is" goes on through a whole lifetime. Around this process one builds up the sheltering tradition of "scientific objectivity." And the empirical study of how things *have changed* operates to save one from having to ask the troublesome question: "Where are our institutions taking us, and where do we want them to take us?" If one strips culture of inner, ordained teleology and regards it as the fumbling mass of lags, inconsistencies, right and wrong inferences, and clear and confused motivations which every culture is, then the social scientist who steps within a given institutional area and accepts *its* statement of its problems as *his* may be largely surrendering that very objectivity which makes

[120]

science potentially useful to man in confronting his dilemmas.[7] In so doing, the social scientist may take on the

[7] The objection may be raised here that the essence of objectivity is scrupulously to observe and to analyze a given culture-trait only as it is presented to the observer-analyst by the culture; and that the importation of a "something else" by him into his observation marks him off at once as no scientist. (This point is discussed at greater length in Chapter v.) Science without hypothesis is sterile, however beautifully "objective." At least three types of hypothesis are in use in current empirical research: (1) That suggested in Professor Mitchell's statement regarding the work of the National Bureau of Economic Research, quoted in footnote 6 above in the present chapter. This type of hypothesis reduces the rôle of hypothesis in the research situation to the minimum. Granted that hypothesis and data are engaged in a continuous game of leapfrog, in which hypothesis prompts the collection of pertinent data, which in turn prompts the sharper statement of hypothesis, and so on indefinitely, those who use this first type of hypothesis prolong the initial leap indefinitely; the whole game tends to be constricted to this initial stage in which, starting with an initial very elementary hypothesis such as, "It is necessary to know more about such and such a phenomenon," the game consists in gathering, analyzing, and presenting data. The belief that facts automatically tell their own story disposes largely of the necessity to sharpen the hypothesis and carry on. Those who content themselves with this first type of hypothesis tend to rest back on one or more of the following value-judgments: they may assume that the more or less indiscriminate gathering of data on anything at all about which we do not know every last detail that can be known is intrinsically self-justifying; they may assert that we do not yet know enough (as we frequently, but by no means always, do not) to formulate a more actively directive hypothesis; or they may, and frequently do, also rest back implicitly upon the second type of hypothesis below. (2) The second type of hypothesis assumes implicitly or overtly that the going institutional system at a given point under analysis is fundamentally right and adequate or, in any event, should be saved, and that more knowledge about the incidental weaknesses in its essentially right operation will enable us to make it operate better. (3) The third type of hypothesis involves no concern for the saving or ⁕ scrapping of the going system as such. Thus liberating hypothesis to run free, it offers a basis for discovery of the attributes of that kind of institutional set-up that would perform a given humanly needed function as effectively as the full range of our present and obtainable knowledge permits.

The first of these three types of hypothesis may be called naive objectivity with a general bias in favor of the going system; the second, frankly biased objectivity; and the third, true objectivity, in the best tradition of science.

The point being made here is that, while the understanding of a culture-trait or of a complex of traits must of course include full analysis and understanding of the trait or traits *as the culture is wont to view them,* analysis and the hypotheses that evoke analysis must not stop there; the hypothesis must be unfettered by the casually developed pressures of the culture; it must also wrench analysis clear nearsightedness which is such a marked aspect of a culture of "practical" men floundering in the search for little remedies for large troubles. Examples of this are all about us, e.g., in the economists' efforts to heal "the sickness of an acquisitive society" by such things as "pump-priming" or "manipulating the price level" in order to "stimulate business."[8]

From one important point of view, it may be said of the social sciences, as of philosophy, that: "The history of human thought . . . is the record, not of a progressive discovery of truth, but of our gradual emancipation from error."[9] To the extent that social science accepts more or less uncritically the definition of its problems as set by tradition and current folk-assumptions, and views its rôle as the description and analysis of situations so defined, it forfeits thereby, if these problems are wrongly defined, its chief opportunity to contribute to the "emancipation from error." More data avail us little if they are data on false or misstated problems.

---

of the popular pattern of acceptance and rejection and set the phenomenon under study in a wider context of relationship and meaning. Thus, an anthropologist who goes to the West Indies to study Negro voodoo analyzes the latter in two ways: first, as a system of imputedly true and reliable causal sequences in which those who practise it earnestly (if they do) believe, and second, as sophisticated science knows it to be. It is the failure so largely in current social research to take this second step of seeing an institutional area in relation to other known things, a wider scheme, that is here questioned.

[8] Lewis Corey gives an instance of this in his *The Decline of American Capitalism*. In speaking of a contemporary economist as an example of that group of economists who have urged during the present depression that wages must be lowered in order to bring about recovery, Corey says: "[He] is an 'objective' economist whose objectivity completely accepts and justifies capitalism. He considers economics a 'science,' but a science which refuses to go beyond the relations and needs of capitalist production. It is an interesting phenomenon that the more 'objective' the economist, the more he is an apologist of capitalism." (New York: Covici-Friede, 1934, p. 105, n.)

[9] Norman Kemp Smith, "The Present Situation in Philosophy" (his inaugural lecture delivered at the University of Edinburgh in 1919), *Philosophical Review*, January 1920.

A pronounced characteristic of our current social science world is the dismay and disillusionment of many empirical scientists who have built their professional lives on the analysis of problems accepted largely at their face value as viewed by the culture. Recent events have, for the social scientist, "heaped theoretical terror on the top of practical panic." One may cite those analysts of international relations who accepted the problems of international comity as primarily political and solvable on the political level through international law and treaties; those economists who thought the problem of business cycles could be solved by leaving current individualistic business enterprise throughout the world basically unchanged; those who have believed that the problem of the Supreme Court could be solved by appointing "better men" to the bench; and those students of public administration who have sought to cope with the growing demoralization of urban citizenship and public administration by drafting new charters and re-shuffling administrative units. It is by no means intended to minimize the importance of work on problems as defined by the conventions of the culture. But although empiricism is conducive to realism, it is also deceptively conducive to a kind of over-preoccupation with immediacies which may distract attention from critical larger questions. It is the frame of reference of the problem to which empiricism is addressed, and not simply the fact of empiricism, that gives significance to close, factual analysis. The all too frequent aloofness between social science theorists and empiricists is unfortunate because neither can afford to get along without the other. If empiricism represents a healthy revolt from unfounded theorizing, it in turn invites criticism at many points by its naive concern with the collection of data on problems too casually stated.

The empirical method, learned from the natural sciences, has imported into the social sciences an undue emphasis upon certain kinds of assumed hidden orderliness and impersonal causality in the datum of social science, which it becomes the task of the scientist simply to discover and to describe:[10] Under the early influence of evolutionary doctrine, it was assumed that every culture goes through certain stages of development in the same order and sequence; then, under the influence of individual psychology and Freudian analysis, it was assumed that study of the laws of individual behavior (as if these could be isolated from a specific cultural setting) would tell us all we need to know about the processes involved in people's living together; finally, the preoccupation with the operation of institutions in Western Europe and the United States in the phase of expanding economy during the last century and a half has led to the imputation of a non-existent orderliness to this particular set of institutions. All three of these procedures seek order and sequence in an inadequate setting. In the last of the three, the dominant one in current social science, the error lies in seeking to derive the laws of social science from study of sequences observed in a single set of historically conditioned *institutions, qua institutions*, rather than from study of the *full range of behavior* around the functional cores these institutions

[10] Lawrence K. Frank has stated this problem in his article on "The Principle of Disorder and Incongruity in Economic Affairs" in the *Political Science Quarterly* for December 1932:

"In the physical sciences," he says, "the basic conceptions have been those of order, regularity, and constancy as they were revealed in the earliest of scientific explorations, astronomy. With the aid of mathematics, itself a series of implications predicated upon postulates of order, the physical sciences made great progress with these conceptions in the fields of physics and chemistry, where confirmation was found on every side. . . .

"When we turn to human affairs and social life, we cannot invoke these principles because we are dealing with human behavior, which is learned or acquired by the individual through experience. . . . Instead, we face a social life and a congeries of economic activities which are chaotic and disorderly, for which we must imaginatively create new patterns of behavior whereby some order, regularity and constancy may be introduced."

express.[11] Thus, we social scientists tend to begin by accepting our contemporary institutions as *the* datum of social science; we then go on to view them as a "system"; this, in turn, endows the system, by definition, with *its* laws; and then we seek to discover these laws as the laws of social science. Actually, the datum of social science is the entire range of human behavior, as revealed in other (including primitive) cultures as well as in our own. If social science ✳ is to be science, it must discover order and sequence wherever they exist, but there its task only begins. It must discriminate between the kind of orderliness that exists within the biological life-processes within the individual organism and that which culture exhibits. For when these biological life-processes interact with the complex and uneven thing that a cultural setting is, order fans out into disorder. To be sure, each going culture exhibits a minimum pattern of order of some sort, because some kind of *modus operandi* among its unevenly historically conditioned parts is necessary to the continuance of human life. But there is no basis for assuming that any given culture, particularly a complex and casually developed one like our own, has a fundamental orderliness or exhibits a degree of orderliness that is either rational or humanly most serviceable. If such order is to exist in culture, it must be *built into it by science*, and not merely *discovered in it*.

One may, then, attempt to state the task of social science ✳ as follows: to discover what kinds of order actually do exist in the whole range of the behavior of human beings,

[11] As Lewin points out, any adequate formulation of laws must include "irregular" and disorderly individual cases. The Aristotelian emphasis upon the antithesis of individuality and law no longer maintains in modern science, for instance, in physics and psychology. Frequency is not the ultimate criterion and expression of lawfulness. The particular case must be included within scientific law even though it occurs but once. (*Op. cit.*, pp. 6*ff*.)

what kinds of functional relationships between different parts of culture exist in space and over time, and what functionally more useful kinds of order can be created in our contemporary culture.

Working within the traditional assumption of orderliness, statistical manipulation is the spearhead of current empirical research. It has been remarked that it is almost impossible to overestimate the significance of sex in human affairs, but that this impossibility Freud has achieved. In much the same sense, one may say that it is almost impossible to overestimate the significance of refined statistical procedures for social science, but that some current researches are achieving that impossibility. If social science has tended to acquire humility as it has shifted from *a priori* theorizing to empirical observation and analysis, it is by way of reassuming its lost assurance through its erudite devotion to statistical manipulation. The beautiful precision of this procedure, as more and more variables are drawn within its intricate net, may, and does in some cases, operate to distract attention from the need for candid, and if need be radical, revision of implicit assumptions.

Dr. W. F. G. Swann of the Bartol Research Foundation has effectively described this all-too-common process, in the course of a discussion of the change in point of view to which we have to adapt ourselves in passing over from the Newtonian description of motion to that adopted in Einstein's theory of gravitation.[12] He does this by taking as illustration a fanciful causal explanation of a physical phenomenon. The scientific observer, he says, may look down from an airplane, whose height flattens out the unevenness of the terrain, and observe a traveller wending a wide, circuitous course around a house. Searching for an explanation of the traveller's failure to travel in a straight

[12] "The Trend of Thought in Physics," *Science*, April 24 and May 1, 1925.

line, the scientist-in-the-airplane draws upon the "law" that a body moves in a straight line unless a force acts upon it; he concludes that the house repels the traveller, and develops the hypothesis that the house contains a man who plays a stream of water from a hose upon travellers, compelling them to keep away from his property. Swann then goes on to show how, as new data are brought to the attention of the scientist, the latter clings to his assumptions and elaborates new explanations around them to make them fit the situation as he has defined it. He clings to the central hose explanation but begins to modify it slightly. "I shall say 'Naturally this is no ordinary kind of hose.' . . . The hose which I shall have to picture will be radically different from any hose which I have ever seen. I shall go on in this way, modifying and adjusting the hose, making it more and more difficult to understand; and, forgetting that the original justification for its introduction was its apparent power to explain what was observed in terms of something which I thought I knew all about, I shall soon be in the position of expending 99 per cent of my ingenuity in trying to understand the hose, leaving only one per cent for the law of the traveler." At this intricate and disheartening impasse, someone jogs the elbow of the scientist and tells him that there is no hose at all, and that the traveller pursues his circuitous path because the house is really situated in the floor of a valley, unobservable from the airplane, and the easiest path across is around the level surface of the rim of the valley.

One has an uneasy feeling that far too many of us social scientists are preoccupied with elaborate manipulations of data within the terms of the hose-theories that we have inherited![13]

[13] Preoccupation with inner niceties and refinements in a period of transition is not unique to the social sciences. Professor Wendell Bush describes the same

Without applying it too literally, the devotee of statistical refinement may nevertheless find a useful warning in Jonathan Swift's description of the Grand Academy of Lagado.[14] In one part of the Academy a professor had perfected a device for improving knowledge by practical and mechanical means, whereby "the most ignorant person at a reasonable charge, and with a little bodily labour, may write books in philosophy, poetry, politics, law, mathematics, and theology, without the least assistance from genius or study." A framework twenty feet square stood in the middle of the room with the forty young assistants standing in ranks about it. Fitted to the frame were square bits of wood on which were pasted papers bearing "all the words of their language, in their several moods, tenses, and declensions, but without order." At the professor's command the forty young men each gave a sudden turn to his iron handle [read "Monroe machine"] and "the whole disposition of the words" on the wooden blocks "was entirely changed." The professor "then commanded six and thirty of the lads to read the several lines softly . . . and where they found three or four words together that might make part of a sentence, they dictated to the four remaining boys who were scribes . . . and the professor showed me several volumes in large folio already collected, of broken sentences, which he intended to piece together, and out of those rich materials to give the world a complete body of all arts and sciences."

No informed person questions nowadays the indispensability of objective data-gathering and of the exhaustive statistical analysis of those data for all they are worth. The only question that is being raised here concerns the
✳ need to ask, "*What* are they worth for *what?*" Objective

type of procedure in the field of philosophy in "The Emancipation of Intelligence," *Journal of Philosophy*, March 30, 1911.

[14] *Gulliver's Travels*, Chap. v.

empiricism can become as much of a blind alley as can logical speculation. And if the social sciences are to be judged by their adequacy in helping man to resolve his difficulties, they will be only weakened by a policy of rationalizing one's way out of blind alleys by asserting that "more knowledge about anything is a self-justifying pursuit and there is no sure basis for saying that any one datum is more important than another." One of the perplexing commonplaces of the university lecture hall is the fact that whole courses and batteries of courses leading to advanced degrees are "passed" and dissertations are written without the question's ever being raised as to what is to be done with all this knowledge—other than to give more lectures and to supervise the writing of more dissertations. A student may sit through an entire year of admirably analytic lectures on the structure and functioning of an important current institution—e.g., our economic productive system—without the lecturer's once raising the direct question: What do we human beings — want this particular institutional-complex to do for us, what is the most direct way to do it, and what do we need to know in order to do it?

History is the most venerable of the social sciences. ✳ Man's future may be obscure, his present confused, but his past, though continually reinterpreted, stands firm. To the extent that this past is honorific, we may be proud of it and employ the sentiments it inspires to stiffen men's wavering current loyalties; to the extent that it reveals man confronted by typical human dilemmas and finding serviceable paths through them, we may cautiously canvass past precedents as possible dress rehearsals for coping with the fumbling present; and, in so far as it represents irreparably spilled milk, we may learn from it how to avoid past errors. Each human being is his telescoped past experience in culture pressed by vital impulses against present circumstances; and history enables him to extend this experience beyond his personal life-span. If the sciences of human behavior in culture must be continually aware of the present circumstances, including the rhythms, motivations, and growth-processes of the human stuff that drives them, they must also just as surely deal with the rôle of past processes and events in shaping the character of the present, and with the implications of these past things for present action. The place of historical analysis in social science is, therefore, basic and beyond question. And this is reflected in the prevalent assumption in our culture that "the more history you know, the better"— an assumption which is apparent in the large place of this discipline in popular education.

But tradition has its limitations as well as its solid advantages. In a culture which constantly cripples its grasp upon current problems by a proud mystical adherence to a written Constitution, to legal precedent, and to inherited folklore, the impact of a whole discipline—the most strongly entrenched social science in American education —devoted to the teaching of the past *qua* past tends to be decidedly conservative. Without disparaging "the lessons to be learned from the past," one may still urge that our problems, however much conditioned by the past, *are in the present*; that the present is an era of the widest, most rapid, and most complicated cultural change in our national history; that our chances of coping successfully with current problems depend to no small extent upon our ability to throw off tradition and to handle our problems freshly in the light of new knowledge and techniques; and that the analogical appeal to past situations tends to blur precisely those elements of greatest hope or perplexity, namely, the new factors which were not present in the earlier situations. There probably never was another era when "the appeal to history," uncorrected by the multiple new variants in the situation, meant less.

No minor part of the value of man's history lies in its explosive implications for present action. Only psychology, with its undercutting of the falsely assumed psychological bases on which many of our most revered institutions are reared, rivals history in this respect. For history, with authoritative finality, preserves eloquent evidence of the dead hand of custom and class coercions, as well as the record of the stubbornly recurrent insistencies of human nature. As James Harvey Robinson pointed out,[15] "History has been regularly invoked to substantiate the claims of the conservative, but has hitherto usually been neglected by the radical,[16] or impatiently repudiated as the chosen weapon of his enemy. The radical has not yet perceived the overwhelming value to him of a real understanding of the past. It is his weapon by right, and he should wrest it from the hand of the conservative." Elsewhere Robinson pointed out that "The present has hitherto been the willing victim of the past; the time has now come when it should turn on the past and exploit it in the interests of advance."[17]

It is precisely this recapture of the past in the service of — present action that makes such a book as Professor Beard's *An Economic Interpretation of the Constitution of the United States* so relentlessly applicable to our present problem of political democracy within private capitalism. And yet historiography, with some notable exceptions, has been largely unprepared or unwilling to play such a forthright rôle among the social sciences. This is due to a number of factors, principally within the discipline itself.

[15] *The New History* (New York: Macmillan, 1920), p. 252.
[16] Robinson footnotes the Marxian socialists as an exception.
[17] *Ibid.*, p. 24.

The essence of things past is that they cannot be changed. They can be misinterpreted and reinterpreted, but the datum itself is immutably there, like the natural phenomena with which the natural scientist deals. Hence historians who aspire to regard themselves as scientists, rather than colorful interpreters, have been scrupulous sticklers for scientific objectivity. Since it only works havoc to impose one's belated wishes upon the past, the historian has rightly insisted that it is his business to hew rigorously to the line of the facts as he finds them, regardless of human predilections and regrets.

This insistence is indubitably necessary. But it has led to other less desirable tendencies. History, thus voyaging forth with no pole star except the objective recovery of the past, becomes a vast, wandering enterprise. How much so may be gauged by leafing through the logbook of current historical research in progress.[18] Here one sees a gigantic industry of recording and annotating things assumed to be *worth knowing for themselves* because they are part of the hitherto unknown. Even the ample robe of scholarship might find difficulty in giving dignity to such an amorphous procedure, were the whole not bolstered by a heavy implicit reliance upon an assumed automatic transfer of the knowledge so gained to pragmatic current situations.

But this automatic transfer of "the lessons of the past" is a large assumption. Transfer of learning depends upon the relevance of the thing learned to the new situation. In order to count upon such automatic transfer in the case of history, one would have to assume that the historian goes

18 See *List of Research Projects in History, Exclusive of Doctoral Dissertations, Now in Progress in the United States and the Dominion of Canada*, published as a supplement to the *American Historical Review*, April 1934. Also *List of Doctoral Dissertations in History Now in Progress at American Universities*, December *1937*, issued by the Division of Historical Research, Carnegie Institution of Washington, 1938.

to the past with a thorough analytical knowledge of a present problem and quarries the gigantic pit of the past with the intricate niceties of this problem that confronts us precisely in mind. Stated concretely, this would mean that the historian of democratic processes in an earlier era would know to its roots the field of conflicting power forces in which our *present* democracies labor to operate, and, selecting a sharply defined aspect of a relevant problem, would go back to the past to ask what elements in a past situation or situations were similar to and what elements were different from the ones we face today, how significant these similarities and differences are in the present *Gestalt* of the problem, and what concrete guidance the past affords. Despite some tendency continually to rewrite history in the light of current problems, historical analysis tends to be so largely preoccupied with the past for the past's own sake that the comparability of the historian's re-creations with present situations is more often gross than refined. It was precisely because Karl Marx, commencing as a philosopher of history, mined the past for its specific implications for the operation of the capitalism of his day that he gave to historiography one of its most important hypotheses, and to social technicians an historically-edged instrument for confronting their contemporary problems. If the record of the past is to be usable in the present, it is not enough to "re-create the past"; it must be re-created in sharp orientation to the specific intricacies of present problems.

Another obstacle to the automatic transfer of knowledge about the past to present situations inheres in the fact that the great majority of historians are not equipped with an adequate knowledge of psychology. The past becomes a dynamically projective reference for present behavior only when it, too, is viewed as behavior. One cannot equate events analyzed on the level of *things, events, forces,* or even *the processes of things, events, or forces*, with current behavior by *persons*, because the two halves of the equation are incommensurable. Lacking an adequate set of theoretical postulates as to how human nature behaves, historians tend to take over implicitly either (or alternately both) of two theories—that men are governed by hedonistic rational choices, or that they do what they do because they have to. These two views represent the oversimplified extremes of a complicated situation. Man is not predominantly rational. And, on the other hand, human motivation, however conditioned and determined by the past, always operates in the present; and at the white-hot edge of decision, the stuff of behavior which the historian finds so rigid when cold, is continually bent and directed into new forms. Choices, limited to be sure by past conditioning and by the momentum of movement along habitual grooves, but still choices to an important degree, *are* being made as man lives along. And these choices, including the factors determining their constriction and their potential range, are a central part of the business of social science. Uneasily aware of the inadequacy of either rationality or determinism as an explanation of how things have come to be as they are, some historians turned to the "great man" theory or to the theory of intruding events as explanations of the dynamic element in past behavior, only later to abandon these, too, as inadequate. Other historians, eschewing the search for any grand formulas, have settled down to the empirical recording of "the small, the common, and the obscure" as the pebbles out of which the process of gradual accretion will in time build useful structures.

Like economists, historians for the most part elect to avoid any open commerce with the intricacies of modern psychology. The following incident from the oral examination of a candidate in American history in a leading graduate school reflects this situation. The candidate in question was regarded by her department as unusually well trained and promising, among the pick of the crop. She knew an amazing number of facts. The closing examiner from the History Department asked her two questions: "Miss ———, what persons can you name in American history whose surnames were Johnson?" The second concerned persons whose surnames were Wilson. And the candidate knew lots of Johnsons and Wilsons! An examiner from another discipline then asked what was apparently regarded by the historians present as a freak question: "Miss ———, you are going out of the university as an unusually well trained specialist in interpreting the behavior of man in the past. What working theory of human nature, of how people behave, do you use in your historical analyses?" The answer was, "I have none." "But you must have," protested the examiner, "or you cannot explain what happens, can you?" She not only stood her ground, but went on, under further questioning, to deny to psychology the status of a science and to insist that it has nothing that will help the historian. This incident is here set down as typical rather than as unusual, in the experience of the writer. It suggests a serious limitation upon the value to fellow social scientists of the product of the historical scholar.

These are limiting factors within the discipline. But it should not be overlooked that what has been said of the coercive influence of such things as economic pressure-blocs on the selection of problems for research by the academic economist applies also to the historian. The pressure on the historian is not so close and constant, since he is concerned with the past and therefore not so immediately dangerous; but the pressure is there nevertheless. Such things as class conflict in the United States have been studied too meagerly by academic historians, and then only with a retrospective implication and a monographic paleness that tends to cloak past conflict with the connotation of isolated protest against *"then* intolerable conditions." It is not surprising that it was long after the large rôle of economic circumstances in history began to be recognized that Frederick Turner, in 1894, became the first American historian to point to the need for an economic interpretation of American history.[19]

✳ So in the main historiography contents itself with recreation of the past as "scholarship," i.e., as a self-justifying procedure carried on for its own sake in a general mood of disinterested curiosity. This has tended to impart to the historian and to his product an excessive reserve, which operates as social quietism. Over the urgencies of present social confusion is thrown the blanket of the lessons of history, which show that "Time is long, man has met and survived many climactic eras, and he will continue to do so." This is, to be sure, a useful reminder to the social-scientist-in-a-hurry, but it also operates to prompt the historian to move among his perplexed fellow-scientists like the conservative described by John Morley, "with his inexhaustible patience of abuses that only torment others; his apologetic word for beliefs that may not be so precisely true as one might wish, and institutions that are not altogether so useful as some might think possible; his cordiality towards progress and improvement in a general way, and his coldness or antipathy to each progressive proposal in particular; his pygmy hope that life will one day become somewhat better, punily shivering by the side of his gigantic conviction that it might well be infinitely worse."

Historiography, like everything else, is changing. Such men as Turner, Robinson, and Beard have stressed the

[19] Cf. A. M. Schlesinger, *New Viewpoints in American History* (New York: Macmillan, 1922), p. 69.

need not merely to understand the past but also to aid —
in problems of present control. History as a social science,
however, confronts the question as to whether the leisurely
process of casual change now going on within itself pre-
pares it to play this more active rôle in our present era of
extraordinary change and confusion. Casual change is forever "missing the boat"; and, certainly, needed changes
within a *science* should not have to exhibit the tortuous,
lagging movement that characterizes change in culture-
complexes in which the persons involved are less aware of
the goals toward which they move. We can count upon
academic controls and the strong tradition of objective
historical scholarship to guard the rear against slipshod,
partisan defection in the writing of history, but they will
not implement the advance. Even the vast army of present
and future historians is inadequate to recover and to
analyze the myriad details of the past; for modern social
science is discovering in social concepts and institutions
new complexities and bequeathing voluminous new kinds
of statistical and other records to complicate the work of
the historian who will try tomorrow to fit today into "the
stream of history." Selection by the historian is increasingly
necessary and unavoidable. Criteria of relevance must be
discovered and stated that will enable historiography to
determine whether, e.g., the elaborate analysis of "The
Shield Signal at Marathon" in the *American Historical
Review* for April 1937 is a warranted expenditure of scientific energy. As will be shown later, we do not lack bases
for such criteria. Only in a highly artificial and academic —
sense do we need the history of *everything*. What we do
need from the past is the selection of *some things*, seen in
relation to other relevant *some things* in the past, and the
whole analyzed for their relevance to specific broad and
narrow *some things* pertinent to vital current decision.

[137]

There are signs that the other social sciences, instead of waiting for history to give them what they require, are themselves going to the past and writing their own history around the need to know specific things about the past in relation to current institutional problems. Thus the earlier rôle of history as general surrogate in charge of the past is being undercut. Specialists in the intricacies of sharply defined problems, as science knows these problems today, are challenging the adequacy of history-in-general. And history finds itself uncertain whether it is a "subject-matter" or a "method." While the writing of the old *Kulturgeschichte* of a broad, summary type will remain and will continue to perform a highly useful integrative function, it appears not unlikely that the main body of historical activity, like that of philosophy, may be in process of absorption by workers in the special sciences who are thoroughly oriented technically to contemporary needs for focused genetic analysis of specific problems.[20]

After history, the oldest of our current group of sciences is political science, the science of government. J. N. Figgis[21] pointed out the momentous significance for modern thought of the secularization of political theory. "The State" became a subject of matter-of-fact speculation, supported by a body of law that was bursting the constraints of ecclesiastical rules. But, closely allied to the law and to history, and developing in the center of the intellectualist tradition, the science of government long tended to be one of the most formalistic and taxonomic of the social sciences. Political theory and public law constituted the solid, dignified backbone of the discipline. Academic political scientists lived in a genteel world apart from the rough-

[20] Discussion of this point is carried further at the close of this chapter.
[21] *Studies in Political Thought from Gerson to Grotius, 1414-1625* (Cambridge: The University Press, 1907), Chap. I.

and-ready ward-politician. The study of government and politics, accordingly, tended to be safely historical, or, when working with the contemporary, it reached gingerly down toward Tammany Hall from the clean upper atmosphere, with a sense of deploring the presence of such an unsavory thing as ward finagling and vote-buying.

With the second decade of the present century the great empiricism set in. A large body of political scientists now devote themselves to the workaday details of public administration. There is some tendency for the public law and political philosophy men to disparage mildly these workers in public administration as the handy men of the science; and the latter are not entirely free from responsibility for this, for they often exhibit a nearsighted preoccupation with minor changes in the going system. Another group of political scientists, stimulated by such realistic books by men outside the academic fraternity as Lincoln Steffens's *The Shame of the Cities* and Arthur F. Bentley's *The Process of Government* and by Graham Wallas's *Human Nature in Politics*, turned to factual analysis of pressure politics in specific situations. A growing list of studies is resulting, including E. P. Herring's *Group Representation before Congress* and *Public Administration and the Public Interest*, Peter Odegard's *Pressure Politics, the Story of the Anti-Saloon League*, E. E. Schattschneider's *Politics, Pressures and the Tariff*, Belle Zeller's *Pressure Politics in New York*, D. D. McKean's *Pressures on the Legislature of New Jersey*. Harold Lasswell's *Politics: Who Gets What, When and How* reveals the candid mood of these studies, and the same author has also contributed a valuable impetus in the direction of the study of the psychology of political leadership. A related body of similarly realistic work on our legal institutions is also coming from leading law schools.

Political science exhibits a situation common in present social science: a traditional body of inherited theory, and a growing body of empiricism somewhat disregardful of theory. The technicians in public administration are tending to overreach themselves in assuming that effective administration in the public interest can be achieved by small administrative adjustments of the going system; and the students of such things as pressure politics tend to work ahead in that happy state in which there is so much to describe that theory seems unnecessary for the moment. These latter are working at the central political reality of our culture, namely, the actual structuring of power relationships among our institutions; but they tend to describe it with the aloofness of a reporter covering a fire in a warehouse. They show us the blaze and the damage, but they leave largely untouched the questions: "Is democracy workable in a world of unequal men, and where, and how?" and "Can political democracy survive in a culture dominated by the power of concentrated private wealth?" As Professor Laski has pointed out, "The Industrial Revolution brought the middle class to power, and they evolved a form of state—capitalist democracy—which seemed most suited to their security. . . . It offered a share in political authority to all citizens upon the unstated assumption that the equality involved in the democratic ideal did not seek extension to the economic sphere. The assumption could not be maintained. For the object of political power is always the abrogation of privilege; and that abrogation can only be postponed when the conquests of the new régime are so great that it can offer a constantly increasing standard of life to the masses."[22]

[22] *Op. cit.*, p. 53.

We lack a philosophy of the place of Power in modern — institutional life, and development of this philosophy and the blueprinting of the way ahead under it are allowed to fall neatly between the fields of economics and politics. And if our shortcomings are in general traceable to the relative newness of social science, there is also good reason in the *Realpolitik* of academic life why each group should prefer to avoid this particular problem.

The rise of economics as "an objective and passionless science" followed belatedly after the secularization of political theory. "It was not till a century after Machiavelli had emancipated the State from religion, that the doctrine of the self-contained department with laws of its own begins generally to be applied to the world of business relations, and even in the England of the early seventeenth century, to discuss questions of economic organization purely in terms of pecuniary profit and loss still wears an air of not quite respectable cynicism."[23] All vestiges of such squeamishness have long since disappeared, drowned in the opulence of the commercial and industrial revolutions. The growing science of economics has followed breathlessly after the amazing conquests of technology harnessed to the purposes of money-making. The task it has accepted has been largely that of rationalizing a *fait accompli*. In the fascinating upsurge of material advancement during the past hundred years, the hope of civilization seemed to lie clearly in the hands of the businessman left free to pursue his own private profit; and if the political scientist retired from leadership in favor of the businessman, the economist went him one better and,

[23] R. H. Tawney, *Religion and the Rise of Capitalism* (New York: Harcourt, Brace, 1926), p. 7.

in the main, placed himself and his science at the service of the businessman to try to solve the latter's problems.

Ours is a culture nominally built upon the foundation stones of individualism and *laissez-faire*. John Maynard Keynes has shown in his brilliant Oxford essay on *The End of Laissez-Faire*[24] how this doctrine has been revitalized and kept in authority:

"By the time that the influence of Paley and his like was waning, the innovations of Darwin were shaking the foundations of belief. Nothing could seem more opposed than the old doctrine and the new—the doctrine which looked on the world as the work of the divine Watchmaker and the doctrine which seemed to draw all things out of Chance, Chaos, and Old Time. But at this one point the new ideas bolstered up the old. The Economists were teaching that wealth, commerce, and machinery were the children of free competition—that free competition built London. But the Darwinians could go one better than that—free competition had built Man. The human eye was no longer the demonstration of Design, miraculously contriving all things for the best; it was the supreme achievement of Chance, operating under conditions of free competition and *laissez-faire*. The principle of the Survival of the Fittest could be regarded as a vast generalization of the Ricardian economics. Socialistic interferences became, in the light of this grander synthesis, not merely inexpedient, but impious, as calculated to retard the onward movement of the mighty process by which we ourselves had risen like Aphrodite out of the primeval slime of Ocean.

"Therefore I trace the peculiar unity of the everyday political philosophy of the nineteenth century to the success with which it harmonised diversified and warring schools and united all good things to a single end. . . .

[24] London: Hogarth Press, 1926, pp. 13-15.

"These reasons and this atmosphere are the explanations, whether we know it or not—and most of us in these degenerate days are largely ignorant in the matter—why we feel such a strong bias in favor of *laissez-faire*, and why State action to regulate the value of money, or the course of investment, or the population, provoke such passionate suspicions in many upright breasts."

In summarizing the position of economics regarding *laissez-faire*, Keynes quotes a few pages later Cairnes's statement that "The maxim of *laissez-faire* has no scientific basis whatever, but is at best a mere handy rule of practice." "This," says Keynes, "for fifty years past, has been the view of all leading economists. Some of the most important work of Alfred Marshall—to take one instance —was directed to the elucidation of the leading cases in which private interest and social interest are *not* harmonious. Nevertheless the guarded and undogmatic attitude of the best economists has not prevailed against the general opinion that an individualistic *laissez-faire* is both what they ought to teach and what in fact they do teach."

Here one is witnessing the predicament of a science shaped by the very institutions about which it is supposed to be "objective." One of the most dramatic and momentous conflicts in our current American culture—a crisis crowding insistently onto the front pages of our newspapers—is that between the advocates of the old doctrine of *laissez-faire* and those who propose centralization, planning, and control. The conflict is rendered the more confusing by the fact that those who shout the loudest for uncontrolled individualism are engaged in operation of highly organized corporate business units which gain such advantage as they hold over their competitors chiefly through their sedulous use of planning and control. A science which largely limits its view to the norms congenial to the folkways it studies is unequipped to offer forthright guidance out of such a maze of customary freedoms and controls.

Economics can defend its liaison with business by pointing to its substantial accomplishments. The work of such men as Wesley C. Mitchell and Frederick C. Mills at the National Bureau of Economic Research is unexcelled anywhere in the social sciences for its careful, analytical integrity. Young economists the country over accept this research as a model for their own work. Here is current economic research at its best. It makes no overt assumptions; it is "objective analysis." But it tacitly assumes that private, competitive business enterprise, motivated by the desire for profit, is the way for a culture to utilize its technical skill to supply its people with needed goods. Such things as "prices," "production," "distribution," and "economic processes" are accepted as given, subject only to such small changes as the outcome of these researches may suggest. This type of economic research asks no questions that fundamentally call into question or go substantially beyond the core of the folkways. The general attitude is ameliorative, and the economist's task thus becomes the study of how limited adjustments can be made, within this dynamic process of business enterprise, to decrease the amplitude of disjunctions and increase profit to all concerned. Now all of this may be sound procedure, for our cultural folkways may have stumbled on the ultimate, essentially most effective way of producing and distributing commodities. It may be correct, as the culture believes and as John Bates Clark asserted, that "competition is an inextinguishable force"[25] and "If nothing suppresses competition, progress will continue forever."[26] The culture may be right in assuming that the profit motive is the inevi-

[25] *The Distribution of Wealth* (New York: Macmillan, 1899), p. 441.
[26] *Essentials of Economic Theory* (New York: Macmillan, 1907), p. 374.

table mainsp ng which must operate the provision of the goods and services desired by man. But a science jeopardizes its status as science when it operates uncritically within the grooves of traditional folk assumptions. Furthermore, private capitalism the world over appears to be laboring along so heavily as to make it the urgent responsibility of the social sciences to include within their scope the systematic canvass of all possible far-reaching adaptations or outright substitutes for it. Individuals differ in their hypotheses as to what such a systematic canvass would reveal. The task of science is to remove all tenable hypotheses from the limbo of uncertainty.

If there is serious question as to the adequacy of economic science in dealing with present perplexities, this would seem, therefore, to be due not so much to any inadequacy in the detail of its work as it is to the constriction of its focus. When leading economists in the field of labor problems say that "wages are out of line" at the present time and that "this is holding up the return of prosperity," they are speaking through the closed iron visor of a particular set of economic folkways and a particular, historically-dated theory of "marginal productivity." For "out of line" means out of line with labor's contribution to total product, assumed to be set by "natural laws" which apportion the incomes in a culture among the different claimants. It is this kind of theory and pronouncement,[27] relying tacitly upon the existence of impersonal economic laws congruent with business enter-

---

[27] For typical examples of this sort of theorizing see statements by J. B. Clark in his *The Distribution of Wealth* such as, ". . . The distribution of the income of society is controlled by a natural law, and . . . this law, if it worked without friction, would give to every agent of production the amount of wealth which that agent creates." (p. 3.) Or his justification of private property on the ground that "property is protected at the point of its origin, if wages are the whole product of labor, if interest is the product of capital, and if profit is the product of the coordinating act." (p. 9.)

prise as we know it, which blocks the posing of fresh questions and confirms the *status quo*.

The kind of problem our culture faces is not solvable by debating wage theory pro and con implicitly within the rigid framework of "marginal productivity," but by using science to discover how several million unemployed persons can be put at humanly constructive work and the standard of welfare of the population raised. As this is being written, the Department of Agriculture is seeking a way to make surplus food resources available to the many millions of our families who need this food—e.g., millions of oranges allowed to rot on the ground because they cannot be sold at existing prices. Arrayed against such a move stands the grocery business, wholesale and retail. This is the type of problem that requires the help of economic science: we have the food and we have the hungry people; and all that prevents getting the two together is a set of economic rituals that act as a bottleneck between the people and the food. Again, the constriction of focus within economic science appears in the claim of leading statistical empiricists that they substitute "dynamic process" for the "static equilibria" of the Marshallian school. This aim represents an important gain, but here again the iron visor clangs down, for a dynamic system of analysis should use variables which are as dynamic as the changing processes it seeks to analyze; but the "new economics" employs the old static system of variables—Marshall's stout "engine of analysis"—applying these static variables at each particular point in the time series it seeks to analyze. At point after point economic science curbs its potential effectiveness by the uncritical, and therefore unscientific, device of allowing the traditions of business enterprise to define the situation for it. Thus, the studies by the Brookings Institution of *America's Capacity to Produce* and *America's Capacity to Consume* cramp "capacity" within boundaries relevant only to a kind of economic theorizing antedating and out of step with modern technology. It is in general a safe tentative hypothesis for science that ideas are to be suspected and reexamined when extended beyond the domain in which they arose.

The position of consumption in economic science is a crucial instance of how important problems are crowded out of view in a science which defines its field as economics does. It is one of the inevitable commonplaces that everyone accepts as "right in theory" that all our economic processes are not ends in themselves but instrumental to the ends of human living; and, within this broad generalization, production is not an end in itself but instrumental to the use of commodities to serve the ends of living. Adam Smith stated this unequivocally when the science of economics was setting out on its long career: "Consumption," he said, "is the sole end and purpose of all production; and the interest of the producer ought to be attended to only so far as it may be necessary for promoting that of the consumer. The maxim is so perfectly self-evident that it would be absurd to attempt to prove it."[28] And so it is. Subsequent economists have rarely challenged this statement. They have, in the main, said "Of course!" and turned to the business in hand. For they and their science are but children of a culture. And in Adam Smith's time, as today, that culture was engaged in the grand adventure of growing rich. Smith goes on to point out in his next sentence the contradiction between theory and practice: "But in the mercantile system, the interest of the consumer is almost constantly sacrificed to that of the producer; and it seems to consider production, and not consumption, as the ultimate end and object of all industry and commerce."

[28] *The Wealth of Nations* (London: Methuen, 1920, 2nd Cannon ed.), Vol. II, p. 159.

In a culture stressing money-making, the earlier expansion of money-making meant more production and consumption; but, under modern conditions, it means the contraction of production and consumption *relative to our ability to produce and to consume*. Crop restriction under the Agricultural Adjustment Administration is simply the flowering of a familiar modern weed in a new field. The Industrial Revolution gave man for the first time in his long history the prospect of vanquishing scarcity. It was a heady prospect. No wonder men were fascinated, the "objective" economists along with them. The formula is simple: "You can't have what you don't make. You can't make things if men can't make a profit from producing them. Therefore, profitable production is the key to welfare and the freest rein should be given to such productive enterprise."[29] In the century and a half since Adam Smith, all orthodox economic theory has either followed John Stuart Mill in dismissing the consumer from the picture or has retained him as a faithful servant called Demand, who could be counted upon to be unostentatiously and infallibly present when needed. And the Federal government has enacted tariffs, built up Supreme Court precedents, and established administrative services in Washington to favor the ends of more and more profitable production.

Economists have gained in prestige from their close affiliation with money-making, and the research funds they

---

[29] A recent statement of this need to give priority to the needs of profitable production was made by E. R. A. Seligman as a witness in the suit by the Federal government to dissolve the Sugar Institute for alleged violations of the anti-trust laws. "Both interests [those of the producer and those of the consumer] are important," testified Professor Seligman. "If there were no producers, there would be no consumers; only stagnation and death. Therefore, as between the interests of consumer and producer, the producer should be, if need be, favored." (Quoted in New York *Times* for September 22, 1932, in a news item headed, "Seligman Cites Stock Exchange as Example of Free Market at Sugar Institute's Trial.")

can command are the envy of the other social sciences. What the culture has lost thereby we are only glimpsing today as we struggle in the chaos of the depression with the problems of a capitalism seemingly in decline. The distortions of a hundred and fifty years of economic theory do not make it easy to restore production to its "perfectly self-evident" rôle of instrument to the human needs of consumers.

We know what our machine technologies can do—that they can produce far beyond the capacity of our economic institutions to distribute the product of their "progress." The question our American culture poses for economic science is: How do you propose that we bring our economic institutions abreast of our technological skills? What is your documented blueprint for changing our institutions so as to achieve the optimum use of our resources for the welfare of our population? As Bridgman remarked in the address to his fellow scientists referred to above, "The game of getting the right answer is a hard one"; and "The only thing in [the scientist's] control by which he may command the situations which confront him is his intelligence." But the fact that a problem is difficult and the manifest need continually to cross-cut accumulated folk-practice with intelligence are the only reasons we bother to have social science. In view of the grip of economic institutions on the rest of our institutional life, the "failure of nerve" by a crucial social science like economics endangers the entire culture, including science itself.[30]

[30] One of the characteristics of our immediate era is the extent to which workers in the natural sciences are becoming apprehensive as to the degree to which current institutional chaos, inviting the rise of totalitarianism, threatens the freedom of all science. As a result, physicists, biologists, and similar specialists are beginning to interest themselves in problems that lie in the field of the social sciences.

Sociology has inherited an impossible rôle. Newest among the social sciences, it lives in a twilight zone of qualified respectability which much of its sprawled current work does little to clarify. It came into being in a world in which its elders, political science and economics, were immersed in the abstractions at the secluded inner core of their respective fields as they had elected to define those fields. There was obviously a "something more." Neither the "political man" nor the "economic man," singly or collectively, described the whole of social reality. People lived in families, neighborhoods, communities, whole societies, and they exhibited an inveterate propensity for associating themselves in a variety of functional groups which were not confined to the economic and political sections of their lives. What was needed was a frame of reference within which the discrete special social sciences could be viewed along with these other relevant things. So a Science of Society was born. Some sociologists still think of their field in these broad terms, as a kind of holding company for all the special social sciences. Others regard such a pretension as a delusion of grandeur; they fear the level of generality to which this leads and insist that a science must be focused and grounded in a growing body of integrated, first-hand empirical work. The building of a science of society, these latter claim, is but another way of stating the common field of all the social sciences, and the effort to train young scientists in a special discipline which encompasses so gross a field leads to superficiality.

The need to study the total culture as an interacting continuum, stressed in Chapter II, confirms the essential soundness of sociology's attempted inclusive aim. Actually, the islands of emphasis of the special social sciences leave vast areas of the everyday life of men and women unaccounted for. And even within such concepts as "demand," "the market," and "majority rule" are unexplored areas of social interaction sufficiently great to invite application to them of the statement by a psychologist regarding his own field, that "between the two terms of the sensori-motor circuit there is more *terra incognita* than was on the map of Africa sixty years ago."[31]

The relative newness of sociology and the fact that it has scattered its energies over many problem-areas, where awareness of the existence of problems has come but lately and factual data are therefore scant, have added to its apparent superficiality and disorder. Here is the staggering congeries of subject-matters covered by present-day sociology: Social Theory, Social Organization, Social Classes and Social Groups, Social Change, Social Evolution, Social Legislation, Social Pathology, The Family, Crime and Delinquency, Urbanism, Human Ecology, Rural Life, Leisure, the Press and Communication, Population Problems, Race Problems, and a large group of "sociologies of" Religion, Thought, Language, Occupations, War, and other special subjects. All of these are useful problem-areas for the social sciences, some of them crucially important, and most of them are far under-worked as yet. What sociology is here attempting to do is to play Old Woman Who Lived in a Shoe for a crowded brood of emerging special sciences.

As such, sociology does two serious disservices, one to itself and the other to the older established social sciences. Its ambitious effort to develop singlehanded this omnibus load of diverse fields renders its training of young scientists and their resulting research attack more superficial than the complexity of these problems warrants. This boomerangs back upon the validity of sociology as a science. The disservice this over-wide program of sociology does to the other social sciences is no less real. The effort of sociology to cover the whole range of the "social" fortifies

[31] Wolfgang Köhler, *Gestalt Psychology* (New York: Liveright, 1929), p. 54.

the tendency of the special sciences to shrink away from marginal problems. Confronted with the "social aspects" of a given problem, these special sciences find it over-easy to wash their hands of these, saying "It's not *our* problem. Sociology will deal with it." This claim, therefore, of sociology to study the social aspects of things encourages the perpetuation of such primitive dichotomies as "economic *and* social" or "political *and* social"—as if the "economic" or "political" could usefully be regarded as entities apart from the "social." It is this kind of false segmenting of problems that enables the economist, for instance, so largely to exclude such things as class conflict from among the variables he employs in his purportedly dynamic analysis.[32] If the emphasis upon culture as a unifying device for the social sciences means anything, it means that the way ahead must involve the viewing of each problem in the full context of every relevant part of the culture, including the economic *and* the political *and* the social *and* the psychological.

It is appropriate to insert here comment on the use of the related terms "social" and "society" in the social sciences. As the reader will have observed, the present volume avoids the use of the term society, save as a loose, handy term of reference to the group of people who

[32] An illustration of this is pointed out in Dr. Paul M. Sweezy's review of *Full Recovery or Stagnation?* by Professor Alvin H. Hansen, of Harvard University, in the *Nation* for November 19, 1938: "If Professor Hansen's analysis is brilliant and profound, his proposals for policy are disappointing. The fault does not lie with him as an individual but with the tradition of thought—orthodox economics—with which he is identified. The economic system, according to the orthodox way of looking at things, can be analyzed and its ills prescribed for in complete abstraction from the kind of society to which it gives rise. Whether capitalism will survive, says Professor Hansen, 'is not so much a question of class struggle; it is rather a question of the inherent workability of the system.' But the basis of the system is a set of property relationships which, in turn, inevitably give rise to the class struggle. Here again it is not a question of whether we like it or not; to attempt to understand capitalism in abstraction from class struggle is to miss the nub of the problem as it exists in the real world."

live in and carry a culture. Whereas it is common practice ✳ to employ the conceptual trilogy "the individual," "society," and "culture," the analysis has here confined itself to the first and last terms. Present-day thinking is still heavily influenced by the folkways of an earlier era when it was common to think of the individual as an entity apart from society. This was dictated by the view of the individual as one possessed of a private "soul," "mind," and "will." Thus endowed, he was independent, deriving his motivation from within himself through esoteric, rational, hedonistic processes;[33] and when he learned something from the world about him, or when he acted as a member of a group, these things were acts of rational choice of a different order from the isolated integrity of his life as an "individual." It is because the sciences of economics and government grew up in this world of assumed independent, self-starting willers and doers that the subject-matters of these sciences could be treated as an objective set of reified things *out there* (prices, law, the State, etc.), rather than as the fluid behavior of individuals in culture. And this same weather of opinion required that another fictitious separate thing *out there*, called "society," be invented to account for men when they ceased to act as discrete minds and acted with and in relationship to each other. Hence sociology has called itself "the science of society."

Modern science has discarded this earlier conception of a discrete, autonomous individual, save in the biological sense. There are no Robinson Crusoes, no "individuals" apart from other individuals, and it is a tautology to speak

[33] For an illuminating description of the working of this assumed internal personal "brain trust," see Wesley Mitchell's paper on "Bentham's Felicific Calculus" in the *Political Science Quarterly* for June 1918, reprinted in his collected essays, *The Backward Art of Spending Money, and Other Essays* (New York: McGraw-Hill, 1937).

of "the individual *in* society." To speak of the individual is to speak of a something living among and interacting with other individuals; and, save in the biological sense, the term has no other meaning. It is for this reason that the line of analysis suggested in the present volume drops out "society" as a working concept for the social sciences, leaving only the two concepts, "culture" (the more or less patterned totality of behavior, including ways of thinking, feeling, and acting, and such physical things as tools, books, buildings, etc., whose meanings for use we have learned from our forebears) and "individuals" (the private versions of the common culture, always operating in a network of relationships to other persons).

Even psychiatry is having to give over the effort to build a science of "the individual as such," and, in the same sense, the effort to build a separate science of "social relationships as such" is barren. Social relationships do not exist as a separate datum, but only as a part of doing something. To attempt to view them as things apart is to lose sight of the only thing that can given them meaning. Institutions are the behavior of always and inevitably interrelated and interacting individuals. The effective study of any institution necessarily includes, therefore, the analysis of the number, size, prestige, leadership, and interfunctioning of constellations of interacting individuals as they form and re-form within and around the given area of institutional behavior. Thus economics may well come to deal more and more realistically with the variously structured constellations of persons related to each other in making and selling things (employers, employees, social classes, corporations, trade associations, and so on) and in buying things (the market, the pace-setting innovators with high incomes and the mass of lower-income buyers who strain after them, consumer cooperatives, and so on); political science may come to concern itself, as the monographs cited earlier suggest that it is already beginning to do, with the class and other relationships of those who vote together and apart in ward, city, and nation; and those specialists who deal with the family, leisure, religion, and other institutional areas will similarly include these formal and informal combinations in interaction within their analysis. It is a disservice to the social sciences to attempt to abstract a special, separate science of social relationships as such; for there is no social science other than the – science of persons interacting in groups.

Sociology has performed a distinct service historically in emphasizing among the unsocial social sciences the basically group aspects of all institutional behavior. It has also been a useful incubator and brooder in which numerous important baby sciences have been hatched and started toward maturity. But its future as a contributor to the common task of the social sciences appears to lie in its surrender of the claim to be "the" science of society, of social organization, or of social relationships as such. The time would seem to be coming, in the ragged evolution of the social sciences, when sociologists may reenlist their energies among the workers in either of two general fields. – Those who are primarily interested in the processes, forms, and dynamics of group-wise behavior may cease to study these *in general*, by synthetic, largely second-hand abstraction from the data of other sciences; they may enter and learn to know intimately a special area of institutional behavior as specialists in that given area, be it economic, political, or other; and they may then concentrate on the relevant dynamic processes of group formation, leadership, and interaction as these affect behavior *in that concrete area*. In this way they would remove two standing reproaches that haunt general sociologists interested in the social system, social forms, and the processes of social interaction: that they generally have no precise techniques, but must largely just "talk about" their subject; and, second, that they are woefully lacking in a precise, first-hand body of close, empirical data in any single field of group interaction. The second group of sociologists, those not now primarily interested in processes of inter-action in groups but preferring to work empirically as specialists in any one of the emerging new areas of scien-tific concentration—such as the family, crime and delin-quency, urbanism, leisure, communication (the press, etc.), population and vital statistics, race, and so on—may go ahead to develop these new areas as valid bodies of theory and data within the growing family of the special social sciences.

If sociology thus loses its traditional separate identity, the things it has sought to do may go forward with new vigor. The analysis of social interaction would then assume greater specificity and meaning, because it would derive intimately from the living context of political behavior, organized labor, business organization, and so on; and the emerging new fields of scientific study would take on the dignity of valid new areas of scientific exploration. And how would the old rôle of sociology as integrator of "the whole of living" be taken care of? As this multiplication of knowledge about the social organization in specific institu-tional areas occurred, the common focus of each specialized area of knowledge upon analyzing appropriate phenomena as integral parts of the total culture would supply the unification which sociology has sought to contribute in the past.

Anthropology, like sociology, is a relative newcomer among the social sciences. It has had a priceless advantage over the other social sciences—though this has also operated adversely to lock it within itself as a discipline. Just as sociology has capitalized on the neglect of the "social" aspects of everyday things by the older disciplines, so anthropology has developed as a science by tilling the overlooked field of primitive cultures in the backward corners of the world. It has thus had an invaluable monopoly on an indispensable raw material of the social sciences. If, for instance, the economist cannot put human beings into a test tube to see what would happen if they were boiled free of all the accompaniments of a capitalist economy, the anthropologist can approximate this by studying cultures where our type of economy does not prevail. Anthropology is, therefore, potentially the science – which provides for all the rest of us exact data on the range of human tolerance for institutional ways different from our own.

Actually, the enrichment of the other social sciences from anthropology has been slow. The use of its data and concepts has recently begun to spread rapidly; almost too rapidly, in fact, for there is a tendency for the workers in the other social sciences to abstract from their setting in a primitive culture colorful single details, which are used uncritically. Both the lag in application of anthropological materials to our own culture and the ensuing tendency to quarry them for piecemeal details are traceable to certain historical circumstances in its growth as a new science. Beginning under the stimulus of the theory of evolution, early workers in anthropology were fascinated by the taxonomic arrangement of cultures from the "lowest" to the "highest." As this impulse began to wear thin, the science shifted emphasis to empirical description of culture traits, and to tracing their distribution and paths of diffusion over the surface of the globe. There was good reason for this descriptive empiricism, for, in the world of the last century, advanced cultures have been rapidly blurring the original characters of primitive cultures. Anthropology as a science has accordingly been engaged in a race to salvage its subject-matter from under the feet of colonial traders and missionaries. This preoccupation with description of as many cultures as possible before they are lost has contributed heavily to three things: the routine character and lack of significant theoretical inventiveness of many ethnological monographs; insufficient fertilization of anthropology by the rapidly growing body of new knowledge regarding the psychological and related aspects of human behavior; and the almost complete disregard by anthropologists, in their literal, trait-by-trait empiricism, of sophisticated social science concepts and of problems of our own culture on which comparative data from primitive cultures are badly needed. Thus anthropology has tended to go along as a separate esoteric mystery, and all of us have been the losers thereby. There are, of course, exceptions: Margaret Mead approaches primitive cultures with a rich orientation to sophisticated analysis of human personality, as does also Edward Sapir; while Hortense Powdermaker's *After Freedom*, a study of Negro culture in a community in the Deep South, and Lloyd Warner's forthcoming study of Newburyport, Massachusetts, reveal the growing interest in our own culture among younger anthropologists. And yet, it is significant of the centripetal tendency of the science that an important fresh effort by Dr. Mead (in her *Cooperation and Competition among Primitive Peoples*) to utilize comparative data to throw light on an urgent problem of our own culture has been greeted by a sarcastic review in the *American Anthropologist* which rejected it almost *in toto*.

If one asks any anthropologist what his science is all about, he will say that it describes and analyzes cultures and culture processes; and if one pushes the questioning farther and asks why one wants to do this, the answer is, "So that we can the better understand and control our own culture." But one has only to scan the remote table of

[158]

contents of the *American Anthropologist*, with its meticulous articles on pottery designs, dance forms, kinship systems, and linguistics, to see how aloof and self-preoccupied the great mass of anthropological endeavor still is.[34] Anthropology has taught us to study the whole culture as a functioning unit, and it is rendering us more cautious about generalizing about man and his culture solely on the basis of Western Europe and the United States. But the collection of data is not an end in itself, and it takes on meaning only when these data are seen as relevant to significant problems. And the significance of problems in the social sciences is to be judged not only by their relevance to the technical demands of their subject-matter, but also by their ability to implement us in getting ahead with the effective control of our own cultural forms.

A heavy handicap which anthropology faces is the physical remoteness of much of its field from workers in our culture, and the consequent heavy cost of field research. This has tended to confine the first-hand study of comparative cultures to anthropologists, with consequent loss of fertilization of other social sciences. If factors of remoteness and cost argue for the continuance of anthropology as a *separate* discipline, the need is nevertheless great to implement current field work in appropriate cultures with specialists from other disciplines. This will save the anthropologist from his present embarrassment of trying to be a specialist in all the complicated aspects of behavior at once. It is not so much a reflection upon anthropologists as upon the impossibility of this situation, that they have tended to resolve this embarrassment by

[34] It should, however, be noted that, under the strong urging of its veteran dean, Professor Franz Boas, the American Anthropological Association passed at its 1938 annual meeting a strongly worded resolution asserting the fallacy of Nazi racial theory.

simply turning their backs upon so many of the problems of behavior posed for answer by our culture.

Psychology is unique among the social sciences in that, its announced field being the study of individuals, it has not been so tempted as have its fellows to overlook individual differences and to concentrate upon derivative generalizations of the by-and-large-and-other-things-being-equal sort. With its field thus fortunately concentrated on the central powerhouse of culture, individuals, it is in the strategic position of having the other social sciences turn increasingly to it for the solution of realistic problems—mental health, education and child development, labor problems, advertising and market research, public opinion and propaganda. It is a safe prescription to almost any young social-scientist-in-training to "get more psychological underpinning." And yet psychology, working in close contact with the biological sciences and solicitous to maintain its status as a natural science, exhibits its own centripetal preoccupations that do not always make contacts with the other social sciences easy. Social psychology has tended to be the poor relation of this austere world of animal experimentation and "brass-instrument research." Though this playing down of social psychology is decreasing, students in the other social sciences tend to find the offerings of departments of psychology somewhat repellent and difficult to adapt to their needs as economists, political scientists, or historians.

Additional factors have deterred the other social sciences from ardently embracing psychology. Their concern with problems viewed on the institutional level—in terms of money, balance of trade, political parties, sovereignty, society, and so on—has already been noted. Another important deterring factor is the confusion of rival schools in current psychology. This science, which has shot up like a skyrocket within a half-century of intensive development, has embraced and then discarded instincts; is in conflict over the varying emphases of the several psychoanalytic schools, and over the biological, as against the cultural, genesis of behavior; and exhibits many other uncertainties. When doctors disagree, the patient inclines to postpone the operation until they make up their minds. This, in general, is the attitude with which the other social sciences confront psychology. They are encouraged in doing this by the fact that some of them have burned their fingers badly in the past by accepting psychological theories that were later discredited. The outstanding instance of this is the long involvement of economics in a hedonistic psychology which based motivation on the calculation of pleasure and pain. By the time Alfred Marshall wrote his *Principles of Economics*, this theory was discredited; yet so firmly was it written into the structure of economic science that his effort to avoid use of "pleasure" and "pain" by substituting "satisfaction" and "dissatisfaction" amounts to little more than a change in surface labels. Again, though not so seriously, some economists involved themselves in the brief upsurge of the instinct theory, following the publication of McDougall's *Introduction to Social Psychology* in 1908—only again to beat a retreat from psychology. The sour impression made by these involvements in a science "too new to know its own mind" resulted in the attitude that economics should have nothing to do with psychology. Men like H. J. Davenport simply turned their backs upon psychology and the study of behavior and announced that economics is confined to the study of those things that can be measured in terms of prices, and is concerned with these prices only *after* they have been set in the marketplace.

The retarding effect of all this on sciences which pretend to be, and inevitably are, sciences of human behavior is —

too obvious to need elaboration. Such men as Wesley Mitchell, as noted above, recurrently emphasize the need for the social sciences to recover a realistic emphasis upon human behavior and to work more closely with psychology. But one of the ironies of the situation is the cumulative coerciveness of the formal concepts and methods of a science which tends to prevent even those who recognize the need from embracing it in their research. If social science is to handle its problems as behavior, i.e., in terms of the dynamic sources of institutional events, the need cannot be met by hitching a psychologist onto an occasional joint research project; rather, the very statement of its problems needs to be shot through with psychological awareness.

The way ahead would appear to lie through a clarification of the present ambiguous status of social psychology. At least three things would seem to be involved in this:

1. There is need to make more explicit and to implement further the present tacit assumption that all psychology is social psychology. During recent years psychological research has made increasingly apparent the fact that, however much laboratory techniques and research into the biological basis of behavior may contribute to the understanding of emotional and mental processes, these can be comprehended only if they are also studied as social phenomena. Inasmuch as every individual grows up in culture among other people, such things as perception, memory, reasoning, and the other psychological processes are socially conditioned and can be fully understood only in their specific social setting.

2. The focus of the problems that psychologists attack needs to be sharpened and, at the same time, given more continuity by the close, continuous identification of the psychologist with the various other social scientists engaged on a given problem-area. This calls for specialization

by social psychologists and the division of their labor among the various fields that engage social science. It is as impossible for social psychology to attempt to build a separate science of the psychology of social interaction as for sociology to attempt to develop alone a science of social organization and relationships, or for history to stand off as an isolated discipline and seek to give us the precisely applied knowledge we need as to how complex current problems came to be as they are. At present, the social psychologist, like the sociologist, tends to be a jack of all trades. The things he works on sprawl all through the special sciences devoted to the several institutional areas of behavior. They involve studies of motivation in voting, in retail buying, in work, in having children, in leisure, and everything else; of public opinion touching business, religion, race issues, politics, and everything else; of the efficiency of radio and advertising techniques; and, in short, the measurement of almost any kind of behavior in culture. What the social psychologist has is an invaluable growing body of techniques for measuring behavior in culture, and more or less disparate chunks of knowledge derived by applying these techniques here and there. But techniques useful for a diversity of purposes do not make a science; and technical proficiency, divorced from close, continuing identity with analysis of the larger meanings of a related body of institutional problems encourages an amorphous empiricism which can too easily be bent to other interests than those of science.[35] The present situa-

[35] The wholesale exploitation of these techniques by advertising agencies and market research bureaus is too well known to require elaboration here. In doing such work, the social psychologist tends to sell merely his technical proficiency, with only casual knowledge of, and often with a disregard for, the task of analyzing the functioning serviceability of man's economic and other institutions. The recently developed polls of public opinion, now being widely employed in the analysis of public opinion on many topics by the American Institute of Public Opinion, represent an important new instrument for democracy, as does the

tion in such an eclectic social psychology, divorced from the whole context of the problems on which it works, resembles somewhat that existing in the field of child development a dozen years ago, when "norms" for height, weight, intelligence, and other isolated factors were highly developed, but there was little work on the nature and processes of growth itself and on the variations in pattern of growth from child to child.

3. Out of the preceding grows the need for clarification of the kinds of training required to fit social psychologists specializing in the several areas of institutional behavior to operate effectively in these fields. For some years it has been recognized that the psychologist attacking clinical problems needs training in biology and medicine as well as in the social factors involved in maladjustment and adjustment. More recently, child psychologists have begun to receive training in physiology, nutrition, and a wide group of selected subject-matters bearing on mental and emotional development and growth in social participation. It may be expected that social psychologists dealing with other areas of behavior will in time become less psychologists-in-general, and more richly trained as specialists in the many ramifying aspects of the areas of institutional behavior to which they elect to devote themselves.

recent perfection of techniques for the "management of public opinion." But the importance of techniques depends upon the context in which they are used. When the director of the American Institute of Public Opinion declared before the National Association of Manufacturers in New York, on December 7, 1938, that his sampling studies establish the fact that "the public is the real boss," he was correct within the limited meanings of his techniques and tabulations; but only a scientific technician who does not know, or does not choose to bother with, the pressure forces within American economic and political institutions could content himself with such a partial and confusing statement.

That social psychologists are aware of this exposed position of techniques unidentified with a philosophy of social science is apparent in the recent organization by a group of them of a Society for the Psychological Study of Social Issues.

Equipped with training both in psychology and in the intimate details of the specific institutional segment on which he proposes to work, such a social psychologist would employ his talents continuously and coherently as a member of the team of diverse specialists exploring that segment of behavior in culture.

The above analysis attempts only to suggest tentatively some of the difficulties that confront the social sciences as they find themselves in a position of enhanced responsibility for developing usable tools for the resolution of man's current dilemmas. These sciences represent a division of labor which we are wont to regard optimistically as roughly covering the field. But their respective rôles and emphases have not, for the most part, been developed scientifically, but casually, subject to the uneven pressures of changing circumstances. One science concentrates upon the past, another upon the individual, another upon society, another upon comparative study of the cultures of remote, primitive peoples, two more upon specific institutional areas, and a final one (if statistics be included as a separate science) upon a particular type of methodology. The assumed division of labor lacks the value of division of labor directed to a common end, because these several emphases have no common focus. Only in the very loosest sense may they be said to be engaged in the common study of behavior within the single continuum of culture. This explains the crude articulation of the several sciences and limits the possibility of interchanging concepts and findings.

It is customary for social scientists, when confronted with such considerations as the foregoing, to plead the relative youth of the social sciences and to urge that changes for the better are actually taking place. It may be that our only course is to wait and see how things develop.

But, in view of the urgency of the public need for prompt, incisive, and reliable direction from social science, it behooves social scientists to make sure that in urging a "wait and see" policy they are not simply following the line of personal convenience. Evolution through casual trial and error may be the way of nature, but it is not the way of science. If one is not simply observing the inner orderliness in nature, the essence of science is to analyze, to draw inferences, *and then to implement action.* The burden of proof would appear, therefore, to rest upon social scientists who elect to follow a "wait and see" policy rather than to move toward making their science more directly projective into action.

Certain desirable steps for the reorientation of social science have already been suggested. These are the explicit acceptance by the several sciences of the culture continuum as the common subject of study; the acceptance by them within this common focus of a shared set of propositions (subject, of course, to change with new knowledge) as to the processes of behavior of individuals; and the viewing of the datum of social science as involving the interaction of these two basic factors: the dynamic biological organism carrying his version of the culture in the form of learned habit-structures, interacting with the culture as presented by the similarly dynamic culture-versions carried by the people about him.

A further step seems indicated: In this process, the several disciplines, as we now know them, would be supplemented and in part replaced by a series of specific problem-areas on which workers with all types of relevant specialized training and technique would be cooperatively engaged. Labor problems would not be the province of economists alone, with only incidental help now and then from psychologists; the study of political behavior would include, in addition to the present political scientists, psychologists, economists, sociologists, and other specialists, concerned with such related problems as the significance of individual differences for the democratic process, motivations in citizenship, political attitudes in relation to social classes, and the relations between economic organization and political power; the study of the family would, similarly, draw together a wide and varied group, including such diverse specialists as economists, anthropologists, and psychiatrists. Present departmental lines in universities would blur, as training was reoriented around the full dimensions of problems, rather than the traditions of disciplines, and as research personnel of a variety that rarely at present joins forces on any problem would build new patterns of research around these problem foci. The new field of child development, drawing together scientists from the biological and social sciences, suggests this new reorientation. Only by making use around each problem of a — varied and coordinated group of specialists, trained to use their specialized knowledge and techniques *on that problem* and jointly to present that problem in its total setting, can science hope to fulfil its necessary task of presenting thoroughgoing analysis of *all* relevant aspects of the phenomena it purports to study.

Objection may be raised to the above on the ground either that a "problem-area" is simply another name for a discipline, or would promptly become indistinguishable from a discipline; or that a discipline as at present constituted is but another name for a problem-area. There is large room here for quibbling over words. The nub of the matter appears to be this: Social science disciplines at present, conducted as internally self-perpetuating academic traditions, tend to confuse such things as being an economist—or a sociologist, or a political scientist, or an anthropologist—with the solving of problems by the multi-disciplined attack requisite for the effective handling of most fundamental cultural snarls. And they are able to go on doing this by assuming an automatic process of coordination of their findings—a coordination which the facts in the situation largely belie.

The weight of accumulated learning carried along by each of the self-perpetuating disciplinary glaciers is so great that the pressure within each discipline is to "teach the facts" to scientists-in-training, rather than to train them to view problems freshly and to develop versatile skills for coping with them. And, because there are so many facts to learn within each broad discipline set up as these disciplines are at present, an economist taking his Ph.D. degree, for instance, though nominally free to do so, is actually discouraged from taking psychology or government or anthropology or sociology as his secondary subject of specialization. Under these circumstances, the proper secondary subject of specialization for a historian is another historical era rather than another social science, while the psychology major is discouraged from attempting labor problems or government as his minor subject. This situation is further complicated by the fact that, in some universities, the social sciences are even broken up under different "faculties" (groups of departments) having different requirements as to internal concentration. At Columbia University, for instance, psychology and anthropology are lumped with philosophy in a faculty apart from the faculty cluster of the other social sciences —and "faculty" requirements are piled on top of departmental requirements to limit the graduate student's efforts to work off the reservation in the other faculty.

Here, again, slow, one-step-at-a-time changes are occurring, for this relatively rigid situation is not viewed with complacency by some social scientists. But habit, departmental prestige, and the mounting total of empirical facts to know within each discipline impart great rigidity to the situation. One may foresee that the proposed device of "roving professorships" unattached to any single department, at Harvard University, may amount to little more than the hitching of another box-car to the existing train; for the need is not for unattached devotees of the old problems stalking our campuses like wistful bad consciences of the academic community, but for new groupings of professors *attached* to fresh definitions of problems. The national Social Science Research Council represents an — important step toward the reorientation of social research. But the large degree of failure to date of its efforts to develop new alignments of research personnel around interdisciplinary research is directly due to the inability of social scientists, trained to work within the grooves of the present disciplines, to grasp imaginatively the possibilities inherent in working closely with scientists trained in other disciplines.

It would be salutary for us social scientists to ask ourselves: Why are we caught at the present time with no *social science* professionals equipped to handle the acute and complicated problem of housing? And what similar problems confronting the culture likewise fail to fall within the boundaries of any of the present disciplines. For each of these maverick problems, as well as for those which are the traditional property of some discipline, there is need to ask: What varied specialties of concept, knowledge, and methodological technique need to be brought together in new combinations in order to enable social science to cope adequately with this problem? Take the field of "labor problems," for instance. How can we focus on this field sustained, coordinated work of the following sorts, now either omitted entirely or treated only sketchily and sporadically: the biology and psychology of individual differences in their relation to capacity to endure monotony, speed, competition, and other aspects of different types of jobs without strain; the psychological accompaniments of different kinds of job strains, in the shop and in the home; sex differences and age differences in relation to capacity to adjust to different types of work; the relation of different leisure pursuits to the rhythm of work and recreation on various jobs; consumption standards and resulting psychological pressures at different income levels; incentives under private capitalism, as compared with other types of economy; the nature of social classes, the conditions of class identification by workers of different types, including the low-salaried middle class, class stereotypes, and the intricate effects of the class structure of our culture upon the worker; other group identifications and symbols of the worker; racial and other antipathies among workers; conditions of urban living affecting workers on and off the job; attitudes toward skill, leadership, old age, saving, the future, children, and authority, and other intellectual and emotional stereotypes among workers; conditions affecting the spread of slogans, rumors, and fear among workers; and the elements of status and prestige on and off the job? Such things as these are the bone and gristle of the "labor problem" in our culture. Similar treatment is applicable to most of the other problems on which social science is at present engaged.

– In any realignment of research personnel around problems, provision must be made for every type of temperament. A body of scientists is not a group of impersonal robots; its most priceless ingredient is the active personal interest in various problems and aspects of problems of each individual member. And at the root of vital personal interest is the dynamic selective factor of individual temperament. The task of training scientists involves the patient discovery of individual temperament and bent in contact with a wide variety of subject-matter and method-ological approaches; and then the systematic orientation of each temperament to the most penetrating problems that can be explored in the cooperative endeavor of science by one of that temperament, and the development of skill in appropriate techniques. None of us engaged as foremen along the assembly line of a great graduate school can view such a statement of our problem without wincing! But the social science of the future must encourage diversity of approach, and this will require in each problem-area the whole range of temperaments—from that which finds itself most happily engaged in semi-routine computations, at the one extreme, to the philosophically disposed theoretician at the other.

The problem of theory in the social sciences is acute, — and this involves the relation of the social scientist to the philosopher. The theoretical structures of the several disciplines is extremely uneven. In economics an orthodox theoretical structure has been developed that is so imposing that it operates at many points as a deterrent to fresh realistic theorizing—as in the case of "value theory," which, as Veblen remarked, is "a theory of valuation with the element of valuation left out."[36] Santayana's warning that "A tradition which erects a screen of professional problems between the philosopher [read here "scientist"] and the natural subject-matter of intelligence is one to be suspected"[37] applies to not a little of the obfuscating theory of economics. At the other extreme, in a science like anthropology, dominated by empirical description, the structure of penetrating theory has been so meager as scarcely to give significant form to the science. Social science,

[36] *The Place of Science in Modern Civilization* (New York: Huebsch, 1919), p. 144.
[37] *Three Philosophical Poets* (Cambridge: Harvard University Press, 1922) p. 177.

viewed as a unity, is making little effort to build a common basic theoretical structure. Here, again, the reliance is upon automatic synthesis.

The empirical social scientist is apt to take satisfaction in saying with some emphasis that he is "no philosopher." But if the theory that guides social science is to be more than a set of literal generalizations about the limited degrees of order and continuity observable in the institutional behavior within the confines of a single culture, this aloofness from philosophy is untenable. This raises the interesting questions of where philosophy comes from, and how the social sciences, as the cooperative science of man in culture, are going to get themselves the common philosophical structure they so patently need? Is philosophy best derived from "philosophers," i.e., from those persons who have taken Ph.D.'s in departments of philosophy? The New York *Herald Tribune* for December 30, 1937, carried an account of the meeting of the Eastern division of the American Philosophical Association in Princeton to discuss, in the presence of Professor Einstein, the question, "Does causality hold in contemporary physics?" According to the press account, "In opening their addresses each [of the three philosophers who spoke on the final day] had conceded that it might seem presumptuous for philosophers to attempt to discourse knowingly on physics, but explained that *were they to be ruled out from a consideration of nature they would have no field.*" (Italics mine.) This suggests the uneasy predicament of the philosopher-in-general in the modern world of vast accumulations of highly specific and technically complex knowledge in the hands of the many groups of specialists. Professor William P. Montague has stated the predicament of the philosopher even more sharply:[38]

[38] "Philosophy as Vision" (the first of his Paul Carus Foundation Lectures), *International Journal of Ethics*, October 1933.

"Disillusionment and a mood of defeatism is making itself felt throughout our entire guild. How can we go on with speculative theories about the constitution of reality when the winds of scientific knowledge in physics, chemistry, biology, and psychology are sweeping around us and covering the once fertile fields of fancy with the arid sands of fact? . . .

"In short, as philosophers we appear to be doomed. — Province after province of our once mighty empire is being invaded. Natural scientists and social scientists, historians, grammarians, and mathematicians hem us in and perform our onetime business better than we can ourselves perform it. Where can we go and what can we do?"

All of this suggests the possible demise of the old philosophy-in-general dominated by the false quest for logically derived certainty, and the scattering of those of philosophical temperament among the many problem-areas of living. If nature, including human nature, must be the starting point of philosophy, then the philosopher must be a person deeply rooted in the empirical knowledge of that particular aspect of nature about which he attempts to theorize. Under such circumstances, the philosophy which would guide the social sciences of the future would be less the work of single minds building logical systems as philosophers, and more predominantly the cooperative product of sensitive minds, each professionally familiar at first hand with some area of intricate empirical data, reaching out from their respective coigns of knowledge in the effort to effect mutual synthesis.

Such a closer identification of philosophy and theory with precise empirical analysis would do much to lessen the present endless bickering between the empirically disposed temperaments and the theoretically disposed temperaments as to which of the two is superior. There is and can be no conflict between sound qualitative and sound quantitative work. As Montague remarked in the address cited above, "Great in vision, poor in proof, philosophy at its highest has ever been." What is obviously needed is to yoke philosophy and empirical analysis together in such fashion that each can contribute its strengths to the common task of discovery. If philosophy bound down to the exigent realities of special empiricisms would appear at first glance to have forfeited much of its glamour, it would nevertheless gain immeasurably in its working ability to perform what is presumably its primary function, the guidance of man in understanding and orienting himself in his world.

In any change in emphasis from disciplines to problem-areas, the position of history, touched upon earlier, needs special consideration. It may be that the historian, instead of continuing to be a historian first and a specialist secondarily, will in the future more commonly reverse that order. He may secure his primary training in a specific field, and utilize history as a method rather than as an independent subject-matter. Such a reorientation of historical analysis would necessarily involve the transfer, from present graduate departments of history to other social science departments, of a considerable body of young would-be historians.[39]

Four objections will be raised to this proposal regarding history: (1) That the "new history" in its monographic

[39] In this connection, it is worth while to note that graduate departments of history, like similar departments of sociology, and for the same reason, draw an unduly large number of students of undefined and miscellaneous interests. One does not require a defined interest in a problem singled out and seen in relation to other problems in order to "go in for" history or sociology. These fields are so broad that they seem especially inviting to the student who goes in, wanders around, and hopes in some mysterious way to "find himself"—and in the course of this to find a career. In this respect, history and sociology are not simply unfortunate victims of circumstances. It is the amorphous character of both disciplines that attracts to them the amorphous student.

studies is in effect supplying more and more contemporaneously focused material of this sort; (2) that this is the sort of proposal emanating from the stubby-fingered over-practical man who would bind down scholarship to immediacies and limit history to the period since 1776, the Civil War, or 1900; (3) that the analysis of the whole, as a whole, is as necessary as the analysis of parts; and (4) that any such procedure would tend to whittle away the objectivity of history by playing straight into the hands of the type of prostitution of science that occurs under contemporary dictators.

As to the first of these objections, the question is not whether history is managing to do some valuable work, which of course it is; but, rather, whether, in view of the precious man-hours of trained energy involved, this work is either as precisely useful or as copious in volume as we have a right to expect. In the judgment of the writer, in neither of these latter respects is history meeting the need.

As regards the second objection, that it is here proposed to limit history to immediacies and to the recent past, no such limitation is, of course, intended. The tough continuities of tradition—for example, the long persistence of Aristotelian modes of thought into our modern era—are too obviously persistent in our habitual ways of defining certain problems to warrant any such arbitrary chopping off of the relevant at any given date. Nothing, however remote, which helps significantly to explain the structure and functioning of current living should be allowed to elude the grasp of the specialists studying why we confront a given problem and what we can do about it.

The third objection is an important one and affords the basis for the original claim of sociology, as well, to be regarded as a separate discipline. "Man," the historian

[175]

insists,[40] "is far more than the sum of his scientifically classifiable operations. Water is composed of hydrogen and oxygen, but it is not like either of them. Nothing could be more artificial than the scientific separation of man's religious, esthetic, economic, political, intellectual, and bellicose properties. These may be studied, each by itself, with advantage, but specialization would lead to the most absurd results if there were not someone to study the process as a whole; and that someone is the historian." Some temperaments are peculiarly adapted, as suggested earlier, for particular types of approach to problems. Among these are the synthesizers and systematizers, and they perform a highly necessary service. It is incredible that a substantial number of scientists with a flair for such comprehensive analysis would not continue to perform this useful function. But this does not argue that a separate discipline should be singled out as synthesizer. In fact, the major thrust of modern empirically-grounded science points away from any such effort to build special sciences of synthesis. Interest in a defined area of human behavior not only does not stand in the way of continuous effort to reach out from *this* immediate problem and see it in its *whole* context; but, quite the contrary, depends inevitably for a large share of its meaning upon such synthesis. But it is synthesis *from* the specific knowledge of the component problem, not synthesis *in general*. The effort toward synthesis cannot be the responsibility of any single social science, since no corps of scientists can know enough; but it must be the common responsibility of all.

Finally, the proposal to restate the rôle of history as a function of the search for resolutions of contemporary difficulties evokes the fourth vociferous objection. Here one touches a live nerve—and the patient jumps! Science, it is

[40] Robinson, *op. cit.*, pp. 66-7.

contended, must maintain its objective integrity, must not obscure its vision by emotion or risk allowing itself to be used exploitatively by those who do not live by the scruples of the disinterested investigator. This reservation of ultimate control within itself is the prime factor which insures the continued value of science to mankind. No man who has ever known the excitement of research on the thin edge of the unknown would deny such contentions. They are the stuff of which the scientist's Self is made. It is useful to recall again at this point, however, that a science is itself but a bit of culture. And every going culture, even our own "free" culture, actually operates as a selective screen that tends to set the scientist to work on certain problems and to distract his gaze gently but coercively from others. No area of living is devoid of hazards; no important gain is ever made without risks. The issue confronting science is not—at least not as yet in the United States—one between aloofness and slavery. Science gives away aces from its hand when it so states its case. If ✳ social science today feels itself unable to engage intimately on problems of moment to the world of affairs at their points of acute controversy without becoming contaminated and unscientific, then here is the first and most crucial problem-area of our culture which social science should set itself to explore scientifically. Social science will — stand or fall on the basis of its serviceability to men as they struggle to live. If it plays safe and avoids risks, it will find itself ridden down and cast aside. For the one sure fact in the present confusions of our culture is that the issues will be confronted by some means of control in some fashion. If social science is timid, it may have to endure the eclipse German science is now experiencing. Here, as at so many other points, the need is to state the problem positively, not negatively: of course science can be abused, but it can also be used.

A social scientist has no place, *qua* scientist, as a party to power-politics. When he works within the constricting power curbs of a Republican or of a Communist "party line," or when he pulls his scientific punch by pocketing more important problems and accepting a retainer to work as an expert for the partisan ends of a bank or an advertising agency, he is something less than a scientist. In a positive sense, when he does such things he is actively inviting the Hitler-type of open control over science by whittling away the crucial claim of science that it is objective and cannot be bought for the use of unscientifically defined versions of the public interest. But, also, when the social scientist hides behind the aloof "spirit of science and scholarship" for fear of possible contamination, he is likewise something less than a scientist. We social scientists need to be more candid about ourselves and our motivations. We should be more sensitive and realistic about what our evasions do to ourselves and to our science.

A final word may be said regarding the relation of the social sciences to the humanities. There are numerous evidences already of the sense of community between the two groups. Novelists, artists, and poets provide valid insights into our culture that go beyond the cautious generalizations of social science and open up significant hypotheses for study. And a scholar like Parrington, a professor of English literature, stands as a permanent symbol for the inescapable importance of studying special problem-areas in relation to the total culture. In his three great volumes the polite world of letters mingles familiarly and authentically with the jostling world of the businessman and politician. We are becoming increasingly aware of how the arts of our people reflect, react against, interplay with the pressures generated by the institutions with which the social sciences deal. In the study of these responses, the emotional mood in which modern man avoids or reaches for these arts, the quality and degree of popular diffusion or constriction of art and literature, social science has the most sensitive index to the qualitative human adequacy of operation of our economic, political, familial, religious, educational, and other institutions.

Attention was called in Chapter 1 to the ominous emerging tendency, under the stress of our times, for certain university administrators, fearful of the controversial possibilities in the social sciences, to play them down in favor of the humanities. Such efforts should be stoutly resisted, even by the humanities. For, while humane letters may live a dubious dependent existence as an incidental ornament of Caesar, the possibility for the mass of mankind to appreciate and live the values for which the humanities stand depends directly upon an ever more realistic and fearless social science.

V

VALUES AND THE SOCIAL SCIENCES

THE rôle of the learned man in earlier times may have been to stabilize custom and to conserve the past; but the social scientist, as his modern counterpart in today's world of rapid scientific discovery, is bound more closely to the moving front edge of man's experience. "Personality," as Santayana vividly phrases it, "is a knife-edge pressed against the future"; and, as instruments by which man works his way ahead in this atmosphere of accelerated change, the social sciences partake of this projective quality in human life. While human behavior exhibits large conformity to habit, one of its most signal features is also the thrusting insistence with which it uses the sticks and stones of culture to get ahead. Motivation, though conditioned by the past, is always contemporary and colored by the immediate situation.[1] Each individual is constantly going from a unique, concrete present to a unique, concrete new situation. This means that, granting all due weight to the institutionalized past as it conditions present behavior, the variables in the social scientist's equation must include not only the given set of structured institutions, but also *what the present human carriers of those institutions are groping to become.*

The social sciences are, therefore, engaged in analyzing a process of change which, at least in certain important respects, presents real options, and these options are of paramount significance. For social science to overlook this

[1] See Gordon Allport, *op. cit.*, p. 194.

is largely to sterilize its functions. At the risk of seeming to overplay the amount of option that actually exists, one may say that the social scientist works constantly in terms of the kind of universe the natural scientist would face if the latter held the power to postpone or to prevent its possible collapse as a place tolerating human life.

The social sciences exhibit reluctance, however, to accept this full partnership with man in the adventure of living. They tend to mute their rôle as implementers of innovation. So one observes these grave young sciences hiding behind their precocious beards of "dispassionate research" and "scientific objectivity." They observe, record, and analyze, but they shun prediction. And, above all else, they avoid having any commerce with "values." Values, they say, may not be derived by science, and therefore science should have nothing to do with them. Social science prefers to urge that all the fruits of scholarly curiosity are important, that there is more than enough work to do in filling in the infinite odd bits of the jigsaw puzzle of the unknown, and that science has no criteria by which to allot priorities in importance. It prefers to say that for science the word "ought" ought never to be used, except in saying that it ought never to be used.

There would be no social sciences if there were not perplexities in living in culture that call for solution. And it is precisely the rôle of the social sciences to be troublesome, to disconcert the habitual arrangements by which we manage to live along, and to demonstrate the possibility of change in more adequate directions. Their rôle, like that of the skilled surgeon, is to get us into immediate trouble in order to prevent our chronic present troubles from becoming even more dangerous. In a culture like ours, in which power is normally held by the few and used offensively and defensively to bolster their instant advantage within the *status quo*, the rôle of such a constructive troublemaker is scarcely inviting. But that is simply another way of stating the predicament of the social sciences in our type of culture.

Nature may be neutral. The sun and lightning descend upon the just and upon the unjust. But culture is not neutral, because culture is interested personalities in action. The social scientist's reason for urging the neutrality of science in such a world of bias is understandable, but it has unfortunate results that curtail heavily the capacity of social science to do precisely the thing that it is the responsibility of social science to do.

Nobody questions the indispensability of detachment in weighing and appraising one's data. But in other respects, as a matter of fact, current social science is neither as "neutral" nor as "pure" as it pretends to be. On the negative side, it avoids many issues that the going culture would view as either impertinent or troublesome, and it allows the powerful biases of the culture to set for it the statement of many of the problems on which it works. On the positive side, it works in a general spirit of modest meliorism, seeking to make small changes for the better in the various institutions to which it applies itself. Thus economists try to "increase welfare" by "bettering business conditions," making business more "efficient" and "profitable," "reducing the amplitude of the business cycle," "stabilizing prices," and "lessening labor trouble." Political scientists seek to "improve" public administration and international relations. Sociologists, likewise, try to "improve" social organization, urban conditions, the family, and so on. Such aims, here and elsewhere in the social sciences, apply not merely to the social scientist as technician but also affect the selection of problems for research.

"Pure scientific curiosity" is a term to which students of semantics should turn their attention. There is "idle" curiosity and "focused" curiosity, but in the world of science there is no such thing as "pure" curiosity. No economist collects the dates on the coins passed over the counter of a soda fountain, or the precise hours of mailing of letters received by different types of retail stores on Monday and on Saturday, and no sociologist interested in urban problems counts and compares the number of bricks in the buildings on a slum block and on a Park Avenue block. Why do we train scientists? To give them refined techniques of observation, analysis, and control, to be sure. But, even more important, the outstanding characteristic of a well trained scientist is his ability to distinguish — "significant" from "insignificant" problems and data. Good scientific training sensitizes one to important problems; it deliberately sets up before the imagination of the scientist a screen which lets through one type of data and bars another—in short, it gives the scientist a selective point of view. Research without an actively selective point of view becomes the ditty bag of an idiot, filled with bits of pebbles, straws, feathers, and other random hoardings. If nobody goes about endlessly counting throughout a lifetime the number of particles of sand along infinite miles of seashore over all the coasts of the world, why is this? Because there is no point to it, no need to complete this particular aspect of the jigsaw puzzle of the unknown.

The confusion that exists between the social scientist's professions to eschew all questions of value and what he so patently does is a confusion in the point at which valuing is applied. Values may be and are properly and necessarily applied in the preliminary selection of "significant," "important" problems for research. They may be but should not be applied thereafter to bias one's analysis or the interpretation of the meanings inherent in one's data. It is a commonplace that the man who cannot train himself to curb his personal concern in a problem so that it does not bias his appraisal of his data has no business in scientific work. But this does not justify social science in its wholesale official rejection of values. Actually, values are always present in the initial selection of a problem. If they are not overt and announced, they are none the less latent and tacitly accepted.

"Those who boast," says Morris Cohen,[2] "that they are not, as social scientists, interested in what ought to be, generally assume (tacitly) that the hitherto prevailing order is the proper ideal of what ought to be. . . . A theory of social values like a theory of metaphysics is none the better because it is held tacitly and is not, therefore, critically examined. . . .

"Because it is thus impossible to eliminate human bias in matters in which we are vitally interested, some sociologists (for example, the Deutsche Gesellschaft für Soziologie) have banished from their programme all questions of value and have sought to restrict themselves to the theory of social happenings. This effort to look upon human actions with the same ethical neutrality with which we view geometric figures is admirable. But the questions of human value are inescapable, and those who banish them at the front door admit them unavowedly and therefore uncritically at the back door."

In the current social science world, but newly escaped from the era of over-easy theory-building into the world of patient empiricism and quantification, and overwhelmed by the number of things to describe and quantify in an era of rapid change, the prevailing tendency is heavily on the side of accepting institutional things and their associated values as given. The modern professor confines himself to professing facts, and radical criticism and generalization must wait "until all the data are gathered." If the social

---

[2] *Reason and Nature* (New York: Harcourt, Brace, 1931), pp. 343, 349.

scientist does not content himself simply with describing and analyzing what *was* or what *is* in terms of last year's statistics, he is apt to confine himself to short "next step" ameliorative research. No one denies the utility of slum clearance, of predicting recidivism in crime, of relocating the geographical boundaries of administrative units within the Chicago metropolitan district, or of reducing the wastes in distribution. But the little values implicit in myriad such researches on the next step here, and here, and here in the institutional system are not discrete and complete in themselves. Each of these next steps is important only as part of a more inclusive, long-term value to which it is relevant. By refusing commerce with such more inclusive values, the social scientist does not escape them. What he does is, rather, to accept tacitly the inclusive value-judgment of the culture as to the rightness of the "American way" and the need for only minor remedial changes. Whether and at what points this optimistic value-judgment is warranted should be a subject of inquiry by science, rather than a thing taken for granted.

When the empirical analyst says, as in the statement of the National Bureau of Economic Research quoted earlier, that "We confine ourselves to stating the facts as we find them. With opinions about the promise or the danger to American life from the growth of trade unions we have no concern as an organization of investigators," he is staying his hand at the point at which the culture is most in need of his help. One cannot assume that the meanings of "facts" are always clear or unequivocal. Somebody is going to interpret what the situation means, because the character of man's dilemmas is such as to brook no stay. When the social scientist, after intensive study of a problem, avoids extrapolating his data into the realm of wide meaning, however tentatively stated, he invites others presumably more biassed than himself—e.g., the National

Association of Manufacturers, the American Federation of Labor, the advertising man, the American Legion, and so on—to thrust upon the culture their interpretations of the meaning of the situation.

The depression has stepped up like a loudspeaker the dissonances generated in the attempt to operate a complex culture by these casual values tossed up by special interests pretending to speak for the public interest. Never before in our culture has the contrast between the casual and customary *and* the intelligent and humanly valuable been thrown into such unmistakable contrast. Perhaps never before have we had such an urgent sense of the difference it can make to know what current tendencies mean, to know what to value and why, and how to materialize those values. The culture is proceeding to this unavoidable assignment after the blind, shambling fashion of cultures. At this point the social sciences, the instruments for appraisal and direction-finding, plead immunity from the responsibility to guide the culture. It is not the business of social science, they claim, "to care," "to value," "to say what ought to be done." To which the rejoinder should be: Either the social sciences know more than do the "hard-headed" businessman, the "practical" politician and administrator, and the other *de facto* leaders of the culture as to what the findings of research mean, as to the options the institutional system presents, as to what human personalities want, why they want them, and how desirable changes can be effected, *or* the vast current industry of social science is an empty façade.

The point is not that social science should go in for pretentious soothsaying. Man's guess into the future is fragile, even when implemented by science. But the stubborn fact remains that we sail inevitably into the future, the sea is full of dangerous reefs and shoals, and drifting is more dangerous than choosing the course that our best intel-

ligence dictates. If, then, social science should take the —
wheel, what does it know by which it can steer?

It was stated above that it is essential in the training of
the social scientist to help him to discover a point of view, —
a selective screen which lets through the "significant" and
eliminates the "insignificant." Scientific judgment and
imagination cannot be taught, but the young scientist
can learn them, if anywhere, from a great teacher-scientist
who knows how to fill his laboratory and classroom with
his conception of the significant.[3] What social science
evidently needs is to seek to make explicit its tacit criteria
of the "significant."

[3] In these days, when social science is increasingly being drawn into the
controversies that beset our culture, the statement is frequently heard within faculty groups that "It is not the duty of our universities to reform the
world." No claim is made throughout the present book that an entire science,
university, or department of a university should be placed behind the effort to
effect any given single change in the economic or political structure of our culture; still less that classroom lectures should use hypotheses as accepted fact and
propagandize for them. Either of these procedures would be an intolerable
affront to education and to science. It is a subterfuge, however, when the individual social scientist employs such a statement to avoid his personal responsibility as a scientist to set his analysis of data in the long view, to "make up his
mind" in terms of long-run hypotheses, however tentatively held, and to teach
and to carry on research in an atmosphere of constant endeavor to clarify and to
test these hypotheses. Hypotheses are an indispensable part of good teaching and —
research. A good scientist has a point of view. He holds it subject to constant correction, but without a point of view he is no scientist, and as a teacher he becomes simply a walking equivalent of an encyclopedia or a colorless textbook. A
prevalent protest by alert students in the social sciences is that the immediacies
of facts and data tend to operate in the university classroom as a monopolizing concern shutting off the listener from the ripe wisdom of many a mature
teacher. It is the boast of some able professors that they handle controversial
subjects in the classroom in such skilful manner that the students are never able
to know "what the professor himself really thinks about the problem." This
amounts, in the judgment of the writer, to sabotaging the inner meaning of social
science and of education. Of course, no university should have a staff all the
members of which think alike on a given problem. But the blurring of explicit
statement of sharp and divergent hypotheses within a faculty is almost as
dangerous.

The most general criterion in current use is "a new contribution to knowledge." This criterion receives support from the honorific status of "knowledge" in our traditions; also from the empiricist's faith that, if each worker adds his brick of data to the heap, the whole will automatically build itself into a useful structure. But this vague reference of social science to the quantity of knowledge leaves unanswered the question of what it is to which knowledge is relevant.

Another criterion of relevance is often stated in such terms as "economic welfare" and "social welfare." But, again one asks, "welfare" defined in what terms and with reference to what? In this connection the concrete incident with which Floyd Allport begins his *Institutional Behavior*[4] is illuminating:

"At a meeting of the faculty of a certain large university a proposal for a new administrative policy was being discussed. The debate was long and intense before a final vote of adoption was taken. As the professors filed out of the room an instructor continued the discussion with one of the older deans.

" 'Well,' observed the latter official, 'it may be a little hard on some people; but I feel sure that, in the long run, the new plan will be for the best interests of the institution.'

" 'Do you mean that it will be good for the students?' inquired the younger man.

" 'No,' the dean replied, 'I mean it will be for the good of the whole institution.'

" 'Oh, you mean that it will benefit the faculty as well as the students?'

" 'No,' said the dean, a little annoyed, 'I don't mean *that*; I mean it will be a good thing for the institution itself.'

[4] *Op. cit.*, p. 3.

" 'Perhaps you mean the trustees then—or the Chancellor?'

" 'No, I mean the institution, the *institution*! Young man, don't you know what an institution is?' "

Evidently such terms as "economic welfare" and "social welfare" leave us still, therefore, with our point of reference blurred; and they accordingly invite the lack of common focus and articulation of data which now cripples the functioning of the social sciences.

Since it is human beings that build culture and make it go, the social scientist's criteria of the significant cannot stop short of those human beings' criteria of the significant. The values of human beings living together in the pursuit of their deeper and more persistent purposes constitute the frame of reference that identifies significance for social science. But the situation is confused by the fact that the social scientist at work on any single culture confronts in the behavior of people two sets of emphases upon what is significant: those stereotyped emphases which human beings *enmeshed in that particular culture* exhibit as they live toward the goals sanctioned most prominently by *that culture's* traditions and the example of its conspicuous leaders; and a more general order of emphases, common to human beings everywhere as persons living with their fellows, around which the selected emphases of single cultures oscillate. These latter may be characterized as the deeper and more primitive cravings of personalities.

This is not to suggest that there is a "natural man" independent of culture; but simply that human beings, structured and functioning organically alike, subjected at birth and in early infancy to many broadly common types of experience, and growing up inevitably dependent on each other, develop a set of roughly similar underlying cravings. The point here is that, in addition to their more

[189]

immediately biological life-processes and in addition to their culturally conditioned ways of behaving, human beings develop needs that are less directly referable to either of the above than to certain bald and unescapable *human experiences*. All of us are born helpless infants into a world too big for us, where there are hunger and humanly unmanageable things like the weather. In our helplessness we have no choice as regards dependence upon other human beings. From our first moments in life we experience deeply and imperatively the need of living in certain ways, for instance, intimately and securely with other persons. We begin at once to cry out for other persons to succor our needs, we are active when the tides of energy run full, and we lapse into latency and sleep when they run low. We undergo certain experiences that make us feel comfortable and happy, and others that frustrate us. As a result, we acquire from earliest infancy certain very broad cravings *as human beings* which, while not independent of culture, are common to the situation of living on the earth rather than precisely referable to the particular qualities of any single culture. Our culture enmeshes us from birth in its specificities. It may have a structure that actively furthers many of these cravings in its own balance of emphases; or it may have class or other structuring that operates to insure satisfaction to some persons or classes and largely to cramp satisfaction in others. But the growing personality tends to carry along these primitive cravings, echoing and re-echoing within him as he conforms to or resists the precepts of those about him in his culture. The behavior one sees in any single culture is a kind of contrapuntal adaptation between the historically conditioned special emphases of that culture and these less special and more persisting cravings of persons.

Social scientists are wont to stress the *culture's* (institutions') special emphases as defining for them the significant, and to assume that this comprises the whole of the significant. This results in the tacit assumption that the special emphases in a particular culture, e.g., our own extreme emphasis upon competitiveness, are "natural," "inevitable," "what people really want." The task of social science tends, then, to become defined as helping to do and to get these things. These emphases upon the significant within any *single* culture are a less sure guide for social science than generalizations derived more broadly from the behavior of persons in all cultures. No protestations of scientific objectivity and ethical neutrality can excuse the social scientist from coming down into the arena and accepting as his guiding values, *in selecting and defining his problems*, these deep, more widely based, cravings which living personalities seek to realize. The day has passed when ethics could be regarded as a comfortable thing apart, given at the hands of God as an inscrutable "moral law implanted in the hearts of men," a thing to which social science could hand over all its problems of values. The old, aloof ethics has evaporated, and ethics today is but a component of the cravings of persons going about the daily round of living with each other. And the science of human behavior in culture, as a science charged with appraising man's optional futures in the light of himself and of present favoring and limiting conditions, can no more escape dealing with man's deep values and the potential futures they suggest than it can avoid dealing with the expressions, overlayings, and distortions of man's cravings which appear in the institutions of a particular culture.

What, then, are these values and cravings of the human personality? Adequate answer to this question awaits further research by a wide group of specialists, ranging all the way from biochemistry to each of the social sciences, the arts, and the humanities. But life does not wait upon the perfect formulation. One must take one's awareness at

1. The human personality craves to live not too far from ✳
its own physical and emotional tempo and rhythm. While
capable of large adjustment in these respects, the personality suffers strain when the institutional demands of
the culture cut too coercively across this personally
natural tempo and rhythm. One may not assume that the
standards of performance worked out in a culture at any
given time represent the best possible, or even a desirable,
adjustment. In a culture like our own, which employs such
impersonal devices as machines, time- and motion-studies,
and cost-accounting to determine the profitable (defined
in terms of dollars) competitive rate of "efficiency," the
resulting demands for speed, energy-sustention, concentration, and tolerance of monotony in office and factory may
have only the inescapable minimum of relevance to the
cravings of the workers.

As a part of this craving to maintain a tempo and
rhythm natural to it, the personality craves periods of
latency and private recoil during which time, space, and
other persons can be taken on its own terms without coercion.[6]

2. The human personality craves the sense of growth, of ✳
realization of personal powers, and it suffers in an environment that denies growth or frustrates it erratically or for
reasons other than the similar needs for growth in others.

The more precise definition of degrees of necessary
deference to "similar needs for growth in others" is a major
task for social science; and it needs to be worked out
in different types of situations and with full recognition
both of individual differences in capacity and of the inescapable necessity for leadership. Our culture defines this
situation at present with such exaggerated tolerance that

[6] See Chapters v and vi of Plant's *Personality and the Culture Pattern* for a
description of the "barriers" the urban personality in our culture tends to set up
to ward off the pressures of too many other people pressing too closely upon it.

[193]

it equates indiscriminately the need for a free hand by the finance capitalist or employer with that of the laborer. Due regard for the rights of others to grow in their capacities and achievements obviously stops considerably short of tolerance of the rights of vested power agents, even in an allegedly "free country" like ours, to give or to withhold or to obstruct opportunity. Dollars have no conscience, and they may not properly be made the arbiters in such situations.

✶ 3. The human personality craves to do things involving the felt sense of fairly immediate meaning. This sense of immediate meaning may derive from the interest in doing an intrinsically interesting new thing, i.e., the exhilaration of "getting the hang of it"; from the fun of doing something that *is* fun; from the sense of personal power involved in exercising one's craftsmanship; or even from doing something possessing slight intrinsic meaning but with a heavy, reasonably sure instrumental relationship to something else that has great immediate meaning. But immediate meaning tends to be dissipated when the activity in hand is too distasteful; or when the line of instrumentalism from doing something with little or no intrinsic meaning to the something else that has immediate meaning is over-prolonged or too markedly unreliable.

In our culture this craving is put in jeopardy by the fact that so many of us work at highly specialized, semimechanized, and routine tasks which we undertake primarily on the basis of their sheer availability and income yield, rather than because they are peculiarly adapted to us; by the fact that so much of our work goes into the struggle "to make both ends meet"; and by the unreliability of many of the chains of instrumental actions leading to the future, as suggested in Chapter III. The present widespread confusion as regards the hitherto taken-for-granted virtue of "saving for the future" derives from **the** undermining of its immediate meaning by the "big money" era of the 1920's and the subsequent helpless evaporation of savings in the depression.[7]

✳ 4. The human personality craves physical and psychological security (peace of mind, ability to "count on" life's continuities, and so on) to the degree that will still leave with the individual control over the options as to when to venture (for the fun of it, for the values involved) into insecurity.

✳ 5. But the human personality is active and cherishes in varying degrees the right to exercise these optional insecurities. It craves novelty (the learning and doing of new things), provided this can be taken on the personality's own terms, i.e., "in its stride." It craves risk as exhilarating —when it *is* exhilarating. But risk is exhilarating only at the points of peak energy storage in the individual's rhythms of personal living; and when risk is continuous or forced upon one the personality is put under unwelcome strain which invites discomfort, demoralization, and regression. The human personality dislikes to "go it blind" into important risks, but prefers to have its options implemented by the fullest possible information as to the precise nature of the risk and as to the best chances of minimizing that risk.

Our current American reliance upon individual offense and defense, upon living as untied-in, competitive ants in urban ant-heaps, upon casualness and *laissez-faire*, and the widening gap between the knowledge of the trained sophisticate and that of the masses—all of these things tend to force the individual to try continually to stabilize life on the wavering edge of chronic and often quite unnecessary risk. The sheer fact of living ahead into new experience inevitably entails risks. But, when such necessary

[7] See *Middletown in Transition*, pp. 477-9.

and desirable risk is complicated by a mass of avoidable hazards created by the crude structure of the culture, by over-dependence upon individual rationality, and by lack of popular diffusion of relevant knowledge, energy is inevitably diverted to these needless risks that should go into the exhilarating risks of creative living.

※ 6. As a corollary of the preceding, the human personality craves the expression of its capacities through rivalry and competition, with resulting recognition of status—but, again, under the same circumstances as noted in 5 above: only when energy and interest are ready for it and the personality is "set to go" and to go on its own terms. The small boy's spontaneous exclamation, "I'll race you to that tree!" and the friendly rivalry of two farmers in completing the mowing of their fields are fresh and unforced expressions of this desire for spontaneous rivalry. But the human personality does not crave competition when the latter is continuous, enforced, or too threatening. It seems safe to say that most human personalities do not crave as pervasive and continuously threatening competition as they tend to be subjected to in our culture.[8]

※ 7. But if rivalry and the status it yields provide some of the arpeggios of living, the more continuous melody is the craving of the personality for human mutuality, the sharing of purposes, feeling, and action with others. The personality craves to belong to others richly and confidently and to have them belong in turn to it. It craves the expression and the receipt of affection. It craves to be actively accepted and given secure status as a person, *for* the person that it is—as well as for the work it can do. Sympathy is normal to it. Conversely, it suffers when forced to live in physical or psychological isolation. While this desire for mutuality pervades all aspects of living, it is particularly

[8] See the discussion of the prevalence of anxiety in Horney, *op. cit.*

marked in the relations between the two sexes. The personality craves more than physical coitus, although the psychological accompaniments of physical union considered desirable vary markedly in different cultures.

✗ 8. The human personality craves coherence in the direction and meaning of the behavior to which it entrusts itself in the same or different areas of its experience. Contradictions and unresolved conflicts within the rules it learns from the culture create tensions and hinder functional satisfaction. Here is the point at which such aspects of our culture as the dual allegiance to the contradictory values of aggressive dominance and of gentleness and mutuality, noted in Chapter III, throw us continually into tension.

✗ 9. But the human personality also craves a sense of freedom and diversity in living that gives expression to its many areas of spontaneity without sacrificing unduly its corresponding need for a basic integration of continuities. It craves a cultural setting that offers active encouragement to creative individuation in terms of the whole range of one's personal interests and uniquenesses. And, conversely, it dislikes monotony, routine, and coercion that cramp and flatten out the rhythms of living and force a canalization of energy expenditure that deadens spontaneity.

The preceding itemization of persistent cravings of the human personality might be condensed or expanded. Some of these cravings fall into contrasting pairs—security and risk, coherence and spontaneity, novelty and latency, rivalry and mutuality. Confronted with such contrasting tendencies, there is some disposition to dismiss the whole matter and to say that they cannot ever be reconciled. The important thing for the social scientist to note, however, is that these pairs do not represent contradictions any more than sleep is a contradiction of waking. They are but different phases in the rhythm of living. Obviously, no individual craves the independent maximization of each of these values, or of all of them at the same instant. That would involve an anarchy within the personality that would be intolerable. What each of us craves is a pattern of degrees and rhythms of satisfaction of these separate cravings that hangs together in terms of our diverse motivations and "feels right to me as a person living with all these other people." The task of the sciences of human behavior, therefore, is not to "reconcile" these different needs, but to discover the flexible cultural patterning in which their varied expressions in personality can find most adequate expression in the sequences of living.

Individuals differ in bodily endowment and, consequently, in the vigor of their cravings—a weakling may crave security more than his stronger fellows. They differ also in their cravings at different points in the longitudinal life-span from youth to old age. The urgency of craving is also well-nigh infinitely variable, according to the cumulated emphases of a given culture. Life tends to achieve some semblance of satisfaction of these cravings even in cultures where marked degrees of distortion or denial of certain cravings are accepted as normal. What tends to happen in every culture is that, according as certain of these elementary cravings are under strain, or, conversely, are so amply catered to that they are taken for granted, the pattern of the culture exhibits resulting degrees and kinds of compensatory emphases. The heavy institutionalization of our own culture around personal competitive predation and risk gives to the pattern compensatory exaggerations of the importance of property as the source of security and of sex as the source of affection and mutuality. The regimentations and deferred consummations which the culture enforces on individuals also thrust up compensating emphases upon securing the sense of immediate meaning through such stereotyped things as explosive bursts of recreation, asserting one's superiority, being one of the first to wear a new spring style, or moving to a more socially eloquent address. Where the deeper and more individuated forms of spontaneity are denied, personality will write into the culture other forms of self-assertion.

In view of the range of individual differences and of the notorious sluggishness of culture in adapting itself to the modulations of personality, men may not expect even the most flexible and well adapted culture to meet with perfect timing and adequacy all the cravings of personality. It is not likely that all the ambivalences we feel in living may be blamed upon the culture, or that even in our most optimistic moments we can envisage a culture capable of resolving all of these for us. Furthermore, the satisfaction which culture yields to the persons who live by it depends less upon the presence or absence of any universally absolute quantum of emphasis upon a given craving than upon the balance and relationship among available satisfactions of the entire group of interacting cravings; and upon the hospitality of the culture to subtlety of individual patterning.

The situation social science faces is, therefore, complex; but, were this not the case, there would be little need for social science. We need not be staggered by the fact that some occasions giving rise to strain and to such resulting behavior as over-aggressiveness will probably always remain close to the surface of living. Confronted by such facts, the responsibility of social science is to ask: To what extent and how do our present institutions actually encourage such socially disruptive behavior? And how may these aggravating factors be removed or altered? Even after institutions are changed so as to minimize occasions for such behavior, social science still confronts the problem of discovering how the residue of over-aggressiveness can be canalized off through socially harmless outlets, so that it will not be unconsciously and recklessly displaced onto other situations where it does not belong.

※ This chapter has suggested that human cravings are not only inescapably parts of the datum with which social science works, but that they dictate the direction of emphasis of social science as man's working tool for continually rebuilding his culture. So viewed, "institutions," "social change," "trends," "lags," "disequilibria," and all the other conceptualizations of social science become relevant primarily to the wants and purposes of human personalities seeking to live. The central assumption becomes that men want to do, to be, to feel certain identifiable things, such as those outlined in the above chapter, as they live along together; and the derivative assumption regarding the rôle of social science is that its task is to find out ever more clearly what these things are that human beings persist in wanting, and how these things can be built into culture. If man's cravings are ambivalent, if he is but sporadically rational and intelligent, the task of social science becomes the discovery of what forms of culturally-structured learned behavior can maximize opportunities for rational behavior where it appears to be essential for human well-being, and at the same time provide opportunity for expression of his deep emotional spontaneities where those, too, are important.

The problems and hypotheses for research in the chapter that follows derive from such considerations as the preceding. In confronting each problem, the question was asked, "But what do human beings *want?* How do they *crave* to live?" And the resulting hypotheses flow from our knowledge of each problem (how it came to be a problem, what it does to human beings, and so on), seen in relation to the above question. If social science is not to be forever stalemated in the face of the future, some point of reference must be established by which it can get beyond the present paralyzing question, "But how are *we* to determine what *ought* to be? That can be no concern of the scientist." Lacking an answer to that question, there is no firm basis for doing more than following the determinisms of the moment, with such minor remedial improvisations as science may devise. The present chapter has sought to recover the sense of direction within the human stuff of — us all. If such a sense of direction is as yet only partially grasped in such statements of the cravings of human personality, it affords nevertheless a stout instrument with which social science can take up its work of appraising and re-shaping our culture. It enables us to ask: What ones of our current institutions, appraised from this point of view, effectively support men's needs—and how effectively— and what ones block them? And what changes in these institutions are indicated?

VI

SOME OUTRAGEOUS HYPOTHESES

THE controlling factor in any science is the way it views and states its problems. Once stated, a problem can yield no further insights than are allowed by the constricting frame of its original formulation; although, in a negative sense, the data discovered may serve to point the inadequacy of the original frame of reference. The current emphasis in social science upon techniques and precise empirical data is a healthy one; but, as already noted, skilful collection, organization, and manipulation of data are worth no more than the problem to the solution of which they are addressed. If the problem is wizened, the data are but footnotes to the insignificant. In a positive sense, such data may be vicious, in that their very perfection may mislead others into regarding as important the problem to which they relate; for in science, too, "Apparel oft proclaims the man." If science poses questions within an unreal or mistaken framework, data and rival schools of thought begin to pile up behind the two sides of these questions, and the questions assume unwarranted dignity and importance. As Professor Wendell T. Bush[1] has pointed out:

"Theories call forth opposing theories. Now a position taken to resist another position is an alternative position on a certain question. Is the moon made of roquefort or gorgonzola? Do the souls of unbaptized infants go to hell or to heaven? Is the universe one or many? If a certain line

[1] *Op. cit.*

of philosophy happens to be a consideration of merely imaginary [or mis-stated, trivial, or superficial] problems, the criticism which takes that philosophy seriously, which takes it, i.e., for a discussion of real [or important] problems, is itself not a discussion of real [or important] problems. The fact that the former is a well-articulated dialectic does not give its dialectical implications any relevance to physics."

An important question the scientist must continually ask himself is, therefore, "Why do I pose a given problem — and ask the questions I do regarding it?" As has been suggested, the immediate needs of the *de facto* institutional "system" are often too limited, casual, and distorting to warrant their uncritical acceptance as frames of reference by social science. And social scientists are human beings in a culture that provides something less than an atmosphere of pure scientific curiosity. In the face of this situation, social science must nevertheless strive to free itself to discover and to work in terms of an independent and more inclusive frame of reference. Such an orientation was suggested in the preceding chapter, where it was pointed out that a basic datum of social science is the cravings (values) which human personalities living together in culture have persistently sought to satisfy. *If* social science is to be free to be science, it must have the courage to fight for its freedom from the dragging undertow of a culture preoccupied with short-run statements of long-run problems.

Social science must inevitably accept for itself the rôle of bringing the lagging culture not peace but a sword. This inescapable rôle of science was well stated by the late W. M. Davis of Harvard University in a paper in *Science*[2] under the provocative title, "The Value of Outrageous Geological Hypotheses":

[2] May 7, 1926

"Inasmuch as the great advances of physics in recent years and as the great advances of geology in the past have been made by outraging in one way or another a body of preconceived opinions, we may be pretty sure that the advances yet to be made in geology will be at first regarded as outrages upon the accumulated convictions of today, which we are too prone to regard as geologically sacred. . . .

"Of course, this [a specific hypothesis in geology] is 'impossible'; that is, it is impossible in an earth of the kind that we ordinarily imagine the earth to be; but it is not at all impossible in an earth of the kind in which it would be possible. Our task therefore is to try to discover, as judicially and as complacently as we may, what sort of an earth that sort of an earth would be; and then to entertain the concept of that sort of an earth as hospitably as we can and to examine the behavior of such an earth at our leisure. And it may also come to be the part of wisdom to ask ourselves in what way and how far our present conception of the earth must be modified in order to transform such outraging possibilities into reasonable actualities; for that is precisely the way in which the above-listed outrages and many others have gained an established place in our science. Of course, if we do not approve of the necessary modifications we may reject them, and with them the outrages that they countenance."

Would that we all were geologists! "Outrageous hypotheses" in geology were dangerous to their professors in Galileo's day, but today they are taken simply as matter-of-fact science at work at its job. University trustees and Liberty Leaguers do not scrutinize the theories of natural scientists. The word "subversive" has a highly specific reference nowadays, and it points directly at the social scientist. For, whereas an "outrageous hypothesis" in the natural sciences involves simply change in our ways of describing and utilizing impersonal things, such hypotheses in the social sciences may involve the upsetting of personal behavior and vested class interests, and they must usually operate against the hot brakes of personal protest.

This chapter will pose a series of crucial problems confronting us Americans as we live by our culture in the larger contemporary scene. As problems of the culture, they presumably become problems for social science. Accompanying each problem, a hypothesis is proposed for testing relative to that problem. The problems are raised and the accompanying hypotheses suggested in the spirit of Professor Davis's "outrageous hypotheses." One of the difficulties social science has to accept is that we cannot make controlled experiments on phenomena as large as a total culture. In stating these hypotheses, therefore, it is recognized that they cannot be definitely proved or disproved. This does not excuse us from doing what we can. It simply becomes the more imperative to break the hypotheses down into smaller relevant problems, where the predictive value of results can be determined, and then to apply these findings as best we can to the larger situation.

It is assumed that wherever our current culture is found — to cramp or to distort the quest of considerable numbers of persons for satisfaction of basic cravings of human personality, there lies a responsibility for social science. In such cases, the first charge upon social science appears to be to ask: Does the trouble lie in the way we operate our culture, i.e., is it only a matter of relatively small internal changes within the going set of institutions; *or* is the trouble inherent in the kind of culture we have? If the latter, then the questions have to be faced: What alternative kinds of cultural situations would satisfy more directly and amply the cravings that are now starved? What specific research is needed to test out these alternatives? And, if a given alternative, when tested, seems sensible and desirable "in theory, but not in present practice," what techniques and what stages of change would be needed in order to get us from here to there?

In the course of the investigation in Washington of monopoly practices in industry, begun in December 1938, it was stated that it is becoming virtually possible to create technological inventions to order. In the field of human behavior we are likewise learning that it is possible to a marked degree to do the vastly more difficult thing of creating new modes of behavior, if the full resources of our intelligence are applied to the task. It is here assumed that "It can't be done" is irrelevant to social science, if the rigidities of institutionalized habit or human inertia are all that appear to block the march toward desirable cultural change. The problems raised in the pages that follow, accordingly, transcend the present, familiar "going system" and the rights of vested interests; they cut cross-lots (as science always must), regardless of the "Posted: No Trespassing" signs. They are not confined to what we can get tomorrow or the day after. And if such statements of problems are challenged as impractical, the answer is that they possess a realism and practicality of the very highest order; for these questions derive from instant relevance to persisting human needs, rather than to the more or less fortuitous exigencies of an institutional *status quo*. It may be for lack of such ultimate realism that much current social science wanders, and our culture with it. We wander because, setting our course so often only by "the next step," we end by walking in circles. In proportion as the size and ramifying complexity of a culture's problems grow, so must the focus of its analysis and research be projected beyond the immediacies of present snarls in single, narrow institutional details.

Only a nineteenth century liberal can derive much comfort from the passage of an act imposing mild regulation on the securities market or strengthening the anti-trust laws, when the central animus of business enterprise is to circumvent such regulation. Or from the pending bill to reshuffle mildly the Federal bureaus and departments, when citizenship is losing its meaning to masses of our urban population, and when the Senate, in a time of national emergency, is rendered impotent for thirty-one days by a filibuster against such an obvious humane measure as an anti-lynching bill.

A strong deterrent to the overhasty dismissal of any of our all too limited potential options on grounds of "impracticality" or "novelty" is the fact that we are struggling to live today in a contracting world in which novel or upsetting things are happening all about us with startling speed and coerciveness—for instance, totalitarian dictatorships, shrinkage of time and space because of the invention of airplane and radio, 10,000,000 unemployed in the United States, an undeclared Second World War already in progress. If, as seems probable, "capitalism is in decline" and "democracy is on the defensive," the question our culture appears to confront is not "Shall we change?" but "How can we contrive change extensive enough and rapid enough, however radical its innovations, to enable basic human values to survive?" One thing appears highly probable: that *laissez-faire* or even a policy of confining ourselves to casual minor repairs in the machinery will not meet the situation. If praying to the gods for rain does not increase the fertility of our fields, it avails little to redouble our prayers or to make alterations in their wording; we would better turn our energies to the techniques of agriculture.

It is, of course, by no means contended that no social scientists are giving attention to such problems as are stated below. Such problems are implicit, at least, in the thinking of many. But the statement of the program of social science tends to be timid, and its challenge to existing practice is implicit and tangential rather than overt and direct. The candid, sustained, cooperative exploration of problems of this order has not been accepted by the social sciences as part of their central responsibility.

Here, then, are some problems and "outrageous hypotheses" confronting social science. They are stated bluntly in the effort to force attention past the portico of terminology into the central nave of the problem. Terminology is important, but debates over it should not be allowed to stay too long the march to the reality that lies behind. As stated at the close of Chapter v, these problems have been selected not because they represent interesting moves on an impersonal intellectual chessboard, but because they involve frustrations of the urgent cravings of great masses of the American people. And the accompanying hypotheses take the forms they do because they aim to lessen these frustrations as directly as possible.

✳ 1. *The problem*: In our large and increasingly intricate cultural structure, functional adequacy for the ends of living is crippled at many points (a) by disjunctions and contradictions among institutions, and even within single institutions; (b) by the disproportionate structuring of power among institutions and within single institutions; and (c) by the erratic reliance upon planning and control at some few points and upon *laissez-faire*, or casual, adjustments at most others. We confront here not a static situation, but one which is highly dynamic. Conflicts among institutional ways of behaving do not stand still until we get around to resolving them; for life must go on, and the effort to force needed action against friction generates more and more problems. Present modes of coping with our institutional problems appear to be falling relatively farther and farther behind the demands of the situations presented in the culture.

The hypothesis: There is no way in which our culture can grow in continual serviceability to its people without a large and pervasive extension of planning and control to many areas now left to casual individual initiative. It should be a major concern of social science to discover where and how such large-scale planning and control need to be extended throughout the culture so as to facilitate the human ends of living.

To paraphrase Professor Davis's words, our task here as social scientists is to try to discover what sort of culture — that sort of culture would be which utilized its best intelligence systematically at point after point to plan and to coordinate the institutionalized ways of doing things which are important to us as persons. Nobody wants to be planned into the routine status of a robot. But here the problem for social science is to determine which is baby and which is bath, and not to allow both to be thrown away in the frothy suds of indiscriminate "freedom."

A great corporation—General Motors, United States Steel, General Electric, or Sears, Roebuck—does not pretend to operate without close planning and control. It does not leave the fundamental coordination of its many units to chance; the manager of one of its units does not haggle with and obstruct another. Nor are slogans and symbols relied upon to gloss over and to disguise preventable contradictions, strife, and operational inefficiencies among the internal parts of such a corporation. Even less can a whole culture afford to indulge in the costly wastefulness of uncoordinated action. We are slowly coming to realize that uncontrolled complexity generates chaos faster than it can generate order. The cultural lags that *laissez-faire* not only tolerates but augments are not incidental lapses from perfection which time will cure. Some of them are time-bombs which sooner or later go off and cause serious trouble.

We Americans are proud of big things—"the greatest show on earth," "the largest steel plant in the world"— and yet our traditions also warn us against bigness. Anti-trust laws reflect our democracy's experience with the tendency for big, internally controlled units to exploit little, "free" units. No small part of the present predicament of business derives from the attempt to operate it part-planned and part-unplanned. Obviously, it is only the elephant who can afford to say "Each for himself and God for all of us" as he dances among the chickens! And yet, laments by liberals such as Mr. Justice Brandeis against "the curse of bigness" reflect but a wistful nostalgia for an era that can never return. We know too well the utility of coordinated bigness—where it *is* useful[3]— ever to return indiscriminately to the world of little things in endless friction against each other.

We fear "control" and invoke the dreadful specter of bureaucracy. We tend, therefore, to state the problem negatively, instead of asking in a more positive temper

[3] It is not intended here to swallow the desirability of bigness neat. Bigness presents, in fact, a major problem for social science research. This problem is: At what points is it desirable for the culture, in the interest of other, qualitative things, to sacrifice some of the final potentialities of large-unit living and operation? In order to answer this we need to know a great deal that we do not now know, but can find out, about how, under different types of organization and incentive, individuals lose the sense of "belonging" (and thereby lose morale) as the size of the operating unit increases. Or, if belonging is carefully structured to yield emotional tonicity (in neighborhood, school, church, shop or office, and leisure), is the sheer size of a factory or city relatively immaterial? In the analysis of the desirability of bigness in industrial operation we need carefully to distinguish where present efficiencies in such operation are due to mere size (in the sense of facilitating basic technological coordination), to the control over competition that bigness facilitates, to the ability of big industries to control legislation in their favor, and to other similar factors inherent in present modes of operation.

how planning and control can be used to enhance freedom at points critically important to human personality, by eliminating current wastes and insecurities that operate to curtail freedom. We state this problem negatively because we think in terms of the kind of culture we now have. Our kind of culture tends, for instance, to place political control at many points in the hands of the business culls. For our kind of culture awards its greatest prizes to those who make money in private business, and, under this system, our best talents naturally — turn aside from public service. There is little incentive for them to do otherwise in a culture in which motivation is as narrowly channelled as it is in ours. The generally less adequately endowed and less successful who do go into the public services act as second-raters would be expected to act: they are not very efficient, they often emulate their betters by trying to make all the money they can out of their posts, and they prove over-pliant to those with more money or power who seek to exploit them. When we Americans talk about governmental planning and control, therefore, we are talking about these things in a special kind of culture which by tradition and habitual practice scarcely gives planning and control in the public interest a ghost of a chance. It is not surprising that when a political control system of this caliber calls in the "expert," the result usually tends to be unsatisfactory to both parties.

Then, too, control may not wisely be viewed, as we free Americans tend to regard it, as a biscuit-cutter pressed down by an external force upon the dough of private living. Authority is a continuous two-way process, or it is tyranny. Our emphasis upon individualism has made us careless of the inescapable need in a democracy to organize responsibility and authority horizontally at the local base, and vertically up to the apex.[4] Such an integration of individual living is a *sine qua non* of flexibly continuous planning in a democracy. A large culture which does not discover a way of structuring rank-and-file participation in, and responsibility for, authority, in some more active and inclusive way than our pallid American reliance upon the political ballot, invites the loss of even that important check upon authority. It is not the fact of planning and control that needs to be challenged, but its misuse. The question we face is: how much control, where, and how, in order to further the authentic ends of democratic living?

Nobody, not even an anarchist, lives in complete freedom; for complete freedom is impossible in living among other people. As a culture grows in complexity, and chains of causation lengthen, freedom decreases and the need grows for selecting out and institutionalizing those areas where it is desirable to preserve various specific degrees of freedom. Our American culture has written the freedom of the individual into its charter. We explicitly guarantee freedom in religion, in the preservation and disposal of one's property, and against political and personal coercion (e.g., *habeas corpus*). Resting back on the traditions of the close of the eighteenth century, when but 3 per cent of our population lived in urban places of 8,000 or more population, we expect the informal pressures of neighborly life to curb unsocial expressions of personal freedom. In the very different urban world of today these latter pressures are almost non-existent; and, in the resulting welter of unchecked freedoms, workers are free to be dispossessed from

[4] The Nazis, under their "leader-theory," structure authority boldly from the top down. While the Webbs paint too glowingly the present success of the Soviet Union's effort to structure authority along more genuinely democratic lines (see *Soviet Communism*, Vol. I, Chaps. i-iv), the Soviet Union's experiment represents a genuine effort to avoid the two extremes of Nazi over-control from the top and of our own American unorganized confusion at the grass-roots of local living.

their houses and to sleep on park benches because private business is free to work itself into a depression; newspapers are free to suppress and to distort news because of "the freedom of the press"; consumers are free to buy shoddy goods and to be oversold by high-pressure salesmanship because of "free competition"; and the "housing problem" forces all of us to pay too much rent or to live in poor dwellings because of the freedom of the building industry and of the real estate and mortgage-financing businesses to exercise their respective freedoms. We continually sacrifice important freedoms—such as basic peace of mind about our own and our children's future and the ability to choose more freely new experiences and other potentially constructive risks we want to take—for the nominal freedom to exploit and to be exploited and to hang ourselves by our ill-informed and preventable mistakes. Our problem is to discover how control can be used to enhance vital — freedom to live creatively at points important to the human personality, by eliminating current wasteful freedoms that operate in fact to limit these more vital freedoms.

It is an exceedingly narrow and hazardous path we social scientists must here explore. If the way ahead involves the discovery and application of democratic modes of control, the exercise of even this option is seriously curtailed by the shortness of the time available. For, if democratic means of control are not promptly developed, there is no assurance that the shift to another and less democratic kind of control in the United States will come slowly. It may possibly come swiftly, and we may be asked to approve, after the fact, a Fascist-type seizure of power contrived in the name of "anti-Fascism" and "Americanism." For us social scientists, the option remains whether to address ourselves and our research unwaveringly to doing what expert intelligence can do, or to allow ourselves to be surprised by the event with our heads burrowing in the sands.

✳ 2. *The problem*: Democracy, as a frame of reference encouraging recognition of the dignity and worth of the individual and implementing this recognition for political action, is an institutional invention of major importance. It is a value worth struggling to preserve. But democracy is being increasingly ridden down in our chaotic culture under the hoofs of power-agencies bent upon getting things done. The difficulty of running a factory, winning and holding a retail market, winning and maintaining political power, passing legislation, and getting similar things done in a culture as wide and unorganized as ours invites use of undemocratic means to achieve ostensibly democratic ends. In other instances, undiscriminating adherence to the forms of democracy operates to cripple the expert performance of essentially democratic functions.[5] The net result of all the above is that democracy, though generally acclaimed as a symbol, is decreasingly a reality in American life. The present flaunting of democracy under the guise of democracy operates to

[5] Many public issues today are of a highly technical character that should not be disposed of by a show of hands, without far more effective mediating machinery than our casual form of democracy provides. An instance of this is the submission to the voters of a state of the complex issue in its raw detail as to whether the state should increase its bonded indebtedness by $40,000,000 for a specified purpose. In the municipal field, the popular election or political appointment of the public health officer is a case of the application of naïve democratic methods to a technical problem. Likewise, the technical drafting of the details of intricate social legislation by a large legislative body like Congress, composed of miscellaneous small-town lawyers and similar persons of no particular distinction, is open to very serious question. Congress originated in a period when the main tasks of the state were few in number and largely negative in character. It is still a valuable sounding board for the wide discussion of large issues, but for the more precise formulation of policy and drafting of detail, it operates more often than not as a cumbersome device that slows up the work of democracy.

undermine the democratic principle. As Professor Laski remarks in a passage quoted earlier, "There is in America a wider disillusionment with democracy, a greater scepticism about popular institutions, than at any period in its history."

The hypothesis: If democracy is to continue as the active — guiding principle of our culture, it will be necessary to extend it markedly as an efficient reality in government, industry, and other areas of living; otherwise, it will be necessary to abandon it in favor of some other operating principle.

The second alternative will appeal to few as desirable until the full potentialities of the first have been exhausted.

Now the original statement of the problem above may be incorrect. It may be that democracy in the United States is not becoming a decreasing reality. Those who so maintain must shoulder the burden of disproving such seemingly stout facts as the following: Class lines appear to be crystallizing in the United States. We are developing an American proletariat. E. P. Herring of Harvard University asserts that "Never since the rise of modern statehood have there been such great power-areas dissociated so clearly from social control."[6] A Cabinet officer writes, as noted earlier, of "the private ownership [by business] of government." Citizenship probably never meant as little to any generation of Americans as it tends to mean to our massed city-dwellers today. It is becoming increasingly difficult to persuade the ablest citizens to run for municipal office. Thoughtful persons are decreasingly inclined to view Congress as an effective democratic legislative instrument. It looks as if these current tendencies are but the natural extension into an era of greater power-blocs

---

[6] "Logomachy and Administration," *Journal of Social Philosophy*, January 1937.

of the democracy of America's Gilded Age, of which Parrington says:[7] "It was making ready the ground for later harvests that would be less to its liking. Freedom had become individualism, and individualism had become the inalienable right to preëmpt, to exploit, to squander. Gone were the old ideals along with the old restraints. . . . It was an anarchistic world of strong, capable men, selfish, unenlightened, amoral—an excellent example of what human nature will do with undisciplined freedom."

The planning and coordination of a culture to democratic ends, suggested in the hypothesis above, becomes fantastically difficult in such a scene. But for those who accept, however tentatively, the conclusion that democracy is becoming a decreasing reality in American life, the following steps are indicated: To review our democratic assumptions in the light of what we now know about individual differences in intelligence and other personality traits and the degree to which such things are innate or culturally conditioned; to analyze our American culture to discover where the democratic process operates and where it does not, and where it operates naïvely and inefficiently and where it operates effectively; to discover where, and in what form, and with the aid of what new types of social structuring, it should operate; and then to chart the ways of remoulding institutional behavior radically in the light of these findings.

Our culture is increasingly characterized by large-unit participation—for example, in large producing units with employees numbered by the hundreds and thousands, and in large cities (with 45 per cent of our total population in 96 metropolitan communities of more than 100,000). Where and how is it possible to achieve by democratic means and to use for democratic ends the manifest ad-

[7] *Op. cit.*, Vol. III, p. 17.

vantages of large-scale operation? Or do urbanism, mechanization, and the division of labor inevitably involve the loss of democratic participation by the mass of individuals? And to the extent that the latter may be true, where does our choice lie?

A dangerously undemocratic vacuum exists in our culture between the individual citizen and political authority at the top, between the worker and the corporation that hires him, between the person and the city in which he lives. The right of free assembly and organization is an important part of democracy, but, as it operates with us, this represents at best a negative statement of the problem. Denial of the right to *prevent* free assembly and organization does not, in fact, operate positively to establish needed intermediary organizations between the base and the apex of the functional pyramid. Here, again, reliance upon casualness and spontaneous rationality help to shape the situation in which the culture finds itself. There is need to study the present structuring of intermediate organizations— political organizations from the ward organizations within Tammany Hall to the Republican National Committee, economic organizations from craft and industrial unions and local Chambers of Commerce to the National Association of Manufacturers and the Chamber of Commerce of the United States, and so on throughout each functional area of living. We must discover why these particular organizational forms happened to arise, how democratically and how adequately they represent all the needs in their respective fields, and to what extent they actually operate to strengthen, to deter, or to block the public interest, as over against interests of special factions. And then the need is to ask how a more representative and inclusive structuring of organization could be developed by a culture which set out to state the problem of democratic social organization positively.

The C.I.O., for example, has been described by some progressive-minded individuals as the most important development in the United States in the present generation; but the structure of the C.I.O. follows that of individual competing industries, and this organization can become, in its turn, a vested interest supporting a dying individualistic economy. The rise of the American Labor Party inevitably raises the question of how far organization within the philosophy of gradualness can carry us in the direction of desirable social change. And similar questions need to be raised in appraising other current organizations. It does little good to hope that patent needs in the structuring of the culture will in time be met, if, in fact, the odds are found to be against such an automatic process. The fate of social democracy in Germany suggests how fragile and unfounded such hopes can be.

What kind of culture would that culture be which would reverse the present relative statuses of "working for oneself" and "working for the public interest" and would actually enlist its ablest enterprisers to work for the latter? When we scoff at such a proposal are we simply generalizing from prevailing tendencies in the set of cultural institutions we happen to have? To what extent *can* a democracy be built around the private scramble for wealth? Can political democracy be built upon economic undemocracy?

In view of the importance of widespread, accurate, and non-partisan information for the effective operation of democratic institutions, can democracy afford to depend so largely as we do upon privately owned media of public information operated for private profit? It is an established fact that a good newspaper property currently receives two-thirds of its gross income from advertisements and only one-third from its readers. Furthermore, the amount and quality of information printed now depends upon whether it pays a private publisher to print it; and the difference between the amount of news in a New York *Times* and a Centerville *Sentinel* is very great. This question of contriving a more democratically effective means of purveying necessary information is usually answered by pointing to the manifest inadequacies of the press in totalitarian states. But this is but to confront the other horn of the dilemma. Here, as elsewhere, the responsibility of social science is to find a way through. What kind of — culture would it be in which information needed for the democratic functioning of the culture came through without suppression, bias, or curtailment to every citizen and in forms most conducive to effective learning? This is a large order; but it simply states the obvious fact that, if democracy is to work, this can occur only through the most continuous and active application of all the resources of intelligence to the situations we face.

And, following on the preceding, what techniques of — information and what rituals for the strengthening of community feeling do we know or can we discover that might be deliberately employed to strengthen democratic action? And what blueprints do we social scientists have to offer for their application—at what points, in what order, through what channels? The word "propaganda" has an un-American sound because, operating as it now does so largely outside of democratic controls, it is so largely directed to undemocratic ends. In a world bristling with dictators wielding all the arts of propaganda, democracy will no longer be able to survive with a *laissez-faire* attitude toward public opinion. It must take the offensive in its own behalf and use these new and potent instruments for the ends of democracy. Already in the United States the "management of public opinion" for private ends is highly developed. We must either discover a way to democratize this process, or give over the pretense of being a democracy.

The most insistent question of our post-Munich world is: Can democracy set its house in order so as to demonstrate the intrinsic strength and reality of the democratic process in the face of the challenge from the dictatorships before it is too late?

* 3. *The problem*: Private capitalism, which operated with rough-and-ready utility to stimulate raw energy expenditure in the uncouth world of our frontier expansion, is proving a crude, recklessly wasteful, and destructive instrument for creating and diffusing welfare among a settled, highly interdependent population. In a culture like ours, marked by great and continuous personal insecurity, the aggressiveness encouraged by the struggle to get and to keep "a living" is constantly being displaced onto other areas of living. The result is that the disorganizing confusions of capitalism overflow the more strictly economic areas of behavior and tend to coerce the whole pattern of the culture. They appear in the unbalanced structure, in the marshalled resistance to intelligent, needed change, in the lack of effective social organization, in the faltering character of our political democracy, in the elaborate and costly institutionalization of war, and in other similar functional crudities of our culture pattern.

The hypothesis: Private capitalism does not now operate, and probably cannot be made to operate, to assure the amount of general welfare to which the present stage of our technological skills and intelligence entitle us; and other ways of managing our economy need therefore to be explored.

Here the question that social science appears to face is: What kind of culture would that culture be which would use its full array of knowledge and productive resources to maximize the quantity, quality, and useful variety of daily living for the masses of our American people?

Such an hypothesis, however tentatively stated, forces those engaged on research problems within the going capitalist system to ask themselves: "Granted that the utmost change that my data will indicate were brought about, how far would that get us along the road to assuring the maximum of welfare to the mass of the population? And if I add together all the work being done within the going system by researchers like me, how far would *that* get us?" Judgments will vary. For those who believe, after asking these questions, that continuance of the present types of research will equip us so that we can maximize mass welfare, it is their scientific responsibility to demonstrate more clearly than has as yet been done: (1) the precise sequences of concrete alterations they propose to make in private capitalism in order to effect this reform; and (2) their explicit reasons for believing that these changes can be effected before our accumulating disabilities lay us victims to the leprosy of Fascism that is creeping across the present capitalist world. And if they answer the latter of these proposals by claiming to see "good things" in Fascism, or by regarding it as "an inevitable next stage," then their responsibility is to answer two more questions: What "good things" do they see that cannot also be achieved within the framework of democracy? And why is Fascism "an inevitable next stage," and a stage toward what that has relevance to the ends of human personality?

The usual demurrer entered by the objective empirical researcher when confronted by such questions is: "It is not my job to be concerned about whether private capitalism will or will not work. I am studying the facts, and they are equally useful and indispensable preliminaries for anything you want to do with the going system." Are they?

Harking back to the quotation from Wendell Bush near the beginning of the present chapter, it cannot be too strongly stressed that no question can be asked which does not carry an explicit or implicit frame of reference, and that the frame of reference determines to what things the answers are relevant. The current pattern of economic research addressed to problems such as adjusting prices, manipulating the interest rate, changing the price level, stabilizing foreign exchange, adjusting wages to the marginal productivity of the worker, and so on, will yield data and inferences relevant primarily only to an economic system controlled by the mechanism of prices. Accordingly, no amount of research within the framework of an assumed "economic equilibrium" achievable by the price mechanism within a profit economy—however good that research may be—can carry us far along the road to understanding the potentialities of a culture not dominated by the price system operating under the quest for private profit.

It is important to test as thoroughly as possible the hypothesis that private capitalism can be made to work adequately by gradual internal reforms. But such testing must go beyond research on problems as defined by our current practice. Working along at such problems does not necessarily constitute at all the testing of the validity of the hypothesis that private capitalism can be made to work adequately. Empiricism must not be confused with the full-bodied work of science.

For those whose analysis leads them to test the hypothesis of the ultimate inadequacy of private capitalism and of step-by-step remedial adjustment within it, and to search for alternatives, many such questions as the following suggest themselves for research:

Under what conditions could production be dominated by consideration of technological capacity and human

need, rather than by the quest for profit through the bottleneck of the price system?[8] Here research might begin by –
asking how much of a given commodity—e.g., housing—
our population needs, instead of how much it will be able
to pay for at current prices; and then proceed to ask what
is the simplest and most efficient way of producing it by
our mass-production resources, stripped of many of the
costs[9] and competitive wastes that private business enterprise now loads onto the process. A necessarily limited but
nevertheless important application of this technique of
beginning with the question "What goods do people need?"
was made in the *Report of the National Survey of Potential
Product Capacity*, published in 1935.[10]

A large program of research is needed to answer the related question: What is the optimum relation—to avoid
wastes from sub-standard goods at the one extreme and
from luxury at the other—between life-expectancy and
initial cost in the case of each major commodity? It is well
known that the competition for wider markets under the
price system tends constantly, in the case of basic commodities produced under mass production, to sacrifice substantial potential increments in commodity life-expectancy for uneconomical minor savings in initial cost.[11]

---

[8] This is just another way of asking how our culture would need to be changed
to resolve, in the engineer's favor, the conflict between the engineer and the
businessman described by Veblen in *The Engineers and the Price System*.

[9] That the costs of current competitive business are real is revealed by the
following "fair breakdown of the f.o.b. cost of a $500-600 automobile." The
figures are from *Steel*, a trade journal, for April 17, 1933, p. 13:

Platform cost (including materials, parts, and labor for completed car at end of assembly line)	$105–125
Dealer's profits and salesman's commission	150
Advertising	25–30
Overhead, zone supervision, profit, and other items, totalling "almost one-half of the f.o.b. cost"	225–300

[10] New York City Housing Authority and Works Division of the Emergency
Relief Bureau, City of New York.

[11] This point is succinctly stated in the above *Report of the National Survey of*

What are the potentialities of human beings to be motivated by other things than private money-making? Is it true that men would lack initiative, would not be enterprising, if they were not forced by the pangs of need to be so? Is pecuniary self-interest really the mainspring of human action upon which civilization depends? Bertrand Russell insists that men want "power."[12] They also want peace of mind, fun, mutuality, spontaneity, respect, affection, and other things. Men's motivations are diverse; they are also highly malleable by the kind of culture in which they live. It is possible that the extravagant emphasis

Potential Product Capacity: "Ever since the Industrial Revolution, during which production for sale gradually superseded production for use, low price has been the prime market requirement. Even America is largely a 'poor man's' market. Every penny saved in costs is likely to expedite sales. But scalping costs by using the cheapest possible materials is seldom true economy. The use of better materials is likely to add a small percentage to the cost of an item, but it also adds a large percentage to its life. The competition for cheapness is particularly keen in clothing, utensils, household furnishings, and speculative building, and is characteristic of nearly all quantity-production items. A very small addition to the cost of the cloth or of the plumbing, for example, would result in an article likely to withstand a great deal more wear and tear. Unfortunately, under the present system, the additional life that might be built into consumer goods, at so slight an additional cost, would in no way benefit the manufacturer. His pecuniary interest lies in selling a second article to replace the one that has been worn out." (p. xxii.)

A concrete instance of this was brought out in the patent-probe hearings of the Temporary National Economic Committee, as reported in *Business Week* for January 28, 1939. The hearings revealed that the Bell Telephone System has for the past fifteen years made for its own use vacuum tubes that last 50,000 hours, whereas radio tubes on the market not only are built to last well under one-tenth of that time but actually do not last as long as the average life of radio receiving sets. "Technically," *Business Week* reports, "most types of tube (except power tubes which 'run hot') could be made to last the life of the set, at an additional manufacturing cost of a few cents per tube. But since set manufacturers who buy tubes are influenced by price differentials measured in fractions of a cent per tube, additional cost is prohibitive from the industry standpoint." In the face of this situation, "none of the seven manufacturers of radio tubes has seen fit to make such tubes for a very simple reason: there is no demand for them." Of course there is "no demand for them" when the public does not know that it can get them.

[12] *Power* (New York: Norton, 1938).

upon acquisitiveness which we Americans exhibit is a pathology inflicted on us by the historical distortions and current insecurities of our culture. What are the elements of "savor in life" that we are "gambling away," to use Parrington's phrase, and what kind of culture would offer outlets for a richer and more varied set of motivations? All of which simply asks: In what kind of American culture – would the activities involved in getting a living be reduced to an instrumental, rather than their present monopolizing, position?

In what kind of culture would the selection of one's – vocation (one's "calling" in the original sense) not be dominated, as it so largely is with us, by the concern as to which job will pay best? Would an American culture be possible in which status would run with the social service-ability of work, rather than so largely with predatory power and wealth?

Under what circumstances would property not operate as a bar to obviously desirable cultural change? Light is thrown on the problem we face here by the following comment by Professor Laski: "There is, I think, a quite special reason why, in a crisis like our own, the dominant class should find it peculiarly difficult itself to adapt its social forms to new conditions. The type-person of this dominant class has been the business man. . . . For him, all activities are referable to the single standard of profit. . . . Specialisation in money-making has, in fact, gone so far with the business man that he is unable to understand the building of social relationships in which its attainment is not a primary end. By making money the end of all things, he has separated himself from the power to co-ordinate the interests of society at any point where profit has to be foregone. In those circumstances, where the business man, as the master of society, ought to be engaged in the task of unifying disharmonies, his peculiar psychology makes it impossible for him to understand their significance. Unless his opponents can be bought off, the business man has no way, save conflict, of dealing with them."[13]

— How could we devise and operate a culture in which no humanly important service such as health, recreation, education, job-opportunity, family formation and adjustment, and mental health would be subject to class privilege or depend upon ability to pay?

Current developments in the Soviet Union need to be studied closely to discriminate between those elements of success and failure which are related to peculiarly Russian conditions and those which offer bases for prediction of success or failure of a socialized economy in the United States.

Such questioning is heresy where heresy hurts most in our American culture. If social science means anything, however, such an hypothesis and such resulting research problems may not be rejected by the cheap and easy phrase that "they advocate the overthrow of capitalism," or "American institutions," or "the Constitution." Alternatives to capitalism deserve careful analysis, as well as ways of improving the operation of capitalism. One of the things social science knows most surely today is that no culture can be realistically and effectively analyzed by those who elect to leave its central idols untouched; and, if fundamental change is required, it does no good simply to landscape the grounds on which these idols stand. Cultures are not compartmentalized. No student of the American family, of politics and government, of our churches, of education, of our channels of information, of inventions, of the use of leisure, of crime and mental health, or indeed—as was pointed out in Chapter IV—of the social sciences as themselves institutions within a culture, can afford to

[13] *Op. cit.*, pp. 55-6.

disguise or to pretend not to see the long, pervasive fingers of our economy as they reach into the operations of our daily living.

✳ 4. *The problem*: Current social science plays down the omnipresent fact of class antagonisms and conflicts in the living all about us. It studies industrial strikes and analyzes wage differentials and the operation of trade and industrial unions and the machinery for collective bargaining. But it is careful, in the main, to keep the word "class" out of its analysis and to avoid the issue of the possibility of the existence of fundamental cleavages which may not be remediable within our type of economy. Social science does this because the concepts of "class" and "class struggle" lead straight into highly inflammable issues. It is helped in so doing by the tradition that class divisions are un-American and that such differences as exist are transitory and will be eliminated by a rising standard of living and "the general movement of Progress." But such exculpating assumptions may not be justified. There is more than a little basis for assuming, on the contrary, that class divisions are endemic in our type of economy. If, as John Dewey has pointed out, the best way to handle certain traditional metaphysical issues in philosophy is to turn one's back upon them, the same may not be said of such an urgent reality as the class struggle.

The hypothesis: The body of fact and theory around the highly dynamic situation of class conflict will have to be much more realistically and centrally considered if social science is to deal adequately with current institutions.

The issue here does not call for the lining up of social scientists on either side of this conflict situation. The need is, rather, to analyze closely and realistically this stubborn and pervasive complex of factors. There seems little doubt that class lines are stiffening in the United States. Where?

Why? Around what frustrations and grievances? Among what people most and least? How does a class, and the acceptance of oneself as belonging to a class, feel and what does it imply to differently situated persons? And how inevitable are these things? To what extent are people actually motivated, and the course of history determined, by economic factors? And to what extent and in what situations are other motivations involved? If our present economic institutions are found to be creating and augmenting class conflict, what, then, do the social sciences in a democracy propose?

The answers to such problems are not easy. But no aspect of American culture demands more imperatively the best analysis of our social sciences.

✴ 5. *The problem*: The stout assertions of the "equality" of human beings in connection with the original formulations of our American democracy derived from the fact that democracy was a revolt against authoritarian inequality. But since that day biology and psychology have taught us many things about individual differences. And social science is learning that a considerable share of the confusion in our culture arises from the effort to treat human beings as if they were equal. Native endowment, specific cultural settings, and the cumulating course of personal experience in culture—all of these operate to render persons unequal.

The hypothesis: The chance for the survival of democracy and the prospect of increased human welfare would be enhanced by explicit recognition of the fact that men are unequal; by the discovery and elimination of cultural causes of inequality; and, where the causes of inequality are primarily biological, by the restructuring of the culture to adjust freedom and responsibility to ability. Such readjustment would also afford greater opportunity for the expression of qualitative individual differences.

As E. P. Herring remarks,[14] "A modern Declaration of Independence would read that all men are created unequal and that the courts have but aggravated the doings of nature. The existence of great industrial power-units together with the numerous other social and economic hierarchies makes the problem of democratic government essentially one of adjusting their resulting differences. The task, never easy, is made all the more difficult by the undemocratic 'governments' prevailing within the power-units that must be reconciled. From these centers emerges an impatience with the democratic method itself." Symbols and creeds have no meaning apart from the institutions through which they operate. The result of attempting to operate "equality" and "freedom" in the midst of such an institutional situation as Herring describes has tended to institutionalize inequality in the name of equality.

If democracy is to function in a population of widely unequal individuals, social science must show the way to restructure the culture so as to care for these inequalities. There is need to discover, for instance, which differences are so biologically controlled that favorable cultural conditions cannot materially change them; to discover in what precise situations assumed equality among these biologically unequal persons operates deleteriously for the culture as a whole and for specific groups of unequal persons; and to erect at these exposed points appropriate safeguards for the culture and for these persons. In addition to these biologically controlled differences, specific culture settings operate to reenforce and to exaggerate an infinite number of native tendencies to differ, and to create others outright. Persons in the great modal mass of our

14 *Op. cit.* above at footnote 6.

population are endowed with what we call "normal [i.e., most customary degrees of] intelligence." From the moment of birth, the accidents of cultural status—for instance, whether one is born "north or south of the tracks" —begin to play up and to play down the potentialities of each person. As life progresses, culture writes cumulating differences recklessly into these individual lives; until in adult life two persons of generally similar native endowment will differ so widely that one is on relief, reads the tabloids, and follows Father Coughlin, and the other is a manufacturer, is hostile to expenditures for relief, reads the New York *Herald Tribune*, sends his sons to Harvard, and votes for Landon. Otto Klineberg's study of *Negro Intelligence and Selective Migration*[15] reveals tellingly one special aspect of this general problem. We need to discover in one situation after another where the kind of culture we have wantonly creates and augments individual differences, what changes are necessary to eliminate such artificial and avoidable accentuations of differences, and, at the same time, how genuine potentialities for qualitative individuation may be encouraged.

Not only is there need to deal directly with the realities of individual differences, but social science must also increase its attention to inequalities between the complexities of daily living and the abilities of individuals of all levels of capacity to cope intelligently with them. The relative stature of any person, when measured against the mounting size of the forest of problems that surrounds him, is shrinking steadily. In unnecessarily many situations the person is not equal to his problems. This is bad for the culture; for the individual is forced to rely over-much on relatively blind judgment, and, frightened by the number of his mistakes and the strains they entail, he is increasingly

[15] New York: Columbia University Press, 1935.

[230]

building gross, cliché **behavior** back into the culture. As will be suggested later, one may not depend upon educating the individual up to most of these problems, for many of the problems are of a complexity that baffles even the specialist. The need is rather to rebuild the culture so as to — adjust the situation to the individual. Occasions for more or less blind judgment on important matters, and the ensuing strain from avoidable mistakes, must be eliminated through the fullest utilization of two processes: systematic introduction of sanctioned patterns that canalize behavior at exposed points along intelligent lines, and removal from the individual of the necessity for coping with certain issues in their raw complexities—this latter by building into the democratic process a larger place for the intermediary expert.

Our culture suffers continual loss through the futile struggle of unequal people to vindicate the burden of proof they must carry as to their equality to other persons in over-complex situations. In its starker phases, the strain involved may be seen in suicides and in the mounting tide of entrants into our mental hospitals. Less spectacular but even more important is the toll these strains levy upon the quality of American life, a toll measurable in terms of loss of serenity, vital interests, and similar basic freedoms.[16]

The patterning of our culture is directly influenced by — the prevalence of these anxieties in our individual motivations. Any candid person who reads Karen Horney's *The Neurotic Personality of Our Time* finds himself brought up short at point after point with the thought, "But she's talking about me and my friends!" Who is "normal"? And

[16] It is not implied here that there can or should be a Utopian culture in which no inequalities among persons and no ensuing strains will exist. The only thing in question is the possibility of discriminating between avoidable and unavoidable differences and strains and of seeking to reduce as many as possible of the former.

who is "neurotic"? And which of us is not a combination of both? "There is one essential factor common to all neuroses," says Horney,[17] "and that is anxieties and the defenses built up against them. Intricate as the structure of a neurosis may be, this anxiety is the motor which sets the neurotic process going and keeps it in motion. . . . Anxiety connected with a certain activity will result in an impairment of that function." Human behavior institutionalizes itself in four paths of attempted escape from anxiety[18]—each writ large over our American culture. It seeks:

(1) To rationalize anxiety, e.g., by blaming someone. Thus we may say: "Labor trouble is caused by foreign trouble-makers," "It's the presence of too many Jews that is spoiling things," "Human nature is lazy," "The Roosevelt administration is the cause of our troubles." (2) To deny the existence of anxiety, e.g., "Fascism and Communism are un-American and could never get a foothold here," "America can never fail," "There is no basic conflict in aims between capital and labor in the United States." (3) To narcotize anxiety, e.g., by drowning it in hard work, slogans, drink, or excitement, or by purchasing a shiny new car. (4) To avoid anxiety, e.g., by staying away from places and not reading things that "remind you of all these troubles in the world," by hardening oneself against "impecunious friends, beggars, and unpleasant things like that," by playing hide and seek with anxiety by procrastinating about facing it.

When these dodges fail and the anxiety still rides our backs, we individuals build into our culture by our behavior four other dodges:[19]

[17] *Op. cit.*, pp. 23, 57.
[18] *Ibid.*, pp. 47*ff.*
[19] Cf. *ibid.*, pp. 96*ff.*

(1) We may seek reassurance through affection; or (2) we may submissively seek the cover of identification with some traditional source of authority, e.g., we may lean back upon religion or "the spirit of Washington and Lincoln"; or (3) we may have recourse to power-tactics and redoubled aggressiveness; or (4) we may withdraw within ourselves.

In every part of living and at each stage in life, from infancy to old age, the fact of inequality is present. In a culture like ours, which asserts equality in its institutions and yet encourages the gross exploitation of inequality, the struggle is driven underground in neurotic conflicts within the individual, only to burst forth again in ways that render the culture itself more confused. Social science may not dismiss such situations by blaming human nature. Human nature has an inveterate capacity for living more richly if given half a chance.

Attention should be called to one further aspect of the problems generated in culture by inequality among persons: the implications of inequalities in a population for the character of leadership required, especially when extended planning and control are necessary. F. L. Wells of the Harvard Medical School has pointed out[20] that in situations involving normal adults of relatively equal capacities, drawn together by common interests and aspirations, one may find excellent cooperative functioning that largely enforces itself under minimal direction; whereas, in a population more heterogeneous in endowment and interests, a very different situation is likely to exist, and the rôle of leadership is likely to have to be considerably more active. This generalization requires testing in a variety of situations.

[20] "The State School as a Social System," *Journal of Psychology*, 1938, pp 119-24.

✳ 6. *The problem*: Our major institutional forms and accompanying slogans derive from an era which not only viewed men as "equal" but also as "rational." We now know man to be basically emotional in his motivations and only sporadically able to sustain the tensions involved in taking thought in order to direct his actions. Science is daily opening up new dimensions of complexity even in the commonplace situations of daily life—in family life, physical health, mental hygiene, economics, and government. And yet, so great is our reliance upon the rational omni-competence of human beings, that we largely persist, as already suggested, in the earlier habit of leaving everything up to the individual's precarious ability to "use his head." As a result, our personal and cultural dilemmas today are heavily traceable to the irrationality of behavior around allegedly rational institutions. The fact that these institutions have been casually accumulated and are at so many points poorly adapted for the intelligent performance of the functions to which they are applied augments the helter-skelter quality of popular behavior.

The hypothesis: The chance of securing more coherent, constructive behavior from persons depends upon recognizing the large degree of irrationality that is natural to them and upon structuring the culture actively to support and encourage intelligent types of behavior, including inevitably opportunity for creative, spontaneous expression of emotion.

Every parent has seen a child who is "going haywire" in the face of a troublesome situation seize with obvious relief upon a diversion, suggested by an adult, which restores his little world to smooth functioning. No one enjoys continuous dilemmas. We are all children in welcoming escape from them by the best life line within our reach. The hypothesis in the preceding paragraph suggests that it is

[234]

the business of social science to anticipate recurrent, avoidable dilemmas in institutional living and to discover channels of behavior, with accompanying sanctions, that will make intelligent "ways out" easy to come upon.

A culture as careless as ours of the habits of thought, feeling, and action of those who carry it, and tolerating the contradictions and disjunctions that our culture does, cannot expect the judgments of its members to exhibit sustained intelligence when they vote, plan their lives, run their businesses, or rear their children. Public opinion becomes a shambles and private living a network of inconsistencies. What kind of culture would it be which would not expect those who live by it to improvise rational solutions for its own irrational disjunctions? Which would not expect public opinion to pull rational rabbits out of the hat of a ragged and erratic misinformation fed to it by paid propaganda and a business-controlled press? And which would assume direct responsibility for seeing that intelligence was encouraged and supported at every critical point in daily living? What would our American culture need to do if it were to set itself to see that its citizens from birth to death had as little chance as possible to invest their savings ignorantly, to purchase sub-standard commodities, to marry disastrously, to have unwanted children "accidentally," to postpone needed operations, to go into blind-alley jobs, and so on?

Here, again, the structuring of a dull, methodical culture is not the aim. The aim is rather to create a cultural situation which, by minimizing occasions for wasteful mistakes, would free energy and resources for the vital creativities of living. Our present culture's false reliance upon the rational omni-competence of the adult tends to cramp deep, vital spontaneities by institutionalizing superficial whims, and to institutionalize reckless irrationality in the name of rationality as "the American way."

Our culture is a part of the larger world in which such things as war and Fascism are rife. External chaos renders internal order more difficult to achieve. But such impinging difficulties may not be used as an excuse for delaying the setting of democracy's house in order. Democracy as symbol and slogan is weak unless democracy as operating reality is strong.

✱ 7. *The problem*: There is a widespread tendency to steady ourselves in the face of the functional inadequacies of our culture by a comforting reliance upon education. "What we need," we are prone to say, "is to intensify education; and, as education makes people better-informed, many of the problems that now beset us will disappear." This operates, in effect, to justify everyone in continuing to do what he is now doing, while we pass the buck to education. But this great faith in gradualness implies a largely static view of culture; it assumes what may be called the haystack theory of social problems, that is, that our culture confronts a fixed quantum of problems which are being slowly carted away by "progress," each load reducing the total awaiting removal. Actually, however, the culture appears to be piling up problems faster than the slow horse-and-haywagon process of liberal change through education and reform is able to dispose of them. Education does not stand apart from culture, but is a part of it; and when a culture's economic life line is in jeopardy and the culture is accordingly being more and more dominated by privately interested pressure-blocs, the tendency to coerce education to the ends of these pressure groups increases steadily.[21] This operates

[21] The writer found that the heyday of recent freedom in education in Middletown occurred in the late 1920's. With the whole culture "riding to glory" on the swelling tide of prosperity, business relaxed its scrutiny of what the local schools taught. By 1935, after six years of business depression, the culture was

[236]

to curtail further the cultural correction we may expect to get from education.

The hypothesis: If major changes are required in order to cope with present problems in our culture, it is impossible to rely primarily upon popular education to effect such changes.

This amounts to saying that one cannot get an operation performed by setting out to teach the masses about appendicitis. The same point applies to teaching ethics and citizenship, and organizing businessmen in clubs devoted to "service," while the institutional straitjacket is left essentially unaltered. While all possible improvements in education and personnel must be pushed for all they are worth, the basic responsibility remains squarely upon the shoulders of social science to discover where fundamental changes in the cultural structures are needed and to blueprint the ways of achieving them. Only when an intricate culture like ours is better structured to support, rather than to obstruct or merely to tolerate, humanly important lines of behavior, can we justifiably expect secondary agencies like education to carry on effectively.

Our culture is at present proud of its basic hospitality to education. Our definition of education, however, is confused by our undiscriminating adherence to tradition and to democratic slogans. Public education in our schools is largely confined to a traditionally circumscribed area of rather formal knowledge touching only part of the total experience of living. In a helter-skelter democratic spirit, we leave the way wide open to all manner of agencies, commercial and otherwise, to instil whatever habits they find convenient. If our culture is to be controlled more effectively to democratic ends this

tightening its grip on the schools to insure that "only the right things" were being taught. (See *Middletown in Transition*, pp. 233-4.)

mélange of educations must be recaptured and redirected. No important area of public ignorance can be left to freedom of exploitation. Again, in answer to the query, "But who is wise enough to do this?" the answer is that, if social science, working with the humanities and the arts, does not attempt it, then education will occur at the hands of other less adequate agencies. This simply asserts that intelligence is a better director of education than the *de facto* pressure-groups of a casual culture.

Just as social science must be prepared to tell democracy what functions may and may not wisely—that is, in the public interest—be left to various types of democratic action, and under which types of leadership, so it must discover where learning may be left to individual initiative, where and to what extent it should be mandatory in public school education, and what types of learning need to be the subject of constant public propaganda, utilizing the best techniques through all possible channels of information. We need to know what kinds of attitudes and overt behavior may be expected to change at what rates in a given cultural environment under what types of education and propaganda? Also what biassed controls—business, religious, and other—need to be removed from education, so that it may flow freely into any infected area in the culture.

* 8. *The problem*: Religion, in its traditional forms, is a dying reality in current living. And yet no culture can live vitally without a central core of emotionally resonant loyalties widely shared by the mass of the people. As already pointed out, our culture, in its headlong preoccupation with individual money-making, has been reckless of the fate of common values and loyalties; and, as a result, these have been disastrously dissipated, notably in the increasingly prevalent pattern of urban living. Under our

[238]

present culture, common loyalties blur rapidly as they leave "myself and my family" and proceed out into the larger community. In the relative vacuum that "community" becomes under these circumstances, we depend upon various slogans imposed upon us from above, rather than upon loyalties growing richly in the soil of daily living. No amount of patriotism enforced by international insecurity, or of local slogans fostered by Rotary and Chamber of Commerce to fortify My Town's business against Your Town, can supply this need for emotionally rich common sentiments. We have delayed too long the recognition of this aspect of culture, and social science has, in the main, avoided the issue by turning its back upon the whole matter on the ground that prevailing religions and their churches are anachronisms.

The hypothesis: American culture, if it is to be creative — in the personalities of those who live it, needs to discover and to build prominently into its structure a core of richly evocative common purposes which have meaning in terms of the deep personality needs of the great mass of the people.

Needless to say, the theology, eschatology, and other familiar aspects of traditional Christianity need not have any place in such an operating system. It is the responsibility of a science that recognizes human values as a part of its data to help to search out the content and modes of expression of such shared loyalties. In withholding its hand science becomes a partner to those people who maintain outworn religious forms because there is nothing else in sight to perform the humanly necessary function of focusing common values and stiffening life to maintain important continuities under the dislocating pressure of immediacies.

Here, again, the task may not be shirked. Where do some or do all of our people now feel durable values, and how can these be broadened and strengthened? In what situations do what classifications of people now tend to feel themselves "alone," lost in a world too big for them, and set over against others? For instance, we need to know this about urban people and also about farmers as they confront the world of businessmen. Step by step, in the minute processes of neighborhood, shop, and leisure, where are people left hungry to share values together? Where and how does our culture operate to dissipate common purposes, e.g., between rich and poor, employer and employee? Is the maintenance of specific divisively operating institutions worth the price they exact in impaired common morale? And what kind of American culture would it be which set out to build creative common purposes, *not* imposed from the top and dictated by Fascist class-interest, but built upon humanly rich cravings in all the people, and hospitable to qualitative differences among individuals?

✳ 9. *The problem*: War is generally recognized by intelligent people as an impossibly crude, stone-axe device for settling differences. Yet it persists, and, in its present destructive form in a highly interdependent world, it threatens increasingly all the decent values for which civilization stands. It is directly and continuously encouraged by one cultural form, imperialism, based upon another cultural form, capitalism. Freud asserts that there always will be wars because men are sadistic. For those who accept war on this latter ground, the magnitude of the threat of war is so great as to make it obligatory upon them to demonstrate that in *all* types of culture Freud's hypothesis holds—that is, that war is not a function of a special type of culture, a predatory and insecure culture which encourages men to take out their insecurities on others.[22] Those who question Freud's view confront the overwhelming need to test the following hypothesis:

The hypothesis: It is possible to build a culture that in all — its institutions will play down the need for and the possibility of war.

Social science can go far toward discovering what kind of culture that culture would be. The diagnosis is already fairly complete, thanks to a long list of competent studies of nationalism, imperialism, international finance and trade, and other factors within our culture that encourage war. The problem of war, more than most others, has engaged the attention of scientists from several disciplines, and the dissection has proceeded to the point where fairly unequivocal knowledge exists. The causes of war are known and accepted by a wide group of thoughtful students. But the statement of what is to be done languishes because social science shrinks from resolving the austere findings of scholarly monographs into a bold program for action. And each war creeps up on us and is ruefully, or cynically, accepted as "more or less inevitable," because, at the last moment of action, there seems to be no alternative.

In the case of an issue like this, where the problem does not arise from lack of knowledge, what social science appears to need is the will to mass its findings so that the truth they hold will not continue to trickle away as disparate bits of scholarship. We know enough about war and its causes to present these findings, point their meanings, and propose action in a way that will hold this damaging evidence steadily and authoritatively before the eyes of the humblest citizen. But, for social science to do this, two things are necessary: It would have to give over the belief that its function is simply to find the facts and not

[22] See in this connection Margaret Mead (ed.), *Cooperation and Competition Among Primitive Peoples* (New York: McGraw-Hill, 1937).

to point their import for action; and it would have to learn to act collectively, throwing the full weight of its numbers and scientific prestige behind a documented call for action that would leave few loopholes for the timid. The development of such a will and capacity to voice in concert the seasoned judgment of scientists would represent a new stage in the serviceability of social science to man.

In a characteristically clear statement on "Science and the State of Mind," Wesley Mitchell has recently said[23] that "Science is concerned to show only what is true and what is false. By so doing it is of inestimable value in helping men to decide what is good for them and what is bad. But science itself does not pronounce practical or esthetic or moral judgments." If, however, "science" does not pronounce such judgments, *scientists* can; and if they fail to do so, in this world in which the gap between sophisticated knowledge and folk-thinking is so wide, they but aggravate the limitations on the utility of science to man. Professor Mitchell goes on to remark, "The investigator who tries to persuade men that they should choose one course of action rather than another may be drawing sensible conclusions from his scientific findings, but he is certainly not doing scientific work when he does so. . . . For the man who has a cause at heart, however fine that cause may be, is likely to prove a biased observer and a sophisticated reasoner."

It cannot be too often emphasized that the soap-box scientist is a dubious scientist, but that is not the alternative which social science confronts. For the individual scientist or group of scientists to refuse to draw "sensible conclusions from scientific findings" is to place social science in an ivory tower where it does not belong and

[23] Address as President of the American Association for the Advancement of Science before the American Science Teachers Association, reprinted in *Science*, January 6, 1939.

where it cannot remain. In this connection, it should be noted that both the American Anthropological Association and the Society for Psychological Study of Social Issues have recently issued statements asserting the falsity of Nazi race theories.[24] Such careful statements represent science performing its function of trying to do what it can to introduce more order at those points where it is uniquely equipped to afford guidance. In this connection, the rôle of the Science Committee in the important work of the National Resources Committee, whose publications are beginning to appear from Washington as this is written, should also be noted.

✳ 10. *The problem*: Cities are potentially the richest environment for modern living, in that they allow great selectivity in association around special interests and they make possible the provision of the widest range of modern service, educational, and similar facilities. But, as already suggested, as the size of any cultural unit grows in arithmetic progression, the complications inherent in size tend to increase in something like geometric progression, *unless active and continuous planning and control are employed*. Our traditions have prompted us to assume that cultural organization will happen automatically as individuals feel the need for it. This is a largely unwarranted assumption, and as a result urban living represents one of the backward areas of our culture. Only a class-structuring of the culture which thrusts into prominence the homes and other perquisites of living of a favored minority disguises the human unsatisfactoriness of the conditions of life of the mass of our urban population.

[24] See also, R. V. Gilbert, *et al.*, *An Economic Program for American Democracy* (New York: Vanguard, 1938), a proposal prepared by seven younger members of the economics departments of Harvard University and Tufts College.

The hypothesis: Since urban living operates seriously at present to confuse and to devitalize our culture, science needs to discover ways to knit these loose population masses into living communities of interest, before this degenerating tendency renders the culture impotent.

The study of urban problems has been growing rapidly over the past generation. Sociologists, especially at the University of Chicago, are doing indispensable work on urban ecology and related problems; economists and political scientists are providing excellent analyses of urban fiscal problems, services of distribution, and politics and administration; housing problems are analyzed in relation to population movement, tax-rates, and the financing and other costs of building houses; Faris and Dunham have studied *Mental Disorders in Urban Areas*; social welfare workers are providing eloquent evidence of the health and other costs of congested living; and city-planners are re-zoning cities and helping the Federal government to lay out Greenbelt towns on the outskirts of large cities. But this analysis of parts is not giving us guidance in terms of the organized, functioning whole of the urban unit—of the sort suggested by Lewis Mumford's excellent book on *The Culture of Cities*.

Social science is facing here the sort of problem the biological sciences have confronted in their effort to study the problem of organized development within living organisms. The effort in biology has been to separate out smaller and smaller elements in the process of organic development, in the hope that these analyses of parts, when aggregated, would give the key to the whole process of development. As one of these workers has recently pointed out:[25] "The repeated failure of these various attempts to

[25] Edmund W. Sinnott, "The Cell and the Problem of Organization," address as retiring President of the Botanical Society of America, reprinted in *Science*, January 20, 1939.

solve the problem of organized development by cutting up the individual into smaller and smaller unitary elements breeds the uneasy suspicion that here again, as in so many other scientific problems, we have been confusing analysis with solution. The scientific temperament feels much more comfortable when it is breaking down a complex phenomenon into simpler parts than when it is trying to pull together a series of diverse facts unto a unity of relationship. For a solution of the ultimate riddles, however, — synthesis is more important than analysis. . . . It is not an understanding of units which we now seek, but of unity. We are like a small boy who takes the clock apart to discover the secret of its running, but after he has dissected the works into an impressive array of wheels, gears and springs is unable to put them together again successfully and is still as far as ever from an understanding of synthetic horology. . . . It is important to know that a living plant is composed of cellular units, but it is even more important to understand how, through the multiplication and interrelation of these units, the orderly development of an organism is assured."

The need for cooperative work by many types of specialists on the common problem-area of the city, as over against piecemeal attack by separate disciplines on isolated parts of the whole, here stands out clearly. A frequent remark by workers on these separate problems is that "The need, in so far as *my* part of the problem is concerned, appears clearly to be to do so-and-so; but so long as such-and-such other factors remain unchanged, progress in this direction will be slow." The intellectual throttle needs to be opened wide and the question asked, "In what conceivable kinds of urban situations would these obstructing factors be absent and active support be given to the types of constructive change my data suggest?" More specifically, we need, for instance, to ask whether it is possible to build urban people into vital communities in a culture whose economic institutions are operated for private gain by their owners, with little or no acceptance of responsibility for the quality of social living? To the extent that social science believes that this is possible, how does it see that we can do it and what does it propose? And, quite as important, to the extent that social science believes that it is impossible, what specific changes, however drastic, does it recommend?

✳ 11. *The problem*: People dislike the chaos and waste of violent change enforced through strikes, class struggle, revolution, and other such exercise of force. Our dislike of such things does not, however, slow up the pace at which basic conflict-situations ready themselves for explosion. In fact, the history of revolution is one long record of over-long resistance to recognizing the handwriting on the wall. In an era in which cultural change is pronounced, it is important that the mood with which people confront change be as coherent and as integrated as possible; that is, that they not be largely hospitable to change in certain functional areas of living and erratically hostile in others.

Much has been said in earlier chapters of the interfunctioning character of a total culture. As a result, drastic change in one institutional area requires forthright accommodation in other areas, or the culture is thrown into imbalance and acute strains result. One of the marked characteristics of American culture is the eager mass hospitality to technological and to many other types of *material* change. The "new" in machinery, the industrial plants that house machines, in leisure-time devices, in housing and in such things as women's clothing fashions tends to be synonymous with the "good and desirable." The pressure of our technologies has tended, also, to extend this hospitality to newness to many non-material aspects of the related business system, e.g., to various high-pressure selling techniques. But these rapid and pervasive changes are not integrated into the culture, but largely imposed upon it; and they are paralleled by, and because left so largely to run free they invite, marked mass resistances to change in such things as the structure and rôle of government, in traditional attitudes regarding the capacity and responsibility of the individual to direct his life "freely" and "rationally," in the controlling legal system, and in many similar matters. In the resulting situation of strain, the tendency is for the mass of persons to change where they must and to develop a somewhat blind emotional resistance to change at all other points. This tends not only to institutionalize cultural (and individual) chaos but also to deter the process of badly needed change.

The hypothesis: It is necessary to structure into a complex culture like ours a congruent hospitality to change in all institutional areas, in order to prevent the continuous disruption of the culture by changes that occur in single areas.

We know a great deal already about emotional readiness to learn, and also about resistance in situations involving strain. Such knowledge needs to be applied and extended in contact with specific institutional situations. There is evidence that liberal attitudes (i.e., those hospitable to change) are correlated with intelligence,[26] and there is a great deal of evidence of the correlation of conservatism

[26] "There are only the rarest exceptions to the general finding, in recent years, that individuals whose attitudes are currently described as liberal or radical make higher scores on tests of intelligence than do those holding conservative attitudes. . . . The relationship is not, of course, a perfect one, nor in most cases is it very close. . . . [But] the relationship has now been so often and so consistently reported that, for most groups at this time, it may apparently be accepted as a demonstrated phenomenon." (Theodore Newcomb, "Determinants of Opinion," *Public Opinion Quarterly*, October 1937.)

with property ownership.[27] The recent sharp change in public tolerance toward open discussion of the need to check the ravages of syphilis reveals what can be done to change public resistance to the application of intelligent change. Our need here is for systematic and insistent analysis of situation after situation to discover where and how blockage occurs in the application of requisite change; and to formulate the precise steps necessary to eliminate the blockages.

For instance, what, if any, are the common characteristics of the specific changes which Americans in various income, occupational, regional, and other groups view with hospitality or with hostility? What differences in motivation are involved, and why? What attitudes toward specific changes hang together in clusters and derive from a common motivation—for instance, the manufacturer's resistance to government interference, the C.I.O., and to changes in the Supreme Court? At what points is present hospitality to change socially desirable, and at what points —for instance, the acceptance of annual automobile models—is it actually socially undesirable and due to such factors as commercial exploitation or other partisan propaganda?[28] At what points is artificially fostered readiness for change welcomed by particularly circumstanced people as an anodyne for anxieties fostered by conflicts within the culture? At what points does resistance to change generate from what types of insecurity? And which of these insecurities are inevitable in any culture and which are the result of particular features of our present culture? What can be known from the close study

[27] See the nationwide sampling polls of the American Institute of Public Opinion for evidence on this point.

[28] In this connection, attention should be given to the validity in various specific cases of the cloaking of commercial advertising under the name of "educating" the consumer.

of actual changes of different types as to the rôle of leadership of specified kinds in helping to effect change?

✳ 12. *The problem*: Most of the above hypotheses will possibly be accepted by current social scientists as theoretically worth testing; but, in the face of the requirement for bold and precise action, most of us will gently sigh, "O Lord, *don't* send me!" The dangers inherent in making one's intelligence explicit in terms of its full implications for going institutions is immediate and real. It is much safer either to avoid dangerous hypotheses or, when one does touch them, to leave the implications of one's data to be read between the lines, if and as the reader so elects. Most of us social scientists recognize "that men build their cultures by huddling together, nervously loquacious, at the edge of an abyss." Most of us pay at least shadowy deference to the fact that the justification for our earning our keep is that social science is a useful tool for understanding and coping with humanly important problems. Most of us recognize "the lag behind life of the social sciences." If we have not lapsed into acceptance of some such rationalization as that "These are all big problems, and Rome was not built in a day," we are uncomfortable; for the question "What is to be done?" will not down in a world whose institutions are so seriously in discord.

The hypothesis: Social science cannot perform its function if the culture constrains it at certain points in ways foreign to the spirit of science; and at all points where such constraints limit the free use of intelligence to pose problems, to analyze all relevant aspects of them, or to draw conclusions, it is necessary for social science to work directly to remove the causes of these obstacles.

To the extent that social scientists recognize this as difficult or dangerous, they inescapably pose for themselves the problem of discovering and stating what kind of culture that culture would be in which intelligence would be freely and eagerly used constantly to rebuild men's institutions.

To the workaday manipulative man of affairs, the mere posing of such hypotheses as all of the above may seem fantastic. But social science is confined neither to practical politics nor to things whose practicality is demonstrable this afternoon or tomorrow morning. Nor is its rôle merely to stand by, describe, and generalize, like a seismologist watching a volcano. There is no other agency in our culture whose rôle it is to ask long-range and, if need be, abruptly irreverent questions of our democratic institutions; and to follow these questions with research and the systematic charting of the way ahead. The responsibility is to keep everlastingly challenging the present with the question: But what is it that we human beings want, and what things would have to be done, in what ways and in what sequence, in order to change the present so as to achieve it?

If social science turns aside from this task, the way ahead will be a prolonged series of blank emergencies. To the student of culture, such institutional stalemates as the one that occurred at the time of the "bank holiday" in the spring of 1933 are known to be rarely auspicious occasions for effecting needed cultural change, *provided the thinking has been done in advance and the desired course of action is charted*. Without the latter, such emergencies will continue to be capped by nothing more effective than Blue Eagles, forensic exhortations, scattered remedial legislation, and laments over the shortcomings of our institutions in the face of Fascism. With such research and planning, we may yet make real the claims of freedom and opportunity in America.

INDEX

INDEX

Becker, Carl, *The Heavenly City of the Eighteenth Century Philosophers*, 57, 62; *Progress and Power*, 5, 106, 108

Behavior, choices in, 134, 180, 191; datum of social science, 125; distribution of, 28; and historical analysis, 134; interaction of, 15; processes of, in relation to cultural processes, 42*ff*.; *see also* Cravings; Emotion; Human beings; Individuals; Personality

Behavior of Money, The, 34

Behavior of Prices, The, 34

Bell Telephone Co., 39

Belonging, 79, 97; *see also* Aggressiveness; Community, feeling of; Mutuality; Urban living

Benedict, Ruth, *Patterns of Culture*, 56n.

Bentham, Jeremy, 153n.

Bentley, Arthur F., *The Process of Government*, 139

Berle, A., and Means, G., *The Modern Corporation and Private Property*, 74n.

Bigness, 78; American pride in, 210; and casualness, 65; and complexity, 82; differences in, 67; increasing prevalence of, 216; and "little man," 78; utility of, 210

Biology, 244

Birth of Tragedy, The, see Njetzsche, F.

Boas, Franz, 159n.

Brady, Robert, *The Spirit and Structure of German Fascism*, 64n.

Brandeis, Justice, 210

Bridgman, P. W., 8, 149

Brookings Institution, 146

Bühler, Charlotte, *Der Menschliche Lebenslauf als Psychologisches Problem*, 93n.

Bureaucracy, 210; *see also* Government, personnel

Burke, Kenneth, *Attitudes Toward History*, 58n.; *Permanence and Change*, v, 249

Bush, Wendell T., 127n., 202, 222

Business, 60, 61; dominance of, 6, 69, 99; *see also* Capitalism; Culture, Structuring of; Property

Business-enterprise and cultural change, 100

Businessman, 70, 225; orientation to future, 92

Butler, Samuel, 44n.

Capital accumulation, theories of, 36

Capital and labor, 61

Capitalism, 41, 89, 145, 207, 220*ff*.; and democracy, 215*ff*.; and loss of sense of community, 85, 87; *see also* Aggressiveness; Competition; Money-making

Case analysis, 26; *see also* Culture, and individuals

Casualness, 63*ff*., 108; and bigness, 65, 243; normal in culture, 64; and planning, 65; *see also* Laissez-faire; Planning and control; Rationality

Catholic Church, 65, 110

Causality, assumption of impersonal, 124; *see also* Determinism

Change, cultural, 38, 40, 62, 63; attitude toward, 246*ff*.; lags in, 110; liberal attitude toward, 207; in material and non-material culture, 59; obstruction of, 108; possibility of, 206; process of, 64, 107; reliance on education, 236; resistance to, 17; unevenness of, 100*ff*.; *see also* Casualness; Conservatism; Laissez-faire; Learning

Crime, 6, 27

Cross-discipline research, 17, 51*ff.*, 166*ff.*; *see also* Social science

Culture, as active agent, 23, 24; assumed orderliness in, 124; casualness of, 63*ff.*, 186; comparative, 39, 157; complexities and individual capacity to learn, 230; complexity of, 57, 234, 236; concept of, Chap. II, 19*ff.*, 50, 152; a continuum, 32; contradictions and disjunctions in, 5, 11, 49, 58, 68n., 93, 101, 109, 197; definition of, 19, 154; determinism in, 22, 41, 134; directional orientation of, 48; dynamics of, 23, 24, 38*ff.*; frequency as determinant of pattern, 32; functional relationship of parts, 65, 126; functional strength of, 71; imbalance in, 66, 220; and individual differences, 229; and individuals, 13, 21*ff.*, 22n., 24, 27*ff.*, 29, 38*ff.*, 49, 50, 71, 182, 190, 200, 235; integration of, 70; and interpretations of situations, 54; lags in, 20, 38, 75, 106*ff.*, 246; official version of, 28*ff.*, 32; order in, 125; pattern of, Chap. III, 49; concept of pattern, 55; private versions of, 48, 88; problems in as origin of social science, 115; processes, and individual processes, 42*ff.*; and rational behavior, 234*ff.*; rigidities in, 46; and society, 153; structuring of, 65*ff.*, 82, 107, 212; sub-patterns of, 55; two levels of value in, 189, 191; *see also* Change, cultural; Individuals and culture; Institutions; Pattern of culture

Culture of Cities, The, see Mumford, Lewis

Curiosity, pure, 114, 182; *see also* Objectivity

Darwin and *laissez-faire*, 142; *see also* Dewey, John

Data, accretion of, 7, 16; frame of reference of, 123; meaning of, 185; *see also* Empiricism; Objectivity; Social science

Davenport, H. J., 161

Davis, W. M., 203

Decline of American Capitalism, The, see Corey, Lewis

Decline of the West, The, see Spengler, Oswald

Democracy, 60, 85, 207, 214*ff.*; bigness and, 78; and capitalism, 140; decline in, 6; disillusionment with, 68n.; and individual differences, 229; and inequalities in power, 77; and planning and control, 213; structuring of, 216, 217; as symbol and reality, 214; *see also* Equality; Freedom; Government, personnel; Liberty

Democracy in America, see De Tocqueville

Democracy in Crisis, see Laski, Harold

Depersonalizing mechanisms, 91

Depression and social science, 4

Determinism, cultural, 22, 134; economic, 41, 228

De Tocqueville, *Democracy in America*, 81n.

Deviants, place in social science, 28*ff.*, 125n.; *see also* under Culture: assumed orderliness in; and individuals; private versions of

Dewey, John, 227; *How We Think*, 64n.; *Human Nature and Conduct*, 64n.; *The Influence of Darwin on Philosophy*, 119

Dickinson, Z. C., *Economic Motives*, 34n.
Differentiation, 44
Disciplinary walls, 17, 51*ff*., 166*ff*.; *see also* Social science
Dissociation, 45n.
Distribution of Wealth, The, see Clark, John Bates
Dualism in science, 21
Dynamic Theory of Personality, A, see Lewin, Kurt

Economic Interpretation of the Constitution of the United States, An, see Beard, Charles A.
"Economic man," 13, 15, 27, 150
Economic Motives, see Dickinson, Z. C.
Economic Program for American Democracy, An, see Gilbert, R. V.
Economic Tendencies in the United States, 38
Economics, 4, 13, 26, 32*f*., 141*ff*.; basis of as science, 37n.; and business, 117, 141, 146, 148; business cycle analysis, 6, 123; conservatism of, 141, 143, 149, 168; consumption, 117, 147; distribution, theories of, 36; dynamic theory, 146; focus of, 120, 122, 144, 145, 221, 222; labor problems, 169; and laissez-faire, 142-143; and Marxism, 116n.; motivation in, 27, 37n.; objective as apologist of capitalism, 122n.; objectivity in, 144; price theory, 36; and psychology, 33, 134, 161; secularization of, 141; and technology, 147, 149; theory in, 145, 171; *see also* Hypotheses, scientific, types of; Mitchell, Wesley C.; Social science
Education, 66, 67, 69; belief in, 61, 92, 237; coercions of, 100, 236; by commercial agencies, 108, 248n.; content of, 237; liberal, 8; reliance on for cultural change, 236*ff*.
Einstein, Albert, 114
Emotion, *see* Affection; Aggressiveness; Anxiety; Feeling; Frustration; Hardening process; Horney, Karen; Isolation; Jung, C. J.; Love; Neurosis; Plant, James S.; Security; Spontaneity; Strain; Sympathy; Tension
Empiricism, in anthropology, 158; dangers in, 126-129; in economics, 144; in history, 132, 134; in political science, 139; in social science, 119; and statement of problems, 123; and theory, 35, 121n., 173, 202; and values, 184; *see also* Data, accretion of; Statistics; Theory
End of Laissez-Faire, The, see Keynes, J. M.
Engineers and the Price System, The, see Veblen, Thorstein
English "muddling through," 64n.
Equality, belief in, 60, 228*ff*.; rationalization of inequality, 76; *see also* Freedom; Individual differences
Erewhon, see Butler, Samuel
Essentials of Economic Theory, see Clark, John Bates
Evolution, doctrine of, 89, 142
Experimental Social Psychology, see Murphy, G. and L. B., and Murphy, Murphy, and Newcomb
Experts, use of, in government, 78, 211

Fact-finding, *see* Data; Empiricism; Hypotheses, scientific, types of; Objectivity; Theory
Fall of the City, The, see MacLeish, Archibald

Family, 67, 68, 83, 85, 93; cultural disjunctions and, 98; home, 95; as scientific field, 117; world of and job world, 95; *see also* Child development; Father, rôle of; Men and Women; Sex adjustment

Faris, R. E. L., and Dunham, H. W., *Mental Disorders in Urban Areas*, 244

Fascism, 1, 213, 221; *see also* Germany; Italy; Nazis

Father, rôle of, 96

Federal Government, 6n.; growth of administrative machinery, 117n.; *see also* Agriculture, Department of; Congress; Government, personnel; National Resources Committee; Temporary National Economic Committee

Feeling, playing down of, 84, 90; *see also* Emotion

Figgis, J. N., *Studies in Political Thought from Gerson to Grotius, 1414-1625*, 138

"Finer things of life," 97; *see also* Values

Folklore of Capitalism, The, see Arnold, Thurman

Food and drug legislation, 74

Frame of reference in science, 123; *see also* Data; Hypotheses; Objectivity; Theory

France, Anatole, 111

France, "spirit of," 64n.

Frank, Lawrence K., 42n.; 124n.

Freedom, 66, 197; basic and nominal, 213; and cultural change, 63; in contemporary international scene, 105; and control, 210; exploitation of, 100; frustration of, 102, 111; and isolation, 91; in science, 7ff., 178, 249; structuring of culture to support, 66, 211-

212; *see also* Competition; Equality; Frustration; Individual differences; Opportunity; Pressure groups; Security; Spontaneity

Freud, Sigmund, 41, 96, 103, 124, 240

Friendships, 79, 91, 103; *see also* Affection; Aggressiveness; Isolation

Frontier, 81n., 89

Frustration, 101ff.; *see also* Cravings; Culture, contradictions and disjunctions in; Emotion

Full Recovery or Stagnation? see Hansen, Alvin H.

Functional areas of living, 65

Future, businessman and, 92; culture's emphasis on, 58, 87ff.; and motivation, 47; saving for, 194; uncertainty of, 94; workingman and, 92

Gang, The, see Thrasher, Frederic M.

Genius, national and racial, 64

Germany, 71, 177; *see also,* Fascism, Nazis

Gestalt Psychology, see Köhler, Wolfgang

"Getting ahead," *see* Opportunity

Gilbert, R. V., *et al., An Economic Program for American Democracy*, 243n.

Glueck, S. and E. T., 27

Government, and business, 6; municipal, 15; personnel, 211; structure, development of, 117n.; *see also* Congress

Group Representation before Congress, see Herring, E. P.

Growth, craving for, 193; process, 42, 44ff.

Growth of American Trade Unions, 1880-1923, see Wolman, Leo

[258]

Habit, *see* Change, cultural; Conservatism; Culture, lags in; Emotion; Impulse and habit; Learning process

Hammond, J. L. and Barbara, *The Skilled Labourer, 1760-1832*, 44n.

Hansen, Alvin H., *Full Recovery or Stagnation?*, 152n.

Hardening process, 91; *see also* Emotion; Friendships; Urban living

Harvard University, 169

Heavenly City of the Eighteenth Century Philosophers, The, see Becker, Carl

Hedonism, 33, 134, 161

Herring, E. P., 215, 229; *Group Representation before Congress*, 139; *Public Administration and the Public Interest*, 139

Hershey, R. B., *Workers' Emotions in Shop and Home*, 35n.

Herskovits, Melville, 14n.

History, 13, 129*ff.*; amorphous nature of, 132; conservative factors in, 130; and contemporary problems, 133, 137, 174*ff.*; economic interpretation of, 133, 136; historical precedents, relevance of, 2, 130, 132; *List of Doctoral Dissertations in History*, 132n.; *List of Research Projects in History*, 132n.; objectivity in, 132; and other social sciences, 138; and psychology, 133; radical rôle of, 131; rationalization of past, 64; students in, 174n.; and study of wholes, 175; training in, 133, 138, 174; *see also* Social science

Hitler, 85; *see also* Fascism, Nazis

Hobbes, Thomas, 109

Holidays, loss of meaning of, 84n.

Honesty, 61

Horney, Karen, *The Neurotic Personality of Our Time*, 97, 98, 101, 103, 196n., 231

Housing problem, 75, 169, 223

How We Think, see Dewey, John

Human nature, *see* Behavior; Cravings, human; Emotion; Growth; Integration; Individual differences; Instincts; Learning process; Motivation; Rationality; Rhythm

Human Nature and Conduct, see Dewey, John

Human Nature in Politics, see Wallas, Graham

Humanities, 114, 238; social science and, 178

Hypotheses, Chap. VI; geological, 203; scientific, types of, 121n.; *see also* Objectivity; Problems, criteria of importance; Social science; Techniques; Theory

Hypotheses, proposed: capitalism, 220*ff.*; class struggle, 227*ff.*; cultural change, 246*ff.*; democracy, 214*ff.*; education, 236*ff.*; equality, 228*ff.*; planning and control, 208*ff.*; rationality in man, 234*ff.*; religion, 238*ff.*; science, freedom in, 249; urban living, 243*ff.*; war, 240*ff.*

Immediate meaning, craving for sense of, 194

Impulse and habit, 70; *see also* Emotion

Income, distribution of, 74-75

Individual differences, 31, 78, 198, 228*ff.*; biologically caused, 228; culturally caused, 228; and democracy, 216, 229; do not cancel out, 26, 30; in intelligence, 110; need to structure culture for, 231; *see also*

Equality; Freedom; Learning process

Individual solutions to cultural disjunctions, 98, 103

Individualism, 60, 62, 68; and authority, 211; and welfare, 71; *see also* Aggressiveness; Competition; Freedom; Laissez-faire

Individuals, adaptability of, 22n., 113; common human experiences of, 190; cravings of, 189, 191; and culture, *see* Culture and individuals; definition of, 154; differences, *see* Individual differences; identification by stereotypes, 84; isolation of, 91, 94, 97; as locus of culture, 21*ff.*, 27*ff.*; processes of, and cultural processes, 42*ff.*; and society, 153; their values and social science, 189, 191; *see also* Behavior; Emotion; Individuation; Personality

Individuation, 73, 84, 89, 104

Industrial Revolution, 89; *see also* Inventions; Technology

Industry, concentration of, 74, 80; *see also* Bigness; Corporate business; Planning and control; Production

Influence of Darwin on Philosophy, The, see Dewey, John

Inhibition, 44

Insecurity, options as regards, 195; science and, 113; *see also* Emotion; Knowledge, uneven diffusion of; Security

Instinct of Workmanship, The, see Veblen, Thorstein

Institutional Behavior, see Allport, Floyd

Institutions, assumed orderliness in, 124; derivative character of analysis at level of, 24, 25, 50; as distributions of behavior,

28*ff.*; and individual differences, 31; interaction of, 65; as reified entities, 21; relevant to human cravings, 200; viewed as a "system," 125; *see also* Change, cultural; Culture; Culture and individuals

Instrumental living, 194; *see also* Future

Integration, 45, 197

Intelligence, differences in, 7, 230; and liberalism, 247; need to structure culture to support, 231, 234; *see also* Individual differences; Rationality

Inventions, 39, 74, 206; *see also* Culture, lags in; Technology

Investment market, theories of, 36

Isolation, personal, 91, 94, 97

Italy, 1, 71; *see also* Fascism

Job, choosing of, 225; and home world, 95; and social cohesion, 80*ff.*, 83*ff.*; structuring of world of, 68; *see also* Aggressiveness; Competition; Culture, structuring of; Insecurity; Money-making

Jung, C. J., *Two Essays on Analytical Psychology*, 102

Justice, 62, 77, 100; *see also* Law

Keynes, J. M., *The End of Laissez-Faire*, 142

Klineberg, Otto, *Negro Intelligence and Selective Migration*, 230

Knowledge, accretion of, 7, 16; diffused by commercial agencies, 108, 248n.; for its own sake, 2, 114, 129, 132, 188; new, and insecurity, 113; sophisticated and popular, 106*ff.*, 108, 195, 242; uneven diffusion of, 107, 112, 196, 219, 238;

182, 187n., 201, 242; *see also* Curiosity, pure; Social science

Odegard, Peter, *Pressure Politics*, 139

Ogburn, W. F., *Social Change*, 59n.

Old age, 88n., 93*ff*., 94

Opportunity to get ahead, 61, 75, 92, 194

Optimism, 101; *see also* Progress

Orderliness, assumption of, in culture, 124, 125

Organization of culture, 65*ff*., 69, 82, 107, 212; *see also* Culture

Orton, William A., *America in Search of Culture*, 80n.

Our Cities: Their Rôle in the National Economy, see National Resources Committee

Parker, Carleton H., 35n.

Past, rationalization of, 64

Patents, 39, 74

Patriotism, 62, 100; *see also* Nationalism

Pattern of American culture, Chap. III, 105; casual, 63; conflict between rôles of sexes, 95; emphasizes future, 87; marked by differences in power, 74; massed populations with little common purpose, 80; mobility and shallow roots, 79; stresses aggressiveness, 71; stresses youth and years of vigor, 93; uneven hospitality to change, 100; unevenly structured, 65; values dependent on material progress, 99

Patterning of culture, 54*ff*.; casualness normal, 64; concept of "pattern," 55; *see also* Culture; Planning and control; Social science, rôle of

Patterns of Culture, see Benedict, Ruth

Pecuniary standards, 73n.; *see also* Money; Value

Personality, conflicts in, 101*ff*.; differentiation, 44; integration, 45, 197; socially viable types, 73; split, 45n.; *see also* Behavior; Cravings; Emotion; Growth; Human nature; Individuals; Motivation; Personality and culture; Processes, individual and cultural; Rhythm

Personality and culture, as research field, 51*ff*.; *see also* Culture; Personality

Personality and the Culture Pattern, see Plant, James S.

Personality: A Psychological Interpretation, see Allport, Gordon

Philosophy, 13; recovery of for human problems, 119; and social science, 171*ff*.; *see also* Theory

Physics, 125n., 126

Place of Science in Modern Civilization, The, see Veblen, Thorstein

Planning and control, 68n., 71, 99, 208*ff*.; bureaucracy and, 210; in business corporations, 209; and casualness, 65; and cities, 243; positive statement of problem, 210; structuring culture for, 212; un-American, 63

Plant, James S., *Personality and the Culture Pattern*, 72n., 90n., 91n., 193n.

Polish Peasant in Europe and America, The, see Thomas, W. I.

"Political man," 13, 15, 27, 150

Political science, 4, 13, 116, 138*ff*.; empiricism in, 139; international relations, 123; objectivity in, 140; psychology and, 139;

Stern, William, *Differentielle Psychologie*, 12

Strachey, Lytton, *Queen Victoria*, 51n.

Strain, in living and structuring of culture, 66; ratio of susceptibility to, 112; science as creator of, 113; *see also* Culture; Emotion

Structuring of culture, 65*ff.*, *see also* Culture

Studies in Political Thought from Gerson to Grotius, 1414-1625, *see* Figgis, J. N.

Study of Man, The, see Linton, Ralph

Success, 60, 72, 91; *see also* Competition; Money-making; Status

Suicide, 27

Swann, W. F. G., 126

Sweden, 71

Sweezy, Paul M., 152n.

Swift, Jonathan, 128

Symbols, 57, 86

Symbols of Government, see Arnold, Thurman

Sympathy, 90; *see also* Isolation; Mutuality

Synthesis and analysis, 245; *see also* Empiricism; Theory

Tawney, R. H., 100; *Religion and the Rise of Capitalism*, 141n.

Teacher, social scientist as, 9

Techniques *vs.* ideas, 119*ff.*, 163, 201; in relation to problems, 17, 18; *see also* Data; Objectivity; Quantification; Theory

Technological Trends and National Policy, see Stern, Bernhard J.

Technology, 44n., 69, 78, 89, 220, 222, 242

Temporary National Economics Committee, 206, 224n.

Theory, 202; theory-building *vs.* fact-finding, 119, 171; coer-

civeness of, 35, 162; and culture viewed as behavior of individuals, 32; and data gathering, 121n., 173; and empiricism, 35; inbreeding of, 37; *see also* Empiricism; Hypotheses; Objectivity; Problems; Social science; Techniques

Theory of Business Enterprise, The, see Veblen, Thorstein

Theory of the Leisure Class, The, see Veblen, Thorstein

Thomas, W. I., "four wishes," 192n.; *The Polish Peasant in Europe and America*, 192n.; *Primitive Behavior*, 54n.; *The Unadjusted Girl*, 192n.

Thrasher, Frederic M., *The Gang*, 32n.

Three Philosophical Poets, see Santayana, George

Thrift, 61; *see also* Saving

Totalitarian state, 65; *see also* Germany; Italy; Nazis; Planning and Control; Soviet Union

Turner, Frederick, 136

Two Essays on Analytical Psychology, see Jung, C. J.

Unadjusted Girl, The, see Thomas, W. I.

University, administrators and social science, 7, 8, 179; regrouping of departments, 167; rôle of, 9, 187n.

Upper class, pace-setting rôle, 73n.; *see also* Classes, social

Urban living, 117; advantages of, 81; as critical field of cultural disorganization, 243*ff.*; lack of community in, 72, 82; old age and, 94; optional ties of, 79, 83; planning of cities, 82; size of cities, 80, 212; size and complexity, 82; *see also* Community;

Isolation; Municipal government; Neighborhood

Values, 2; attenuation of, 85; class influence on, 114n.; common, 238; dependent on material advancement, 99; money measures of, 37; pecuniary standards of, 73n.; rival, carried by men and women, 98; in social sciences, Chap. v, 2, 121n., 181, 183; surrounding family, 60, 95, 97; two levels of, 189, 191; *see also* Community; Feeling; Hardening process; Hypotheses; Individuation; Objectivity

Veblen, Thorstein, 5; *The Engineers and the Price System,* 223n.; *The Instinct of Workmanship,* 34n.; *The Place of Science in Modern Civilization,* 58, 171; *The Theory of Business Enterprise,* 76; *The Theory of the Leisure Class,* 73

Wage theory, 122n., 145, 146
Wall of fear, 90n.
Wallas, Graham, *Human Nature in Politics,* 139
Wallace, Henry, *New Frontiers,* 6n.
War, 66, 104, 220, 240*ff.*
Warner, Lloyd, 158

Wealth of Nations, see Smith, Adam
Webb, Sidney and Beatrice, *Soviet Communism,* 212n.
Welfare, definition of, 188; individualism and, 71; money-making and, 76, 99; production and, 148; theory of automaticity, 99; under capitalism, 220
Wells, F. L., 233
What's on the Worker's Mind, see Williams, Whiting
White-collar workers, 92
Whitehead, T. N., *Leadership in A Free Society,* 69
Whole, analysis of, 15; history and, 175
Williams, Whiting, *What's on the Worker's Mind,* 35n.
Willis, H. Parker, 6n.
Wolman, Leo, *Growth of American Trade Unions, 1880-1923,* 119n.
Women, 62; emphasis on youth, 93; and men, conflicts in roles, 95*ff.*
Workers' Emotions in Shop and Home, see Hershey, R. B.
Workingman, orientation to future, 92; *see also* Classes, social; Future

Youth, emphasis on, 93

Zeller, Belle, *Pressure Politics in New York,* 139